ADVANCES IN CLINICAL SOCIAL WORK PRACTICE

ADVANCES IN CLINICAL SOCIAL WORK PRACTICE

Selected Papers
NASW National Conference on Clinical Social Work
"Practice Excellence for the 80s" (1982 : Washington, D.C.)
November 18–21, 1982, Washington, D.C.

Carel B. Germain, *Editor*

Associate Editors
Phyllis Caroff
Patricia L. Ewalt
Paul Glasser
Rebecca Vaughan

National Association of Social Workers
Silver Spring, Md.

Designed by Susan B. Laufer

Library of Congress Cataloging-in-Publication Data

NASW National Conference on Clinical Social Work, "Practice Excellence for the 80s" (1982: Washington, D.C.)
 Advances in clinical social work practice.

 Includes bibliographical references.
 1. Social service—Congresses. 2. Social case work—Congresses. I. Germain, Carel B. II. Caroff, Phyllis. III. National Association of Social Workers. IV. Title. [DNLM: 1. Social Work—congresses. W322N269a 1982]
HV40.N255 1982   361.3'2   85-9208
ISBN 0-87101-130-1

Printed in U.S.A.

Table of Contents

Editor's Introduction

In 1978, with the appointment of the Task Force on Clinical Social Work Practice by Arthur J. Katz, then President of the National Association of Social Workers (NASW), the formal process to develop a tentative definition of clinical social work as a base for further elaboration and refinement by practitioners began. The charge was consistent with NASW's earlier effort to achieve agreement on a working definition of social work practice[1] and its later attempts to achieve beginning consensus on a conceptual framework for social work.[2]

The appointment of the 1978 Task Force was also partly a response to the growing demand for increased unity in the profession in order to resist the force of political and economic pressures. More significantly, perhaps, the creation of the Task Force was a response to the changing base of financial support for clinical services. New third-party reimbursement plans had led to or reinforced (1) the profession's interest in licensure or certification, (2) the growth in the full- and part-time private practice of social work, and (3) the invasions into traditional social work domains by competing professions. Mainly, however, the Task Force and its charge reflected the commitment of NASW to the needs and interests of one of the largest components of its membership.

The Task Force, chaired by Jay Cohen, prepared an extensive definition of clinical social work, the distinguishing feature of which was declared to be the historic person-in-situation conception. The definition also specified the elements of a bio-psycho-social-cultural assessment from which clinical interventions are assumed to flow.[3] The definition then provided the base for continuing the deliberations through presentations sponsored by the Task Force at clinical social work conferences, institutes, and panel discussions at NASW's National Symposia and the Council on Social Work Education's (CSWE) Annual Program Meeting.

The first such conference was the NASW Invitational Forum on

---

[1] Harriett M. Bartlett, "Toward Clarification and Improvement of Social Work Practice," *Social Work*, 3 (April 1958), pp. 3–9; William E. Gordon, "A Critique of the Working Definition," *Social Work*, 7 (October 1962), pp. 3–13; Gordon, "Knowledge and Value: Their Distinction and Relationship in Clarifying Social Work Practice," *Social Work*, 10 (July 1965), pp. 32–39; and Bartlett, *The Common Base of Social Work Practice* (Washington, D.C.: National Association of Social Workers, 1970).

[2] "Special Issue on Conceptual Frameworks," *Social Work*, 22 (entire issue) (September 1977).

[3] Jerome Cohen, "Nature of Clinical Social Work," in Patricia L. Ewalt, ed., *Toward a Definition of Clinical Social Work* (Washington, D.C.: National Association of Social Workers, 1980), pp. 23–32.

Clinical Social Work held in Denver, Colorado, 1979, and chaired by
Patricia L. Ewalt. Its two major purposes were "to provide an opportunity
for participants, both practitioners and educators, to share their thinking about the mission, essential competencies, and requisite knowledge
base of clinical social work, and to further the definition of clinical social
work as a contribution to the profession as a whole."[4] The responses of
the 125 Forum participants to the eight invited papers were summarized
and presented at the Sixth NASW Professional Symposium in 1979 in
San Antonio, Texas.

Next, an Institute on Clinical Social Work was held in conjunction with
the 1981 NASW Professional Symposium in Philadelphia, Pennsylvania.
The five papers presented centered on the theoretical and practice issues
generated by the earlier definition of clinical social work, but made
special reference to intervention.[5] The next step was a panel presentation on education for clinical practice, chaired by Florence Vigilante, at
CSWE's Annual Program Meeting in 1982 in New York.[6] The presentation was repeated as an Institute at the 1982 NASW National Clinical
Social Work Conference in Washington, D.C., sponsored by the Task
Force, which by then had become the NASW Clinical Social Work Pro-
visional Council. The theme of this most recent meeting in the series,
of which this volume is an outcome, was "Practice Excellence for the 80s."
The conference was characterized by a marked change in format: A call
for papers was extended that resulted in almost 600 submissions. One
hundred twenty-nine papers were selected competitively for presentation
and were supplemented by 22 invitational papers. A day of pre-Conference
Institutes produced an additional 42 presentations. That some 2,000
clinical social workers attended and discussed almost 200 papers attests
to the participants' sense of shared purpose and professional identity.

It is widely recognized, however, that different assumptions about functions, roles, and tasks and different beliefs about how broad or narrow
the definition of clinical social work should be are held by different groups
of professional social workers. On the one hand, some clinical social
workers might believe that the effort to define clinical social work is
fruitless because a broad definition, which includes all forms of face-

---

[4] Patricia L. Ewalt, "Preface," in Ibid., p. iii.

[5] Phyllis Caroff, ed., *Treatment Formulations and Clinical Social Work* (Silver
Spring, Md.: National Association of Social Workers, 1982).

[6] Patricia L. Ewalt, "Education for Clinical Social Work: Three Issues"; Carel
B. Germain, "The Relationship between Social Policy Content and Class and
Field Courses in Clinical Practice"; Carol H. Meyer, "Research and Clinical
Social Work Practice"; and Bernece Simon, "The Human Behavior and Social
Environment Courses and Clinical Social Work," panel presentation, Council
on Social Work Education, Annual Program Meeting, New York, New York,
1982, unpublished.

to-face practice, does not address the special interests workers now pursue through other membership bodies. On the other hand, some social workers might hold that the effort to reach unity, while retaining diversity, is an imperative of our time and is, indeed, an achievable goal.

That such differences exist should not be surprising in a profession that was established only 100 years ago from segments having various origins and historical traditions.[7]

Internal conflict in a profession or in one of its major segments can lead to growth and further development, or it can undermine solidarity when the profession is under attack. Conflict that is not managed successfully can open the practice domain to eager outsiders waiting to usurp traditional social work functions. The 1982 Conference may have muted our differences only for the moment, but it did clarify the underlying issues that require continuing debate and thoughtful negotiation. Each subsequent meeting dealing with clinical concerns, then, can find us farther along the road toward strengthening our connectedness to one another and expanding our competence as clinical social workers.

Thus the articles in this volume—a sample of all those presented—may be viewed as an affirmation of our shared professional identity and as an authentication of a beginning search for unity-in-diversity. The articles vary in their theoretical bases, the modalities selected, the populations served, the needs addressed, and the practice fields and settings represented. Yet taken together, they describe a richly diversified clinical practice that is also unified in its conception of social work's purpose or mission, its adherence to social work's values and ethics, and its commitment to social justice and excellence.

This volume, then, exemplifies the efforts of clinical social workers to create a vital presence for clinical practice in the world of the 80s—through advances in practice (Part I), advances in service provision (Part II), and advances in theory, ethics, and evaluative research (Part III). What the final decade and a half of the twentieth century will be like is not, of course, predictable. But to some degree, however small, the profession's clinical segment can now choose alternative futures for itself, even as planetary, national, regional, and local contexts continue to change. By its contemporary nature and its timeliness, this volume can serve as a guidepost for clinical social workers to make purposeful choices as they face the practice demands, the shifting contexts, the hostile political and economic forces, as well as the opportunities that lie ahead.

---

[7]A recent analysis of various clinical social work approaches found that the approaches now appear to be moving toward rather than further away from each other. See Carel B. Germain, "Technological Advances," in Aaron Rosenblatt and Diana Waldfogel, eds., *Handbook of Clinical Social Work* (San Francisco: Jossey-Bass, 1983), pp. 26–57.

As a guidepost to the future, the volume beckons the reader to the needs of emergent groups of clientele, provides understanding of the groups, and reports on the special skills found to be effective in meeting the needs. As a guidepost to the future, the volume leads the reader to the broadening range of innovative programs being developed by creative practitioners to serve traditional and new clientele more effectively. As a guidepost to the future, it also points to new directions in our theory base, to a new model for ethical problem solving, and to a rapidly developing set of diverse strategies for researchers and clinicians to use in evaluating practice outcomes and program effectiveness—including the use of computer technology.

CAREL B. GERMAIN
Farmington, Connecticut

March 1985

Acknowledgments

The 1982 NASW National Conference on Clinical Social Work, held in Washington, D.C., was attended by some 2,000 clinical social workers. More than 100 of the 150 papers presented were submitted by their authors for possible inclusion in this volume. Only 22 could be selected because of the limited resources for publication. The selection of a coherent group of papers that would reflect advances in clinical practice across a range of populations, situations, and needs presented a formidable task to the Conference Committee. The papers finally selected for this volume reflect in full measure the conference theme, "Practice Excellence for the 80s." It is expected that many of the other papers presented will appear in the NASW journals and other professional publications.

I welcome this opportunity to thank the members of the committee—Phyllis Caroff, Patricia L. Ewalt, Paul Glasser, and Rebecca Vaughan—for their planning, which resulted in a lively conference. I especially thank them for the thought, time, and energy they devoted to making publication of this volume possible. I also wish to express the committee's deep appreciation to all the presenters—and to the audience of social workers—who demonstrated that advances in clinical social work practice are an exciting reality. We also thank Sheldon Goldstein, Director of Organizational Services for NASW, and his staff, and Ghita Levine, former Director of Public Affairs for NASW, and her staff, for their valuable contributions to the success of the conference. We are indebted as well to Jacqueline M. Atkins, Director of NASW Publications, and her editorial staff, for guiding us through the publication process.

C. B. G.

Conference Committee

Carel B. Germain (Chair), DSW, is Professor, School of Social Work, University of Connecticut, Greater Hartford Campus, West Hartford.

Phyllis Caroff, DSW, is Professor, School of Social Work, Hunter College of the City University of New York, New York.

Patricia L. Ewalt, Ph.D., is Dean, School of Social Welfare, University of Kansas, Lawrence.

Paul Glasser, Ph.D., is Dean, Graduate School of Social Work, University of Texas at Arlington.

Rebecca Vaughan (deceased), MSW, was Lecturer, University of Michigan, Ann Arbor.

PART I
Advances in Practice

Editor's Comments

The articles in Part I describe new approaches to practice with newly defined client populations. The particular problem-situations are themselves not new to social workers, but in the world of the 80s, they present new features and are therefore different. The newness may arise from one or all of the following features: (1) the social context defines the need or problem differently, (2) the members of a population group redefine themselves as a distinctive group facing exceptional life tasks—in addition to the expectable ones faced by all or most people, and (3) clinical social workers recognize a professional responsibility to provide services to the population.

The authors of the first article, Getzel and Masters, consider the clinical issues involved in an old social problem—homicide. The problem is different because of a change in the social context. Violent crimes, especially in large cities, seem to have increased in number and intensified in the degree of violence. In many instances, such crimes are felt to be "senseless" unprovoked attacks on the innocent by strangers.

The need is also different because the families of homicide victims are beginning to define themselves as a distinctive group facing a uniquely demanding situation and its attendant tasks. Complaints among the public reflect a widespread belief that consideration of rights is extended to criminals but not to their victims. Institutionalized responses to those complaints, such as tax-subsidized compensation for victims, have supported the beginning awareness among the families of homicide victims of their special situation.

In turn, these factors have sparked the recognition by clinical social workers of the devastating grief that is exacerbated in such instances by an endless search for meaning. Getzel and Masters present the special knowledge and skills needed by the clinical social worker who seeks to help reduce the stress experienced by these families and to strengthen families' coping resources.

Other families experience a bio-psycho-social problem that has been part of the human experience since time began—hearing impairment. This is the subject of the next article, by Lowrey and Endlich. Despite social work's historic interest in the emotional and social consequences of illness, disease, and impairment, the profession generally has not been effective in its work with the deaf. Perhaps this is because too few of us are able to communicate in a second language, including sign. Also, perhaps, we define the characteristic response of many deaf persons to our offers of service as resistance, or we find the use of an interpreter frustrating.

The social context has changed markedly in the last decade or so through the normalization movement by, and in behalf of, the physically or mentally disabled. Federal and state regulations have mandated mainstreaming in all areas of life. These contextual factors have led the hearing impaired and their families to redefine themselves as a distinctive and self-directing group.

Social work practitioners have been encouraged by the change in context to develop the means for providing, encouraging, or enhancing independent living, new designs for physical and social settings, new educational and work opportunities, and the release of individual and family potentials to the fullest extent possible. Thus the changing context has led to a clearer recognition by social workers of the need for new knowledge and skills to implement social work's traditional value commitment to meet the service needs of the physically or mentally disabled. Lowrey and Endlich present that knowledge in their article and go on to demonstrate the effectiveness of transferring family therapy skills to work with the hearing impaired.

The next article, by Selan, presents the predicament of agoraphobia, largely a woman's affliction. Here, too, social workers have long been aware of and have worked with individuals suffering from this limiting disorder—sometimes successfully, oftentimes not. But the social context has now changed with the advent of new ideas about phobias and new practice and programmatic approaches to them. Many other contextual changes have affected women, in general, and are helping to reshape all clinical practice with women (and, in some instances, with men) across a widened range of issues.

It is not surprising that such developments have evoked a recognition among clinical social workers of the prevalence of agoraphobia and of the professional responsibility for service. Selan describes and analyzes the knowledge, skills, and techniques for treating agoraphobics and demonstrates the use of these in practice examples. She concludes that practice effectiveness with this client population is advancing in all modalities—individual, family, and group.

The next article, by Charnas and Weisenborn, addresses a social problem that displays all three sources of newness. The problem of unemployment has been a prominent concern of the social work profession since its own beginnings in the settlement and charity organization movements of the last century. The concern then was centered largely on the immigrant poor in the cities. Later, during the years of the Great Depression, professional concerns broadened as unemployment struck at all social groups in the nation.

Chronic unemployment has persisted for oppressed groups since the end of the post-World War II boom and is now at a tragically high rate among minority youths in particular. But during the recessions of the late 1970s and early 1980s, heretofore steadily employed workers in the skilled and semiskilled trades and managerial and professional persons were suddenly thrown out of work. The shock was made greater because job loss was unexpected, especially for those who had reached significant levels of seniority.

A newly defined population of unemployed, suffering acute job loss in a totally new context of occupational dislocation, presents a new service responsibility for clinical social work. Charnas and Weisenborn examine the biological, psychological, and social impact on this population and their families. Next the authors specify the clinical skills needed to aid in reducing the severe stress and strengthening coping resources. Recognizing that clinical services are no substitute for work and adequate income, the authors describe the clinician's professional responsibility to participate in efforts to influence social and economic policy and to undertake political advocacy in behalf of those suffering from acute or chronic unemployment.

The next two articles exemplify the influence of contextual change, self-redefinition, and professional recognition of need on two different family structures. Hlenski discusses clinical practice with stepparents and stepchildren. The reconstituted family represents a social structure long known to western society and to social work. It becomes new by virtue of its rapidly growing prevalence reflecting, in part, the rise in divorce rates, the appearance of new norms and values, and perhaps even the influence exerted by the mass media's interest in the fictional and real lives of reconstituted families. Because of many other contextual factors, these families face not only the same expectable life tasks that other families do but also many exceptional ones distinctive to their structure. Hlenski reviews the experiences of members of these families and presents the skills required for helping them meet their newly recognized, unique needs and tasks as well as their expectable ones.

Nelson and Etnyre present a similar undertaking with respect to family structures in which the marital partners differ in their sexual preference. An additional contextual change in this instance lies in the powerful human rights movements directed toward the liberation of previously oppressed groups, including gays and lesbians. New definitions of self and group, and the struggle for equal rights, have created a new and safer environment for coming out to one's marital partner, and others—at least in some instances. Self-aware clinical social workers are beginning to understand the special or exceptional life tasks of such couples and to recognize the corresponding service responsibility of clinical social work. Nelson and Etnyre address the clinicians' need for specialized knowledge and skill if services to these families are to be effective in helping them meet their family tasks, make needed decisions, plan for their future, and so on.

The last article in Part I, by Dunleavy and Misci, covers another "old" social problem—incest and its adolescent female victims. The problem has long been a concern of social workers in child welfare. But it, too, is different now by virtue of changes in context, the beginnings of self-definition by the victimized population (especially among those who are now adults), and a new recognition by clinical social workers (and the public) of its prevalence and the consequent need for new approaches to clinical services—in many settings, not only in child welfare. Dunleavy and Misci address the clinical issues and the knowledge and skill required from the particular standpoint of group therapy as a significant practice modality in service to this client population.

These seven chapters comprising Part I have a common focus on newly emerging human needs, problems, and predicaments. They are dissimilar in populations served, approaches developed, and modalities selected. What unites them most firmly, however, is that all represent advances in clinical social work practice.

Social Work Practice with Families of Homicide Victims

George S. Getzel and
Rosemary Masters

Homicide, more than any other event, symbolizes the imminence of personal crime. Fortunately most of us do not have direct experiences with homicide in our families, yet an inescapable reality of life in inner-city neighborhoods and suburbs is the increased rates of homicide.

In an effort to understand and to serve surviving family members, the Victim Service Agency of New York (VSA), a voluntary agency supported by governmental funds, began the Families of Homicide Victims Project in 1979. This article describes the particular clinical issues associated with homicide that affect the individual's mourning process, family interaction, and reintegration into society. Our work incorporates insights from crisis intervention theory, family treatment, and existential approaches.

IMPACT OF HOMICIDE

The typical homicide victim is a young unemployed male between 15 and 25 years of age. Both the victim and the perpetrator tend to be of the same race and known to one another. The weapon used is most likely to be a handgun. Homicide tends to be an act of passion and may occur as a culminating act stemming from another crime, such as an assault or robbery.[1] Regardless of the circumstances surrounding the homicide, the impact on the surviving family is devastating.

Homicide is a classic crisis situation embodying the five components identified by Golan—a hazardous event, a vulnerable state, precipitating factors, an active crisis, and efforts at reintegration.[2] The event of homicide is abrupt and unforeseen, not permitting anticipatory cognitive and emotional preparation. Kutscher noted that anticipatory grief provides the fullest opportunity to develop ways to mitigate trauma because adjustment attitudes are learned before actual loss.[3] Although there are variations of grief responses among survivors of homicide victims, the suddenness and irrevocability of death aggravates and accentuates grief reactions. In addition, because 50 percent of VSA clients are mourning the death of a child, it is not unusual for parents to evidence the most profound grief that is continuing and episodic for months and in some cases years, as the following case example illustrates:

> John Santiago's adult daughter was murdered four years ago. He came for help because he was experiencing agitated depression prompted by the advent of spring. He had become very sad because the season brought back memories of the times when he walked with his daughter, who would marvel at the renewal of foliage. Paradoxically, spring, the season of rebirth, became a time of poignant sorrow.

In modern times the death of a child has ceased to be a natural event but is instead an overwhelming loss and betrayal. A homicide of a child only re-enforces the perception that the world has failed the survivor who, in turn, sees herself or himself as a victim of the homicide. We frequently see clients who have lost their fundamental belief in the social order, as they drift into nihilism and despair. For example,

> Susan Richmond's daughter was abducted and murdered a thousand miles away. At one point in treatment, Mrs. Richmond told the worker how difficult it was for her to say the Lord's Prayer. She found that she stops at "Forgive us our trespasses as we forgive those who trespass against us," unable to continue. It became clear that any treatment approach must simultaneously attend to symptom reduction and the failure of belief of the surviving family members.

Golan has defined the precipitating factor of crisis as the specific event or issue that "is the link in the chain of stress-provoking events that converts the vulnerable state into the state of disequilibrium.[4] And Bard noted that following any serious crime, such as robbery, rape, and burglary, the victim is overwhelmed by fear and anger. In desperation, the victim searches for ways to undo his or her mounting sense of helplessness and vulnerability. One common but dangerous reaction to victimization is self-blame; another is to see society as utterly anarchic and menacing. Bard believes that the major issue for any victim becomes the restoration of faith in the social order. An effort must be made to enhance the victim's sense of competence and self-worth.[5]

We have found that recurrent reactions of survivors of homicide victims are precipitated by factors associated with murder as an unacceptable death. Murder transgresses contemporary sentiments toward death, which, according to Aries, seek to lighten the burden of dying through technology and the defense of denial, rendering death "happy."[6]

By any account, homicide is an unseemly tragic event and the stuff of drama even if the players are unknowns. Families are burdened and shamed by the murder of a relative. Murder cannot be sanitized and made beautiful or logical. Family members are preoccupied by the images of disfigurement left behind by their loved ones. It is not unusual for relatives to repeat vivid, almost poetic descriptions of the moment of death (if witnessed) or to describe the details of mortal wounds. Repetitive re-enactments represent the survivor's efforts to magically reverse the tragic sequence, while slowly encompassing painful images and unacceptable realities. We have also found that many families suffer from the absence of the use of ritual as a way of transcending the terror of their loss.

HOMICIDE AND FAMILY BALANCE

Death almost always requires the family to organize roles, implicit understandings, and expectations. Disturbance of family homeostasis is an inevitable result of homicide.[7] We found that families of homicide victims experience a sequence of interpenetrated issues in the course of treatment. The following case illustrates these core issues and the treatment approach used.

The Warren Family

Martin Warren contacted VSA three months after his 25-year-old son, Marc, was murdered. He told the worker that he and his wife were having a terrible time adjusting to the loss. Mr. Warren was initially concerned about the well-being of his surviving daughter, Alice, age 20.

Issue 1: Agitated Search Behavior. During early contacts, the family was allowed to express their rage and guilt over the homicide. Weak and unfocused efforts to understand why the murder occurred reflected the survivors' underlying guilt and deep preoccupation with the past. The worker was prepared to witness a rapid succession of emotional displays and outbursts. Following the initial period of shock, which may last days or weeks, mourners seek for ways to undo what occurred in order to regain their loved one. This "searching" behavior has instinctual sources, as mourners obsessively seek reunion with the dead person.[8]

Mrs. Warren, a thin, pretty woman in her mid-fifties, wept during early interviews. She repeated, "I can't accept it." In one interview she repeatedly berated herself for causing Marc's death, recalling a fight she had with Marc about his playing his stereo too loud three years ago, which occasioned his moving out and living independently. After his death she felt that if she had been more lax about rules, Marc would have stayed home and would not have been murdered. Mr. Warren did not respond but expressed a tone of painful emotional constriction. In helpless resignation, he repeatedly told his wife that "there is nothing we can do; we have to let him rest."

Issue 2: Ambivalent Acceptance of the Homicide. Family members spend a good deal of time going over the circumstances surrounding the homicide. The repetition serves denial and helps to anesthetize painful content.

The homicide is often characterized by obvious ambiguity as to the dead relative's complicity in his or her murder. Rage toward the dead may be displaced onto the criminal justice system, which is perceived as allowing crimes to occur and to go unpunished. Rage toward the criminal justice system further isolates surviving family members from the symbols of societal action and from any painful revelations about the victim. Family members unconsciously seek to establish an alliance with the murdered relative.

The Warrens recounted that their son, Marc, although kind and generous, had been a source of worry to them for years. They recalled his near-fatal automobile accident and a series of unsuccessful jobs. The couple wondered about his business associates and the fact that he was kidnapped and shot at his place of work. The Warrens went over the frightful memory of Marc's decaying body, found in the trunk of a car. Both parents raged explosively at the fact that no one had come forth to say what had happened to him. His killers to this day remain unknown and at large.

Issue 3: Historic Family Interaction. As trust develops toward the worker, differential responses of kin become areas of exploration. Global emotional responses narrow to focus on the marital tie and other familial relationships. The worker assists the family members to look at interactional patterns in order to abet griefwork and to establish a more salutary family alignment.

The extent to which death will disrupt the family equilibrium and the family's consequent ability to reorganize itself is related to the family position of the dead, the timing and the nature of death, and the capacity of the family to express its collective concerns.[9] This became the emphasis of the work with the Warren family.

During subsequent interviews it became clear that Mr. Warren was keeping an emotional distance from the rest of the family, a long-standing pattern. He had always worked evenings, leaving parenting mostly to his wife. During family sessions, Mrs. Warren consistently contradicted her husband on various matters. He deferred to her with a resigned, "I guess you're right."

During one interview, Mrs. Warren shared her resentment about the time her husband spent caring for his elderly parents "at the expense of *his* family." She mused that her family of origin taught her to take care of herself and her children. Alice tended to ally herself with Mrs. Warren, against her father.

The worker helped family members to clarify these patterns, which had become more salient and urgent in the aftermath of Marc's death. This discussion presaged more active reconsideration of the marital tie.

Issue 4: Weighing Current Family Ties. In the case of the death of a child, the bonding between spouses is exposed to tremendous stress, particularly if historic role conflicts have centered around the murdered child. The meaning of a child in the family must be pinpointed by the worker. It is very common for grieving relatives to find substitute love objects as a way to sanctify the deceased. The worker should help family members to understand this phenomenon.

It became apparent that one very important bond that had held the Warrens together was their mutual concern over Marc's escapades, which were a subject of daily concern. Rather than resolve the issues of their own respective rights and needs, they endlessly discussed Marc's problems. It seemed likely that somehow Marc's strivings expressed Mr. Warren's own longing to be rebellious. Clearly, he took pride in Marc's struggles to start his own business, something he wished to do.

In interviews with the worker, the couple consistently refused to admit dissatisfaction with their marriage. When the subject of marital disagreements came up, the topic was quickly changed to the subject of Marc. Their daughter, Alice, seemed somewhat aloof from the marital strains, and tended to immerse herself in relationships with peers, but expressed irritation bordering on contempt at her father for being uninvolved and "weak."

Mr. Warren continued to reassure his wife that it was not her fault Marc died. Mrs. Warren had encouraged Marc's girlfriend to visit frequently. The two spent hours talking about Marc. Mrs. Warren had taken to discussing the well-being of Marc's girlfriend.

Issue 5: Approaching the Irrevocability of the Death. As family members begin to accept the negative and positive aspects of the murdered member, they can psychologically approach the finality of the loss. Long-term family issues are acknowledged more openly.

Over time, the family began to discuss Marc as being "less than perfect." Mr. Warren voiced his rage at Marc for disappointing him so terribly. Both parents to some extent started to face their guilt that Marc was caught up in a family pattern that contributed to reckless behavior. As they explored this traumatic issue, the Warrens filled in their family history, linking it to Marc's problem behavior.

It became clear to the Warrens that by accepting the death as final, they were deciding to get on with their own lives. Psychologically, this felt to the survivors like killing Marc all over again. The decision to enjoy living without Marc provoked guilt feelings. We have found a paradoxical approach that can often help families to recognize and to deal with their intense ambivalence about completing mourning. Rather than urge the client to finish mourning, the worker sides with the part of the ambivalence that wishes to mourn forever. Mrs. Warren was therefore told that "many parents never stop grieving. Some go through the rest of their lives expecting their children to return home. They act as if time stands still." Mrs. Warren was also told that since she so clearly wanted to make that choice, she should do so. Mrs. Warren was outraged at this option. For the first time, Mrs. Warren began to say that she wanted to get on with her life.

Later in the interview, Mr. Warren said that he felt that the time had come to dispose of Marc's personal possessions, which were still in the apartment. The worker agreed with Mr. Warren that this was an appropriate decision "to lay Marc to rest." The worker explored how the Warrens could share this significant task.

Issue 6: The Persistence of Societal Estrangement. Although families over time show adaptation to the traumatic crisis—at least to a reduction of the more troubling emotional symptomology—it is very common for surviving family members to grow more restless, frightened, and suspicious about relating to other relatives and friends as they reenter the flow of community life. Family members often are preoccupied with their needs for vengeance and retribution. They may say that *other* people in the community do not understand how fortunate they are as compared to surviving family members who suffer so much. Their deep and persistent mourning may be actually more than their relatives and friends can accept. Thus, the informal support systems of surviving families become altered and diminished. Outside recognition and consolation are denied them at their greatest hour of need. Family members may turn to the criminal justice system for ritual expressions of justice and retribution, but they often feel rebuffed by bureaucratic impersonality.

The Warren family gave ongoing expression to the belief that no one really cared about the pain they were suffering. People might show cautious interest, but soon this too disappeared. The Warrens became hurt and angry toward others. In later sessions, almost embarrassed, they asked if other clients the worker saw had experiences similar to their own. The worker suggested that they might want to meet with other parents of homicide victims. The Warrens said that they would be interested.

Anger toward the police, the courts, and politicians was another theme that never abated in individual family contacts. With attentive listening, it became clear that the Warrens viewed themselves as not part of the outside world, which is so negatively tainted. The daily chores of life involving contact with others, especially strangers, were an unbearable burden. It was apparent to the worker that no amount of individual comforting or discussion could handle their negative image of society.

RETURNING TO COMMUNITY

From our observation of individuals and families, crisis intervention falls short in dealing effectively with survivors' reintegration into the community. Even after the acceptance of the irrevocability of death, the survivor's rage toward the world, and hopelessness, persist. We have found the concept of survivorship is basic to a reconsideration of how we help these families. The identity of "survivor" places the individual in a position alone in the world, as he or she is filled with a powerful experience that torments with the constant reminder of specialness. The survivor of a catastrophe caused by other human beings can no longer look at other people and their institutions with innocence.

Bruno Bettelheim, himself a survivor of the Nazi Holocaust, captured the dilemma of survivors when he wrote, "The sheer prospect of death is not all that haunts: there is also the anxiety we feel when the social structure we create to protect us from abandonment collapses or when the personality structure we built up for the same purpose disintegrates."[10]

Kai Erikson saw collective trauma as a twin of individual trauma in disasters of human origin. Collective trauma consists of the breakdown of social ties that ordinarily ground people to predictable and secure bonds to one another. Survivors become profoundly depressed at the thought that society no longer has "moral anchors." Victims lose faith in the good protection and support of others.[11]

The survivor, thus, is faced with ultimate questions of death, meaninglessness, and isolation.[12] We felt that support groups would afford a way of engaging these powerful questions with peers who share a unique sense of survivorship. Undergirding the anguish of the survivor is an "unheard cry for meaning," to use Frankl's term.[13]

SUPPORT GROUP

A parent support group was begun 2½ years ago and has continued with an expanding membership of people with varied cultural and socioeconomic backgrounds. The power and almost magical attraction of the parents' group arises out of members' anger at society and need to universalize their plight by finding validation for upsetting feelings and ideas. However excessive and unresolved their grief, members find in the group an arena where they can grieve openly and not be perceived as outcasts. As a matter of fact, the group often turns members' long emotional narratives into ritualistic testimonies to their special identities as survivors of an event that only they can fully comprehend.

Initially, the group focuses on individuals' descriptions of the precise details of their children's deaths. Members listen attentively to the wrenching stories of the last times others saw their child alive or dead. Parents often speak of their wish to look at an article of clothing to remind them of the finality of the death. Little interaction beyond intense long silences occurs in the group at its early phase. An underlying theme is a desire for union with the dead.[14]

In short order, the group begins to vacillate between intense mourning and calls for retribution. The cries for vengeance in the group can be overwhelming to the worker who must accept these expressions; to do otherwise is to be perceived as uncaring and rejecting. Group members' rage is often directed at the court, police, and society in general, "who don't really care despite their self-righteous posturing." Group members subtly and unconsciously compete among themselves to show how hurt and abandoned they are. They discuss topics in a way that suggests that no person or changed condition can ameliorate their loss. The worker seeks to point out underlying themes of guilt and vengeance.

Gradually, group members use the presence of the worker to reach out to each other. A significant breakthrough occurs when members bring artifacts from their children into the group. Exchanging pictures of the dead children gives an outlet for contained expressions of positive feelings toward the dead and the first direct caring interaction in the group. Pictures serve as icons that make losses real yet manageable.

A common pattern in the group is swings between mourning for their children and preoccupation with the wrongs of the criminal justice system. The worker helps the group see how they use the criminal justice system to deny their feelings at critical points within the group. Underlying their interaction is a pervasive feeling of impotence. The worker helps them sort out this highly overdetermined theme. It becomes clear to the group that it is appropriate for them to want justice—an emblem of societal capability and atonement.

The group also serves as an adjunct to family treatment. Members discuss how they cope with the nightmares and phobic reactions. They also begin to call each other on the telephone to support one another when crises come up, particularly during the course of indictments and trials of perpetrators. Most recently, a subgroup of parents have developed a Bill of Rights for Parents of Homicide Victims. They have testified before relevant governmental bodies. Their involvement represents a significant step in positively identifying themselves as survivors and using this new identity to reintegrate into the community.

IMPLICATIONS FOR PRACTICE

The central lesson of VSA's Families of Homicide Victims Project is that the murder of a close relative inflicts a massive and long-lasting trauma on the surviving relatives. Functioning is impaired in a number of areas. The potential for disabling depression, family disintegration, and social isolation is significant.

The responses to homicide are not uniform, however. Not only do such responses vary greatly from family to family, but within the same family over time. Social work, because of its tradition of differential intervention, of responding "where the client is," is uniquely equipped to help lessen the psychic damage wrought by the horror of a violent death.

Despite the professional's understandable desire for some orderly progression of mourning and recovery, the recovery from the murder of a relative is far from tidy or predictable. So many external forces impinge on the family that the process of assimilating and working through the homicide is repeatedly interrupted and often reversed. Events such as the arrest and trial of the perpetrator have the effect of a blow breaking open a partially healed wound. At such times, all the original pain, shock, and rage are reactivated in full force.

Social workers assisting families of homicide victims must be prepared to assess and reassess their clients' needs over time. A family that is functioning well one month may be in crisis the next. Wherever possible, follow-up contacts over the first year of bereavement are useful and desirable. The widest possible repertoire of responses is essential.

In general, VSA workers found that assessment should be made and, where indicated, intervention undertaken on the following range of potential "trouble-spot" issues:

1. *Serious Psychiatric Illness:* Suicidal thoughts are frequently expressed and low-level depression is very common, though only 4 of 350 families seen made actual attempts or gestures. Depression in children is often disguised in poor school performance and isolation from peers. Family members may show a deceptive sense of well-being and adjustment in the first few months, only to be overcome by overwhelming sadness and rage once the defenses of denial and isolation fail after the initial period (frequently after six months). Follow-up during six to nine months becomes crucial.

2. *Economic Crisis:* Assistance with entitlements and an array of concrete services is vital in the process of enabling clients to mobilize their ego strengths and reduce severe panic. Services and entitlements provide a structure for the continuity of at least some basic family functions.

3. *Differential Family Diagnosis:* Not all surviving family members need high-intensity counseling services. Emphasis should be placed on parents surviving children, and spouses or siblings who have a childlike relationship to the murdered relative. Murder of one parent by another always provokes extreme distress, and frequently entails referral for long-term psychiatric management.

4. *Criminal Justice Response:* A central task of the social worker becomes one of serving as a mediating agent between the client and the criminal justice system. The well-being of clients often rests on the openness of communication with that complex system. Efforts must be made to sensitize the criminal justice system to the needs of clients and the etiology of their behavior, which may overwhelm assistant district attorneys and judges.

CONCLUSION

Violence is a fact of modern life. The social worker, like every citizen, is angered and frightened by the chaos, despair, and vulnerability that such violence embodies. The temptation is to succumb to the defense of denial—to look away and to pretend violence and its consequences do not exist. In so doing, we serve to reinforce the isolation and despair of the survivors and by extension of all of us. The VSA experience demonstrates that the pain, rage, and isolation of families of homicide victims can be mitigated. This work demonstrates that survivors can find hope and meaning in the face of dreadful and overpowering events. Work with these clients is both a challenge and an opportunity to face and respond to the deepest questions of human existence.

NOTES AND REFERENCES

1. Harold M. Rose, "Lethal Aspects of Urban Violence: An Overview," in *Lethal Aspects of Urban Violence* (Lexington, Mass.: Lexington Books, 1979), pp. 1–2; and Richard Block, *Violent Crime* (Lexington, Mass.: Lexington Books, 1975), pp. 15–30.

2. Naomi Golan, *Treatment in Crisis Intervention* (New York: Free Press, 1976), pp. 63–64.

3. Austin H. Kutscher, "Anticipatory Grief, Death, and Bereavement," in Edith Wyschogrod, ed., *The Phenomenon of Death: Faces of Mortality* (New York: Harper & Row, 1973), pp. 40–53.

4. Golan, *Treatment in Crisis Intervention,* p. 66.

5. M. Bard, *The Crime Victim Book* (New York: Basic Books, 1979), pp. 76–103.

6. Phillipe Aries, *Western Attitudes toward Death* (Baltimore, Md.: Johns Hopkins University Press, 1974), pp. 85–102.

7. Fredda Herz, "The Impact of Death and Serious Illness on the Family Life Cycle," in *The Family Life Cycle: A Framework for Family Therapy* (New York: Gardner Press, 1980), p. 224.

8. Collin Murray Parkes, *Bereavement—Studies of Grief in Adult Life* (London, England: Pelican Books), pp. 57–76.

9. Herz, "Impact of Death and Serious Illness," pp. 223–240.

10. Bruno Bettelheim, *Surviving and Other Essays* (New York: Alfred A. Knopf, 1979), pp. 10–11.

11. See Kai Erikson, *Everything in Its Path* (New York: Simon & Schuster, 1976), pp. 186–245.

12. See Irvin D. Yalom, *Existential Psychotherapy* (New York: Basic Books, 1980), for a discussion of death, meaninglessness, and isolation in treatment.

13. Viktor E. Frankl, *The Unheard Cry for Meaning: Psychotherapy and Humanism* (New York: Simon & Schuster, 1978).

14. See Paul Antze, "Role of Ideology in Peer Psychotherapy Groups," in Morton A. Lieberman et al., eds., *Self-Help Groups for Coping with Crisis: Origins, Members, Processes, and Impact* (San Francisco: Jossey Bass, 1966), pp. 272–304, for information about parent mourning groups and how they operate.

Family Therapy with the Hearing Impaired

Leatrice A. Endlich and
Janet H. Lowrey

The use of family therapy as an effective form of treatment for families with a hearing impaired child has been discussed by Shapiro and Harris, who concluded that family therapy "seems to have advantages over other forms of therapy. . .and proved most feasible and beneficial when the deaf patient was a child or adolescent."[1] The experience of the authors, who have engaged in therapy with several families having a hearing impaired child, has served to both confirm and amplify the foregoing conclusion. We propose in this article to describe and analyze certain dynamics and techniques that we found to be effective in treating these families.

The defects that deafness occasions tend to eliminate even the minimal requirements for traditional methods of psychotherapy that require direct communication between the therapist and the patient. In addition to the obvious inability to hear verbal communication, there are other obstacles in treating the hearing impaired (see Table 1, p. 18).

The Department of Child Psychiatry at the University of Kansas Medical Center provides multidisciplinary evaluation, diagnosis, and treatment to children and adolescents. Over a period of two years, five families with hearing impaired children were referred to this department for evaluation and treatment. They were referred either by private physicians or schools because of various acting out behaviors of the hearing impaired child. These children ranged in age from 11 to 15, and all had congenital hearing losses that were initially discovered when the children were between the ages of 2 and 3. All had received early training in the oral-aural method and were able to communicate orally. In fact, this was the exclusive mode of communication with their families. Three of the children learned sign language at about 10 years of age; however, no parent knew sign language.

Following a diagnostic conference, it was recommended that all of the families receive treatment. This suggestion was based upon our hypothesis that improved family communication would reduce acting out behavior. We found family members reluctant to share or express feelings with one another. This included the inability to express anger appropriately.

Table 1
Problems Indigenous to Therapy with the Hearing Impaired

I. *Communication Problems*

   A. Limited vocabulary.
   B. Inability to deal with abstract concepts.
   C. Lack of knowledge of sentence structure.
   D. Multiple meaning words, e.g., *run.*
   E. Words that look alike when speech reading, e.g., *mat, pat, bat.*

II. *Disturbance in Social Relationships*

   A. Lack of understanding of the feelings of others.
   B. Limited awareness of the impact of own behavior on others.
   C. Rigid and concrete thinking.
   D. Venting of frustration or anxiety by acting out.
   E. Paranoid behavior.
   F. Egocentric view of the world.
   G. Poor self-concept.

III. *Educationally Retarded*

IV. *Family Dynamics*

   A. Family and/or child is usually experiencing ongoing grief regarding
      the handicap.
   B. Communication is usually infrequent, confused, and/or distorted,
      e.g., humor, teasing, lying.
   C. Communication is usually filtered through the mother.
   D. Mother is enmeshed with child.
   E. Sibling problems.
   F. Hearing impaired child is often scapegoated.
   G. Family members often "speak for" the hearing impaired child.
   H. Marital problems.

Parents often had difficulty praising or complimenting their children. Also, they tended to assume that they knew what the hearing impaired child was thinking or feeling. According to Hersch and Solomon, "It is suspected that when the deaf child begins to feel misunderstood and his family feel they are having difficulty getting through to the child, the dynamic principle of distancing, isolation, and withdrawal takes place both by family and child."[2]

In reviewing the literature, one finds consensus among authors who feel that all families with a hearing impaired child face a crisis at the time of diagnosis and that all subsequently must go through a sequential process of grief work. We found each family to be at a different stage in its grieving over the handicap; it therefore became most important to determine where each family had left its grief work unfinished.[3]

We have observed that even though parents had reached some level of acceptance of their child's hearing loss when he or she was younger, at various developmental stages a repetition of the grief work process became necessary. Each developmental stage is composed of specific tasks requiring mastery of certain skills. When the mastery of these tasks is inhibited because of the handicap, parents are once again confronted with the whole issue of acceptance.

At adolescence parents of hearing impaired children see the discrepancy between their child and his or her hearing peers in areas of social and academic development. One of the tasks of normal adolescents is to become autonomous. Parents of hearing impaired adolescents become fearful and anxious about their children's developing independence; they show concern over the adolescents' ability to drive, to obtain a job, and eventually to support themselves. Another major concern is whether they will marry and be able to take care of children. As a result of these fears, parents often become overprotective and do not allow the adolescents the privileges and responsibilities commensurate with their age group. Consequently, hearing impaired adolescents may often be less mature than hearing adolescents of the same age, and, as a result, become isolated from their peers.

We consistently found that hearing impaired children acted out their anger and frustration in response to isolation in a variety of ways. Some children had expressed anger by physically attacking family members; others by acting out in school, either through academic failure or antisocial behavior; others used compulsive eating, withdrawal, and even suicidal behavior. We also found that all of these behaviors were markedly reduced once improved communication patterns were established in the family.

One of the most important goals in family therapy with this group was to constantly teach and demonstrate successful methods of communication and to block dysfunctional and even nonexistent communication. All transactions were monitored closely. The therapists continually modeled techniques for the family by checking out comprehension with the hearing impaired child and finding ways to rephrase complex statements and/or questions. During the course of therapy, continual interaction between the hearing impaired child and his or her family was demonstrated. In addition, family members were taught basic communication skills, such as using "I" effectively, making feeling and intention statements, and checking out messages before reacting.

In hearing impaired children paranoia is not considered an uncommon phenomenon. However, when the family is forced to communicate with and include the hearing impaired child in conversation, this behavior diminishes significantly. This fact reiterates the need for the entire family to be involved in treatment.

Although it is extremely helpful to have a cotherapist who is knowledgeable about, and skilled in, communicating manually as well as orally with the hearing impaired, there is one inherent problem for the therapist. It is not uncommon for the child as well as family members to continually try to force the therapist into the role of being the primary communicator instead of assuming this responsibility themselves.

In treating the whole family, we used the traditional structural approach. One could characterize all the families that we treated as being "enmeshed" in differing degrees. As with all enmeshed families, subsystem boundaries were weak and poorly differentiated. There was evidence of rigidity, characterized by the tendency toward maintaining the status quo in the family. Parents tended to be overprotective, thus preventing the child's normal development of competence and autonomy. Boundary setting became a necessity, as often boundaries were weak, unclear, or nonexistent. The hearing impaired child was usually adept at manipulating and dividing the parents and often enlisted the aid of one parent to act against the other in the child's behalf. Furthermore, it was not unusual for younger siblings to assume a parental role toward the hearing impaired child. Siblings will often become angry and bitter; they may also feel shame or embarrassment about their hearing impaired brother or sister. In all cases it was necessary to insist on the inclusion of the hearing impaired child when strengthening the sibling subsystem.

Decision making in these families was an exceedingly difficult process. Although the hearing impaired children were often the focus of family decisions, they were excluded from the decision-making process because their input was considered unimportant. As a result, they grew to expect rejection.

Another family pattern was the parents' tendency to use the hearing impaired child as a scapegoat. This served to mask the conflict that really existed between the spouses. Since it was not unusual for the mother to be overprotective and too close to the hearing impaired child, an imbalance in the marital axis was created. Marital therapy was therefore essential after the boundaries were realigned.

TECHNIQUES

In addition to restructuring the family system through boundary changing, altering transactions by changing communication patterns, shifting alliances, and detriangulating the hearing impaired child, further methods of reaching these families were necessary. Our work tended to confirm the usefulness of visual and experiential techniques.[4] We used the genogram; family sculpting; role playing; and the Situation, Options,

Consequences, Simulation (SOCS) Model; plus other creative projective techniques. In addition, we videotaped interviews to play back to the family so that they could observe certain target behaviors.

Genogram

The genogram is a map that portrays the history of a family through time.[5] During a session it is drawn on the blackboard as the family provides the necessary information. The genogram gives deaf children a visual opportunity to understand their family history and to enhance their personal identity and their sense of self. It also gives them a background for following the family sessions because they become aware of the relationships and significant events in their family. As the family provides the information for the genogram, feelings about the diagnosis of the hearing impairment usually emerge. This information is beneficial for pinpointing the grief process.

We found that by using the genogram initially, the family was united in completing a common task. The hearing impaired child was quickly removed from the scapegoat role. In all the cases, the hearing impaired child made significant contributions to the family history. Parents were often surprised to learn that their expectations of the child's input had been so minimal.

> The genogram was used with Family A to pinpoint the source of sadness that was continually being expressed through tears by several family members. The genogram disclosed several important issues.
>
> First, we learned that a daughter younger than D had been born with a heart defect and had died at the age of 18 months. Even though family members denied that this was significant, the parents still felt much sadness over this loss. The parents were amazed to learn that D remembered his sister and could relate certain memories that were prelingual.
>
> In addition, the children labeled their mother as "worried." When asked what she worried about, D volunteered that she worried about dad's drinking. Thus, D was the keeper of the family secret and his revelation of this opened an important issue for the family.
>
> Another family issue that was discussed through the genogram was the father's religiosity and its effect on the family. Certain practices were encouraged as a family that D did not understand and thus could not fully participate in. It was possible to discuss ways to include D in these observances and thus reduce his isolation within the family.

Family Sculpting

Family sculpting is a technique in which family members create a picture of their relationships at a specific point in time by arranging their bodies in space. Alliances, triangles, and cutoffs in the family are demonstrated visually in a tableau. The experience is essentially nonverbal and "derives its impact mainly from kinesthetic, tactile, and visual stimuli."[6]

Family sculpting is a beneficial way to include hearing impaired children in the portrayal of family relationships. It has been our experience that hearing impaired children are excellent sculptors because they are often less inhibited and more comfortable with body language than their hearing siblings. Like the genogram, sculpting demonstrates to the parents the sensitivity and perceptivity of their hearing impaired child while affording an opportunity for the child to observe the resolution of a family problem.

> Family sculpting was used and discussed with Family B, utilizing three sessions. Initially the mother was asked to be the sculptor. Her sculpture portrayed the constant discord between J, who was deaf, and his younger sister. It also portrayed her feeling of isolation and sadness in the family. When the youngest son volunteered to sculpt the family, his tableau was a picture of how he wanted the family to be (that is, in a circle—each member facing each other with their arms entwined and with smiling faces). He instructed the sister who fought with J to look "half sad" because of their frequent arguments. When J was asked to sculpt, he also placed the family in a circle; however, he put himself between his parents. Interestingly, this was his assigned role in the family. It was beneficial for the family to see how he felt being in that position.
>
> The discussion of the various sculptures and of the sculpting process pointed out the manner in which J was isolated from, and was not included in, family discussions. The explanation given was that "he could not understand." This discussion also helped to pinpoint the mother's grief process as she expressed feelings of inadequacy, frustration, and sadness over his deafness.

Role Playing

Because role playing is especially useful with nonverbal individuals, it is an excellent tool for the hearing impaired child to use to report a problem or event. With role reversal it is possible to demonstrate certain social skills and methods of coping with interpersonal problems.[7]

The hot seat and empty chair are useful to enable the hearing impaired child to focus on a discussion involving deep feelings about an individual who is not present in the session.[8] Sometimes this is an individual from the past who is unknown to the hearing impaired child.

> Role playing and reverse role playing were used frequently with Family C, especially in relation to A's denial of his hearing loss. He refused to allow anyone to use sign language with him or even any gestures. He refused to watch a speaker in order to lip-read. Consequently, he frequently missed important communications and/or replied irrelevantly. Through reverse role

play we were able to demonstrate to him that he often appeared unfriendly or even retarded when he failed to respond appropriately. Through role play we were able to rehearse how he might tell people about his hearing loss and what was necessary for him to understand them, for example, face him and speak slowly and clearly.

Early in the course of treatment, there was much turmoil and discord in Family D over the anticipated marriage of the older daughter. There were many heated arguments, hurt feelings, tears, and threats to stop the marriage. B, a hearing impaired child, was very much aware of the arguments, but whenever he asked for an explanation he was told it was not his "business." His disturbance manifested itself in an increase in inappropriate and acting out behavior at school. During one of the discussions about the daughter's marriage, Mrs. D accused her husband of causing so much pain over the approaching wedding because of his feelings about his first marriage. He was certain this contemplated marriage would not succeed because his own first marriage was not successful. The empty chair technique was employed. The therapist asked the father to talk to his first wife who was represented by the empty chair. He was to tell her whatever he felt and had been unable to say to her previously. Through this B was better able to follow the discussion and understand the issues and feelings that were causing his father to object strenuously to his sister's marriage.

SOCS Model

The SOCS Model is a methodology for helping people cope with their social environments. The emphasis is on developing coping skills. This methodology can be used with groups or individuals. It involves examining various alternative options and related consequences in a given situation. It is followed by a simulation involving rehearsal of the specific skills.[9]

In using this model with the hearing impaired, we have found the use of a chart helpful (see Fig. 1). The chart is completed as the problem situation is discussed. Through completion of the chart, the individual is able to examine the consequences of choosing a certain behavior. The goal is for the child or adolescent to make more appropriate choices of alternative behaviors.

Figure 1
Problem: (Situation)

What can you do? (Options)	What will happen? (Consequences)
1.	1.
2.	2.
3.	3.
4.	4.

The SOCS model offers still another visual aid to treatment. It gives hearing impaired children as well as their parents options for choosing alternative behaviors. In demonstrating the SOCS model in sessions with families, hearing impaired children are able to develop specific ways to handle their feelings as well as their problems. Once again parents can begin to develop an awareness of their children's ability to solve problems. This all serves to help parents develop more realistic expectations.

Pictures portraying problematic situations or real-life situations from S's life were used for the SOCS model. S was accustomed to handling all problems by being demanding, angry, and unreasonable. We attempted to pose the possible choices of behavior. One example involved S's protests about coming for treatment weekly. We discussed this and devised the following:

Problem: S does not want to come to therapy any more.

What can you do?	What will happen?
1. Refuse to come.	1. Parents, brother, and grandmother will be angry. They may force S to come.
2. Cry and scream.	2. Everyone will be upset. S will feel awful.
3. Refuse to talk.	3. Everyone will be mad. Family will have to continue coming for a long time.
4. Come and talk.	4. Family will solve problem. Everyone will be happy. Family can quit coming soon.

Videotape

Videotaping family sessions with provisions for immediate playback helps demonstrate distortion or conflicts in communication and is valuable in revealing the nonverbal aspects of interactions. Family members become increasingly self-aware and often make constructive comments on their own videotaped interactions.

Because of B's hearing loss, explaining situations and alternatives was an ongoing problem for his family. B often refused to attend to family members' attempted explanations, by either looking away or talking continually. When this happened, his parents became frustrated and angry and gave up easily. The issue was never resolved. It was decided to videotape a family session in order to demonstrate this sequence of behaviors to B and his parents. During a videotaped session, the boys were reporting an incident that had occurred at a neighborhood shopping center. B insisted that the solution to the incident was to report it to the police. He refused to accept any other possible alternatives. With the use of the videotape, we were able to show B how his behavior was preventing any communication with him, and any resolution of the problem. It was also demonstrated to the parents, through modeling, that a gentle touch on the arm and a soft voice could calm B down. He would then pay attention to an explanation.

Projective Techniques

Projective techniques utilizing pictures can be devised to enable the hearing impaired child to develop the vocabulary for the recognition and expression of her or his feelings. One set of pictures should portray facial expressions, gestures, or body stance depicting various feelings and emotions. The child is asked to identify the feeling. If she or he is unable to do this, and the therapist can label the emotion, the child is then asked to create a story about the person in the pictures. The child is also asked if she or he has ever experienced those feelings and the circumstances in which they occur.

The second set of pictures should portray problem-solving situations and interpersonal interactions. These pictures can be utilized to discuss emotions expressed, social skills, and coping behavior. The situations depicted can be used as the problem to be solved via the SOCS model.

CONCLUSION

Although it must be kept in mind that our observations are based on work with only five children, and caution must therefore be used in generalizing the results to all hearing impaired children, it would appear that once communication skills have been mastered and communication within the family is established, acting out behavior in hearing impaired children and adolescents diminishes significantly. Family relationships in toto seem to improve considerably, and parents are then able to set more realistic expectations and goals for their hearing impaired child.

It seems that sometimes parents have not had the desire to improve these family relationships or that the diagnosis of a hearing impairment became a metaphor for "not communicating." By visually and experientially demonstrating to families "how to" communicate as well as "what to" communicate, we were able to help them grow. This was all possible without parents having to learn sign language.

These cases seem to substantiate the findings that have been reported in the literature regarding family dynamics with hearing impaired children who have been trained orally and/or manually when the hearing parents do not sign. Further investigation would be needed to determine if this would hold true if the parents were able to sign; however, it is our feeling that if the parents learned sign language, it would be another indication of their acceptance of the handicap and of their desire to include the child in family communication.

Although family therapy is a highly effective form of treatment with the hearing impaired, our findings indicate that treatment could be even further enriched by the inclusion of the visual, experiential, and educational techniques described here.

NOTES AND REFERENCES

1. R. J. Shapiro and R. I. Harris, "Family Therapy in Treatment of the Deaf: A Case Report," *Family Process,* 15 (1976), p. 89.

2. L. Brian Hersch and Michael A. Solomon, "A Comprehensive Approach to Understanding Deafness," *American Annals of the Deaf,* 118 (February 1973), p. 35.

3. Allan Sieffert, "Parents' Initial Reactions to Having a Mentally Retarded Child: A Concept and Model for Social Workers," *Clinical Social Work Journal,* 6 (Spring 1978), pp. 33–43.

4. S. Lowenbraun, K. I. Appelman, and J. L. Callahan, *Teaching the Hearing Impaired through Total Communication* (Columbus, Ohio: Charles E. Merrill, 1980); and A. H. Streng, R. R. Kretschmer, and L. W. Kretschmer, *Language, Learning, and Deafness* (New York: Grune & Stratton, 1978).

5. Philip J. Guerin and Eileen G. Pendagast, "Evaluation of Family System and Genogram," in P. Guerin, Jr., ed., *Family Therapy: Theory and Practice* (New York: Gardner Press, 1976); and Ann Hartman, "Diagrammatic Assessment of Family Relationships," *Social Casework,* 59 (October 1978), pp. 465–476.

6. R. M. Simon, "Sculpting the Family," *Family Process,* 11 (1972), p. 50.

7. Ira D. Glick and David R. Kessler, *Marital and Family Therapy* (2d ed.; New York: Grune & Stratton, 1980).

8. Muriel James and Dorothy Jongeward, *Born to Win* (Reading, Mass.: Addison-Wesley, 1971).

9. Jan B. Roosa, "S.O.C.S. (Situation, Options, Consequences, Simulation): A Technique for Teaching Social Interaction." Paper presented at the annual meeting of the American Psychological Association, Montreal, Canada, 1973.

Successful Treatment of Agoraphobia

Bella H. Selan

The term *agoraphobia* was coined by Westphal in Germany over a hundred years ago.[1] It refers to a fear of open places. *Agora* is a Greek word meaning "open marketplace," and *phobia* means "fear, terror, or panic." Today the term *agoraphobia* is used more loosely to describe a multiplicity of fears including a fear of shopping centers, supermarkets, restaurants, churches, expressways, and other places where there are crowds or people. Even the fear of being rejected, ridiculed, or confronted with unpleasantness is incorporated in the term *agoraphobia*.

Chambless and Goldstein suggest that agoraphobics are persons who have learned to "fear the fear" and that this fear is the central component of agoraphobia.[2] Stimuli for evoking fears or panic in agoraphobia are harder to pinpoint than those in simple, circumscribed phobias such as a fear of flying or fears of animals. Agoraphobic persons often say that the fear "strikes out of the blue" and for no good reason they can think of. The difficulty is that fear-evoking stimuli can either be external and quite identifiable, or internal and unconscious. A further complication is that noxious stimuli have a way of generalizing over time to other, originally neutral, situations. Thus, a child who may have witnessed a frightening event while playing near a lake, may soon be afraid of all bodies of water and may refuse to take a bath in the bathtub. By the time such a child has grown up, the fear may have spread more pervasively and extend even into unrelated areas. In this manner, the adult agoraphobic may not be aware of the root of the problem and will, like everyone else, think of the fears as irrational. The onset of agoraphobia generally occurs between the ages of 16 and 35. Sometimes an illness, death, or drastic changes in the lifestyle of the phobic precipitate the first attack. Simple phobias occur in equal ratio for men and women; agoraphobia, however, is overwhelmingly women's territory.

According to DuPont, 60 to 80 percent of all agoraphobics are women. Although this percentage constitutes a significant majority, many other forms of mental disorders such as anorexia, bulimia, and especially, depression are also more prevalent among women, particularly *married* women. Ardent feminists like Dowling indict women's acculturation, their fear of independence, and their sense of powerlessness when confronted by a male-dominated world. Another argument has it that women feel freer than men to express their feelings and are thus more likely to seek professional help when they are in distress. This is a seductive viewpoint adopted by many mental health professionals, who see more women than men in clinical practice. However, well-documented data are available that counter this intuitive and commonsense observation. It seems that more women seek treatment, because more women are emotionally disturbed. Whether this is so because of a biological vulnerability to mental disorders or because of social pressures or both is not now certain.[3] Because the majority of agoraphobics are women, the author uses the female client as the exemplar in this article.

AGORAPHOBIA AND DEPRESSION

Because depressions also occur more frequently among women and appear regularly in association with agoraphobia we need to look at this close relationship. Charney calls the link between agoraphobia and depression a "chicken or. . .egg" proposition. Depressions, he said, may be manifestations of the same biological illness as agoraphobia or may be a reaction to the restriction in lifestyle that agoraphobic people experience. Or depression may appear in people who are prone to depression and who also happen to be phobic and whose phobia then triggers the endogenous depression. In any case, phobia therapists are well aware that depression is an expected fellow traveler of agoraphobia.[4]

Unfortunately these depressions, whatever their cause, will not always yield to the purely behavioral interventions and may require a generic therapeutic approach ranging from drugs to in vivo desensitization and psychodynamic psychotherapy. As yet there is little agreement on the temporal order in which one should treat depression or agoraphobia. Hardy describes the emotional breakthroughs that occur *after* some desensitization treatment.[5] The author has observed the same with mildly depressed people who seemed to have to experience some relief from the oppressive, phobic symptoms before they could tackle their depressive ones. However, it appears that more severely depressed people do not cooperate too well with active treatment programs before some of their depressive features have lifted. Thus a fairly accurate differential diagnosis of the etiology of the depression and the agoraphobia should be made before embarking on treatment.

TREATMENT

During the past decade, great shifts have occurred in the treatment of phobias. Neither psychoanalysis nor other psychodynamic treatment modalities have been particularly successful in helping clients overcome phobic symptoms. Behavioral interventions such as imaginal flooding, implosive therapy, systematic desensitization, and in vivo desensitization have all contributed to the impressive success rates of the newer phobia treatments. Most spectacular have been the experiences of phobia therapists whose programs are based on in vivo desensitization sometimes combined with medications. The Phobia Program of Washington, D.C.; the White Plains Phobia Clinic; Terrap in California; Roosevelt Hospital in New York City; the Temple University Medical School Agoraphobia and Anxiety Center; and the Mount Sinai Medical Center, Milwaukee, all use in vivo desensitization.

In vivo desensitization requires that the therapist and the client leave the office and venture into the community to places that the agoraphobic fears. This treatment is simple to describe but rather hard to do. For example, Marks says, seek the evoking stimulus (ES) and keep the client in contact with the evoked response (ER) until the evoked response subsides.[6] The ES may be a crowded shopping center or a very private thought; the ER may be slight anxiety or sheer panic accompanied by unpleasant physiological and psychological correlates. We thus expose the clients to the most dreaded situations and require that they stop avoiding them as they have done in the past.

Most avoidances serve effectively as anxiety-reducing mechanisms and thus link the evoking stimulus with the evoked response in a tight cycle that treatment must interrupt. In certain cases, we can expose the client to the ES in imagery only (implosion), and this is sometimes effective. Relaxation exercises, however, are found ineffective and redundant by Marks and others.[7]

WHO TREATS AGORAPHOBICS?

Most phobia programs have a supervising psychiatrist, a psychologist, and a variety of therapists on their teams. Social workers, no doubt, have the necessary skills, training, and commitment to render effective treatment for phobias and have already worked in many settings as program leaders and therapists. Social workers can provide the psychodynamic aspects of treatment adequately but they need to update their skills in behavioral interventions. It is anxiety-provoking to some social workers to observe a client in acute distress, struggling to overcome the urge to run, while crying effusively. Social workers have been trained to be supportive and ease the burden of their clients; thus it may not be apparent to them that they are helping their clients by keeping them in prolonged contact with misery. If the client is permitted to leave while in a panic, she may become resensitized and experience another failure. Social workers and other phobia therapists need to postpone their own gratifications until they can honestly reinforce the client positively for "sticking to her guns" during exposure.

Many phobia programs also employ "phobia aides," usually ex-phobics who have graduated from the program and have had some training, or "community therapists," sometimes graduate students of social work or psychology, who also have received special training. Interested relatives may be of help as cotherapists and certainly serve well as companions to an agoraphobic who does "homework" and other assignments on her own. These aides and helpful relatives can also work with those professionals who conduct groups for phobic persons or can serve as leaders for self-help groups. The important thing to remember for anyone working with phobic persons is that what they are treating is indeed treatable.

WHAT ARE WE TREATING?

"Imagine yourself suddenly confronted by a masked gunman on a dark street at night," one of my clients explained, "and then you know what a real panic feels like." Small wonder, then, that agoraphobics have learned to fear the panic that is accompanied by terrifying psychological and physiological phenomena. Heartbeats may slow down or speed up, tremors may affect arms and legs, tension headaches occur, fainting seems imminent, and visual perceptions become distorted. Gastrointestinal responses add to the discomfort, which includes dry mouth, tightening throat and stomach muscles, nausea, diarrhea, and colonic spasms.

Agoraphobics also feel that they are losing control over their minds and lives and wonder if they are not truly crazy. Their avoidances of these dreadful feelings become very elaborate and not infrequently result in their staying home altogether, never venturing out into a world that they see as terror filled. Unfortunately, the more an individual avoids the phobic situation, the more entrenched the phobia becomes. In addition, phobic people are overpredictors and usually see the worst in the future. "What if. . ." is their most repetitive thought and question. What if I faint? What if people think I am crazy, stupid, or childish? What if my husband's boss does not like me? What if I get diarrhea and am on the expressway? There is no end to their "what ifs." Part of treating phobic people is to teach them to insert the word "so" in front of the "what if" changing the expression to "so what if." Anticipatory anxiety is a universal symptom of agoraphobia.

Phobia therapists need to remind their clients to remain in the present and forget about focusing on the future or pondering the past. Clients can be taught to change the thoughts (cognitive restructuring) that cause them so many unpleasant sensations. Clients themselves devise amazing ways of keeping themselves in the here and now. Some of them wear rubber bands on their wrists and snap them; others carry tape recorders and play music or the voice of a trusted person; still others begin to count all blue or all black cars on the road, or count houses as they walk. Others do crossword puzzles in cars or planes. We encourage them to do whatever it takes to bring them back into the situation at hand. We explain that their overpredictions are bad habits that they have learned and that anything that has been learned can be unlearned. We teach them to use rational alternatives to irrational premises.

Phobic persons are often seen as controlling their environment with their phobic maneuvers. Yet they see themselves as being controlled by their phobias and constantly fear being caught.

"If I accompany my husband to a movie or theater at all," Linda said, "I sit in the last row, an outside seat of course. This way I am sure I can leave if I panic and won't attract too much attention." Phobics have an exaggerated sense of importance and think that other people constantly observe what they do or do not do. Part of the treatment consists of assuring phobic persons that most other people think about themselves, just as the phobic does!

Since phobics perceive the world to be so unpredictable, they are always trying to bring some kind of predictability into their own lives. Sudden panics are the enemies that destroy their notion of predictability, so they stay out of situations that may bring on a panic. In this way their world contracts and becomes increasingly smaller until even total avoidance does not guarantee them absence of a panic. Many agoraphobic women are in exactly this position when they seek treatment. Their lives may have been seriously disrupted, their marriages may totter, their children are catching on that something is wrong, and they may have lost their jobs or have no way of getting to a place of employment. They may have had other therapy that had some benefits but did not remove the phobic symptoms. It is at this near zero point in her life that the agoraphobic woman has the necessary motivation to succeed with a treatment modality that stresses active cooperation and puts the control into her own hands. Without this strong motivation, therapy will probably fail. The phobia therapist needs to assess the motivational force and balance it with other phobic personality factors.

AGORAPHOBIC PERSONALITY

Usually female, the agoraphobic person is very sensitive and imaginative and somewhat shy as a child. She may have been overprotected by an anxious parent who may also be phobic. She tends to be very emotional, although withdrawn. She has few, but good, friends, is noncompetitive and unassertive, and fears confrontations and controversy at an early age. She rarely rebels against even outrageous treatment because she must always please others before she pleases herself. She daydreams a lot, but controls her own feelings rigidly or lets other people control them for her. She wants the world to be 100 percent wonderful and wants all people to be perfect, so anything less than that disappoints her deeply. She may have one or more alcoholic relatives, who interfere with her visions of the wonderful world. Early on she may have experienced an unusual number of painful separations or the death of an important person. She probably had to assume an unusual amount of responsibility, maybe for siblings, at too early an age.

In her magical thinking she is learning to overpredict, but she hides the resulting fears like all her other feelings and rarely lets on just how crippling her fears are. As an adult, the agoraphobic person has become so skilled at hiding her phobias that even experienced psychiatric professionals are fooled by the calm exterior and do not suspect the true dimensions of her disorder. Thus agoraphobics are often misdiagnosed and treated for numerous other disorders instead. Even when told of a diagnosis that she knows to be wrong, she is not likely to protest; being a people pleaser, she will not assert herself. The diagnostic interview with a person suspected of being agoraphobic needs to be fine-tuned toward those factors that can establish the diagnosis of agoraphobia with exactitude.

DIAGNOSTIC INTERVIEW

Many clients, having been exposed to the media, now refer themselves for phobia treatment, but not all of those who come and request it are agoraphobic. Other mentally ill or schizophrenic patients may have some phobic symptoms and would rather be diagnosed as having a phobia, which is curable, than as having an incurable illness. If the primary disorder is alcoholism or schizophrenia, phobia treatment by modern-day methods will not alleviate either the symptoms or the underlying illness. A very careful history must be taken and inquiries made about previous treatment, mental hospitalizations, and what medications were prescribed. I also require that the client's primary physician be informed of the type of treatment planned and, if a psychiatrist is already involved, I request that the patient have him or her get in touch with me and give permission to proceed. I also inquire about other phobic persons in the family, and ask about any early separations or deaths of significant others that occurred while the patient was young. I try to establish when the onset of the problem occurred, and I want to know who in the family is helping her to maintain her habit. Who shops for her? Who takes the children to school, the dentist, and the doctor? Who stays home with her when she refuses to leave? Who changes plans to accommodate her? Is someone in her family (preferably a close relative) willing to help her overcome her phobic symptoms? I also want to know the current level of functioning. Can she leave the house, cross streets, drive far distances on expressways, visit sick friends in hospitals, attend the theater or movies, or go to shopping centers? Under what circumstances will she or will she not do required tasks—

only days, only nights, only if the sun shines, only when she does not menstruate, only when alone, or only when accompanied by someone else?

In the second part of the diagnostic interview, I explain our program in detail, acquaint the client with the forms we use for homework and assessments, and explain that her full cooperation is required if she is to get well. I repeatedly assure the client that there is hope for her if she is highly motivated and willing to commit herself to a program that requires time and courage. She is told that we have many techniques that we will teach her so that she can help herself. In exchange for all this effort she will experience more ease and discernible progress in a time span that could be very short. I also forewarn the client that after a few sessions there may be an emotional letdown from the original enthusiasm and that even when the terrifying phobia reactions have stopped, she may be somewhat anxious but will be able to live with it. We discuss setbacks that may occur months or years after treatment has stopped, and the client is told that the techniques she learns *now* will help her to overcome setbacks *later*.

Clients usually ask me whether I think they are crazy and whether I really, truly, think there is hope for them. I again reassure them and then ask them to bring along their partner or husband for the second diagnostic interview. Before they leave, a fear inventory is given to them that they have to bring along for the second session.

SECOND DIAGNOSTIC INTERVIEW

If the phobia itself has not already upset the marriage to some degree, the treatment most certainly will. Involved persons, especially husbands, find the woman's phobia completely mystifying. How can this otherwise sensible, competent person crumble when she leaves the house alone? Why must a relative accompany her to the supermarket and why will she not go to church or a restaurant without suddenly running out and sitting crouched in terror in the family car? I try to explain to the client and the significant other what the agoraphobic is feeling but I do not try to invent reasons for the unreasonable. Instead, I encourage empathy and enlist the aid of the significant other in our undertaking. I give the relative or friend strict instructions about not being drawn into the phobic behavior.

An example of a husband who was drawn into his wife's phobia is Steve, whose wife, Michelle, had a dreadful phobia about bugs.

> Steve was not permitted to enter the house with a suitcase when he came back from a business trip. He had to remove all his clothing in the basement so it could be washed or given to a dry cleaner before Michelle would permit him to bring the clothes back into the house. He loves wearing hats, but Michelle would have none of it, because it meant that he had to try them on before he bought them. She feared that someone who had head lice had

tried on the hat before Steve did. If, as they drove through a neighborhood, they passed a discarded mattress on the street, Michelle would have the car washed before driving home. Steve could not bring home strangers; they might have been near someone who had bugs. And on and on.

Steve was given strict instructions to go right ahead and bring in his suitcases and to buy hats, in fact to make Michelle go with him when he did. He feared her anger. He was told to say, "Your therapist gave me strict instructions not to promote your phobia." In this manner Michelle's anger would be primarily directed at me and we could deal with it in session.

I explain to clients that a husband who permits his wife to interfere with his lifestyle will get angry and resentful, while the phobic wife usually feels guilty, thus starting a vicious cycle that surely will erode many a relationship. Instead, I tell the husband to reinforce his wife even if it is for effort alone and to be unstinting in his praise for successful trials. The cooperation of relatives is instrumental in effecting a cure, provided client and partner have helpful techniques.

HELPFUL TECHNIQUES

The client and partner are given a reading list and I recommend that they begin with Marks's *Living with Fear* and Weeks's *Peace from Nervous Suffering*. Weeks, an Australian physician who has worked with thousands of phobics, explains the physical base of nervous suffering and advises clients how to overcome their fears. Marks includes a complete self-help manual and describes professional treatment. Clients are also given an article by Powell, the coordinator of the White Plains Phobia Clinic, in which she explains how the clinic staff work with phobic people. Because I proceed much along the same lines as does the White Plains Phobia Clinic, I also use the highly sophisticated Task Sheet developed by Zane, director of the White Plains clinic, one of the pioneers in phobia treatment. Zane calls in vivo desensitization "exposure treatment," because we expose the client to the phobic condition and observe both the rise and the fall of phobic anxiety.[8] Zane has developed the Six Steps, which help clients view their condition with less apprehension.[9] My clients are also expected to learn the Six Steps.

1. Expect and allow your fear to rise and accept that you have a phobia.
2. When fear appears, WAIT.
3. Try to remain focused on things in the present.
4. Label your own fear level 1 to 10 and watch it go up and down.
5. Do things that lower and keep manageable the level of fear.
6. Try to function with fear.

Into these simple six sentences, Zane has managed to put everything that is necessary to succeed in the conquest of phobias. My clients must also keep a daily diary of events that relate to their phobic thoughts, sensations, and feelings. Each client is taught thought stopping and thought changing (cognitive restructuring) and is advised to use rational alternatives to irrational thinking. We go over some of the irrational thinking patterns and try to reconstruct them rationally. The client is encouraged to call me if necessary; few clients have abused this privilege.

The third session is our first field trip. Phobia therapists, especially if they are new to the field, are themselves sometimes reluctant to leave their offices, especially in bad weather, and, of course, the phobic would prefer to keep on *talking* forever rather than to start *doing*. I cannot stress sufficiently how defeating it would be to persist in just discussing the phobia instead of attacking it in its context, as the following example shows.

"If you had told me when I first came to see you that I would be riding elevators in a high-rise building during the fourth session, I would have told you, you are crazy," Eileen said. Eileen would have lost her job as an office supervisor had she not been able to ride elevators to her company's new office. During the first field trip, we approached an elevator in a low-rise building, then we entered it, and finally rode it. Then she went alone up to the third floor. During the fourth session she was able to ride up and down a high-speed elevator repeatedly and experienced only mild discomfort. To this day she occasionally experiences this mild discomfort but she is functioning and has retained her job.

During the first field trip, Eileen offered to pay me for the session if I just let her back out and go home. Tears were running down her cheeks, and she announced that she was about to faint. I assured her that if she fainted, I would know what to do.

Calm reassurance and the therapist's taking command of the situation usually alleviates anxiety. Many times a paradoxical suggestion will bring out the client's sense of humor. "Please try to have a heart attack," I instructed Barbara, who had begged me to let her out of the car as we approached the feared expressway. "Just feel my heart beat," she said, "I am sure I will die." Of course she did not, although she was pale and exhausted, but very proud, at the end of the session.

I have no particular advice to give to budding phobia therapists regarding the timing of demands made on the client, except to say that if you err at all, err on the side of asking too much rather than too little. You can always back down a bit, but if you proceed too slowly and carefully, the client will get discouraged with her progress and so will you. You must not, however, let clients leave a situation in a panic without first waiting for the panic to subside. Clients must learn that the peak of a panic rarely lasts more than 20 to 120 seconds, and that panic inevitably subsides even if you stay in the phobic environment. You may distract the client or encourage her to count something or to think of pleasant things, but mainly you should let her rate the panic levels so she can observe the descent. No harm has come to her and she has learned that the best strategy is probably to avoid complete panic by not letting levels exceed 5 or 6 on a scale of 10. In order for panics to be prevented, the client actively works on doing so, either filling out task sheets, changing thoughts, snapping her rubber band on her wrist, or holding on to a can of cold soda. The variety of defenses that phobic patients invent to stave off panics is truly amazing.

There is ample evidence that prolonged exposure to panic situations produces better results than short sessions.[10] Thus, a double session is more effective than a regular session, and clients should be encouraged to practice with relatives or phobia aides for longer sessions than they can afford to do with highly paid therapists. Having different persons help the client also prevents the excessive dependence that many phobia clients develop.

GROUP THERAPY

Group therapy is also used by a number of phobia treatment centers to treat phobias. Groups are cost-effective and also benefit phobia clients because a strong support system develops. Most phobia treatment centers encourage the use of phobia aides, or invite partners and husbands to sit in on the group at no additional charge so that they can help during practice sessions. Terrap in California and the Philadelphia Clinic of Temple University conduct two-week intensive therapy groups in which the clients are totally immersed on a daily basis. Follow-up treatment is then rendered by other therapists when necessary. These clinics report good results. The Department of Psychiatry, Mount Sinai Medical Center, Milwaukee, Wisconsin, conducts phobia groups regularly. We usually interview phobic clients to assess which treatment modality—individual or group sessions— best suits them. Groups each have six-to-eight members and run for eight weeks. A follow-up session after one month and another session six months after termination are scheduled. The assessment of clients prior to assignment to group membership consists of a clinical interview, a psychological testing session, and a psychiatric evaluation. The psychiatrist prescribes medication if indicated. We consider medication to be a helpful adjunct to behavioral treatment in certain types of panic disorders.

DRUG THERAPY

Some agoraphobic clients experience so much anxiety and so many panics that they simply cannot go into the phobic situation at all without some kind of medication. Phobics generally do not trust or like medications and often resist taking them even when they are indicated. But several researchers have suggested the use of imipramine and other antidepressants when panics are excessive or when the underlying depression interferes with the treatment. Zitrin, Klein, and Woerner find imipramine helpful but Marks does not.[11] Many phobic clients have been given diazepam (Valium) by other physicians and a few of them will take it on occasion; others will take a drink or two before going into phobic situations.

THE THERAPIST

A good phobia therapist is a secure, mature, and enthusiastic person who does not have overwhelming fears and who is imaginative and inventive. He or she must be firm and has to be able, in Shakespeare's words, "to be cruel to be kind." The therapist must not let the client manipulate the situation so that a set goal cannot be achieved. The therapist also has to insist that homework be done and should question the client quite seriously when it is not done. If the therapist is lackadaisical, the client will be too. A therapist who is comfortable working with both professionals and nonprofessionals will promote success with teamwork. Phobia treatment is successful and thus social workers, who often work with disenfranchised populations, will welcome the ego boost they receive from clients who improve rather rapidly and enthusiastically express satisfaction. If clinical competence is conceived as the ability to restore reasonable functioning to a once seriously impeded client, then the phobia therapist can expect to see his or her competence confirmed by the results obtained. A little success will go a long way in reinforcing both the client and the therapist.

NOTES AND REFERENCES

1. Carl Westphal, "Die Agoraphobie: Eine Neuropathische Erscheinung," *Archiv fuer Psychiatrie und Nervenkrankheiten,* 3 (1971), pp. 138–161.

2. Dianne L. Chambless and Alan J. Goldstein, "Clinical Treatment of Agoraphobia," in Matig Mavissakalian and David H. Barlow, eds., *Phobia: Psychological and Pharmacological Treatment* (New York: Guilford Press, 1981), p. 109.

3. See Robert L. DuPont, "Introduction," in DuPont, ed., *Phobia: A Comprehensive Summary of Modern Treatments* (New York: Brunner/Mazel, 1982), p. xix; Myrna M. Weissmann and Gerald L. Klerman, "Sex Differences and the Epidemiology of Depression," in Edith S. Gomberg and Violet Franks, eds., *Gender and Disordered Behavior* (New York: Brunner/Mazel, 1979), pp. 381–417; Walter R. Gove, "Sex Differences in the Epidemiology of Mental Disorders: Evidence and Explanations," in Gomberg and Franks, eds., *Gender and Disordered Behavior,* pp. 23–68; Colette Dowling, *The Cinderella Complex: Women's Hidden Fear of Independence* (New York: Pocket Books, 1981); Gove and John Tudor, "Adult Sex Roles and Mental Illness," *American Journal of Sociology,* 73 (1973), pp. 812–835;

and Gerald Gurin et al., *Americans View Their Mental Health* (New York: Basic Books, 1960).

4. See David L. Charney, "Depression and Agoraphobia—Chicken or the Egg," pp. 126–132, and Bella H. Selan, "Phobias, Death and Depression," pp. 133–139, in DuPont, ed., *Phobia.*

5. Arthur B. Hardy, *Agoraphobia: Symptoms, Causes and Treatment* (Menlo Park, Calif.: Terrap, 1976).

6. Isaac M. Marks, "Cure and Care of Neurosis," *Psychological Medicine* (Great Britain), 9 (1979), pp. 629–660.

7. See Thomas G. Stampfl and Donald J. Luis, "Essentials of Implosive Therapy: A Learning-Theory-Based Psychodynamic Behavioral Therapy," *Journal of Abnormal Psychology,* 72 (1967), pp. 496–503; and Isaac M. Marks, "Behavioral Psychotherapy of Adult Neurosis," in Sol L. Garfield and Allen E. Bergin, eds., *Handbook of Psychotherapy and Behavior Modification* (2d ed.; Chichester, England: John Wiley & Sons, 1978), pp. 493–547.

8. See Isaac M. Marks, *Living with Fear* (New York: McGraw-Hill, 1978); Claire M. Weeks, *Peace from Nervous Suffering* (New York: Hawthorne Books, 1972); Doreen Powell, "Phobia" (White Plains, N.Y.: White Plains Phobia Clinic, unpublished); and Manual Zane, "Contextual Analysis and Treatment of Phobic Behavior as It Changes," *American Journal of Psychotherapy,* 32 (July 1978), pp. 338–356.

9. Zane, "Contextual Analysis and Treatment of Phobic Behavior as It Changes."

10. Marks, *Living with Fear.*

11. Charlotte N. Zitrin, Donald F. Klein, and Margaret G. Woerner, "Behavior Therapy, Supportive Psychotherapy, Imipramine and Phobias," *Archives of General Psychiatry,* 35 (1978), pp. 307–316; and Marks, *Living with Fear,* p. 636.

Unemployment:
An Aggressive Approach
to a Pernicious Problem

*Jane F. Charnas and
Anne Weisenborn*

U nemployment during the early 1980s reached the highest rate since the Great Depression. Post–World War II statistics indicate that 9.8 percent of the available work force in the United States was either unable to find full-time employment, was underemployed (doing part-time or temporary work), or had been terminated from previous employment.[1] Optimistic thinking and political rhetoric alone cannot decrease the staggering number of men, women, and children who suffer the effects of uncertainty and anxiety from reduced incomes, rising costs of living at the survival level, and little hope of an immediate solution.

The consequences of social, political, and economic policymaking has exacerbated two major types of employment jeopardy. The first is actual job loss through employment termination (from reductions in force, loss of business, or economic streamlining). The second is the threat of that imminent reality. The casualties of these employment risks are calculated in the millions. They range from among the rank and file, less formally trained, and less economically advantaged to the upper echelons of white-collar management, the more affluent, and the better educated. The most numerous victims are blacks and other minorities, although no social class or ethnic group is exempt.

Heretofore, social work has been limited in its approach to unemployment. Job finding and placement, referral to career counseling, and employment training have been long-standing and important roles of the profession.[2] A basic value underpinning the field of social work is that productive and meaningful work is a basic human right. However, less attention has been given in both theory and practice literature to the intrapsychic, familial, and societal effects of unemployment. An individual who has lost such a major ego reinforcement will have decreased feelings of self-esteem and competence and will suffer profound psychological consequences. The majority of the unemployed are likely to be heads of households and this has a devastating effect on family equilibrium and functioning. Role expectations and their fulfillment are altered, often disturbing the basic integrity of the family unit. Possible linkage between unemployment and family violence has been noted.[3] In addition, unemployment contributes to social isolation and withdrawal; individuals and families often feel ashamed of their lack of economic participation in the community, experiencing a sense of not "pulling their own weight," especially if they need financial assistance.

In this article a theoretical framework and practice paradigm specifically formulated for working with populations at employment risk is proposed. The model draws primarily from Eriksonian and crisis theories, but also utilizes family, cognitive, and social networking perspectives. It is hoped that professionals working with people dealing with the economic, psychological, and social sequelae of unemployment—and this includes all areas of clinical practice—will find it useful.

THEORETICAL FRAMEWORK

Eriksonian theory provides a useful framework for working with individuals at employment risk. All psychosocial life tasks may be reactivated during this period; they have an effect upon each other and reaffirm the epigenetic nature of the theory. A person's capacity to trust in others and in the larger environment (including government and social institutions) can be deeply shaken upon hearing of an unexpected or impending employment termination. This foundation of trust, which enables us to interact affectively with one another, is diminished when our basic survival needs (our expectations to be protected by our economic, political, and societal suprastructures) are threatened. Just as "children become neurotic not from frustrations, but from the lack or loss of societal meaning in these frustrations,"[4] the inability to be a working participant in society becomes for the adult not just a frustration, but an injustice and betrayal as well. In addition, hope, which can be considered an adjunct to trust, is critically impaired when an individual finds that attempts to reach out in the environment will be met with a lack of concern and responsiveness.

When no longer receiving a guaranteed paycheck, an autonomous person feels a loss of control and may develop a perceived demeaned dependence on others. This is especially true if unemployment results in the need for financial assistance or social services. The Eriksonian stage of autonomy versus shame and doubt is illustrated by the humiliation and social withdrawal that many unemployed people experience; the ability to take care of oneself and one's family is threatened.

The task of initiative versus guilt is also reactivated during a period of employment risk. Creativity is reduced and is likely to be replaced by immobilization. Energy is dissipated when efforts toward working are thwarted. It is understandably difficult to mobilize one's physical and mental forces to look for work in a shrinking job market.

Positive work attitudes and habits, established during latency in the stage of industry versus inferiority, help the adult to become a competent member of the work force. And when the ability to be industrious and to be an active participant in the work force is frustrated by factors beyond a person's control, the individual's work ethos is demoralized.

One's identity, formed late in adolescence but continually shaped and refined throughout the life cycle, is the accumulation and blending of life roles. A major function such as the work role is greatly disturbed during unemployment. Because it is such a critical underpinning to one's identity, an individual is likely to feel a loss of inner cohesion and stability as well as outer direction. With prolonged unemployment, the adult will experience role confusion, role diffusion, or the possibility of role negation. Moreover, two important psychosocial life tasks of adulthood—intimacy versus isolation and "generativity" versus stagnation—can be profoundly affected by unemployment. The ability to give to or be sustained in a reciprocal relationship is drastically lessened when self-doubt, practical concerns, and an overwhelming amount of self-need surface. Defining the ways in which an individual can contribute meaningfully to society and its culture comes to a halt when that opportunity is denied. The person is left with the desire to contribute but is frustrated with regard to how. Obviously the longer one remains in this state, the more one's desire to contribute wanes, and the risk is stagnation.

When the crisis of unemployment is evaluated against these Eriksonian life tasks, it is striking how a statistical and social concern changes to a critical and personal aspect of one's adulthood. Earlier psychosocial issues, whether they were resolved satisfactorily or not are activated and if this period of employment loss is not rectified within a reasonable time, one's sense of integrity about life, the belief that one was all he or she could have been, may be unalterably damaged.

The second theoretical base from which the practice model is derived is crisis theory. Crises are defined as events or situations that are perceived to be stressful and do not respond to a person's ordinary problem-solving capacities. Typically, a crisis may be viewed as either a loss, a threat, or a challenge.[5] Crises that threaten an individual's basic survival needs or psychological integrity are experienced as overwhelming and insurmountable and evoke characteristic feelings of anxiety, helplessness, and hopelessness. These reactions may result in immobilization and the inability to utilize one's cognitive strengths for constructive problem solving. Unemployment, when it is not self-initiated or desired, is both a loss and a threat, precipitating a change in economic and intrapsychic equilibrium. It results in a range of inhibiting affect, cognitive distortions, a reduction in coping mechanisms, and in many instances, psychological paralysis.

It is interesting to note that underpinning both Eriksonian and crisis theories is the characteristic of hope. In the former it is considered to be "the earliest and the most indispensible virtue inherent in the state of being alive."[6] It is rooted in the early psychosocial crisis of trust and continues to grow, contingent upon a nurturing environment and adequate resolution of sequential life-cycle tasks. Hope may be lacking in the aftermath of overwhelmingly stressful events. Yet it is crucial that the individual in crisis begin to hope again. Given economic realities and actual job availability, it is often difficult or impossible to find an immediate job replacement. Thus, our primary clinical focus is to help diminish the crisis and to assist the individual to cope with what lies ahead.

PRACTICE MODEL

It is imperative that the professional recognize that unemployment or the risk of unemployment represents significant loss and deprivation and that the reactions to it can be profound. To deal with the psychological, economic, and social consequences of unemployment, four levels of intervention are needed: (1) treatment for immediate and long-term affective disturbances; (2) treatment for cognitive distortions; (3) environmental supports; and (4) advocacy to and for the individual in crisis.

Affective Disturbances

Intervention on an affective level should begin with a rapid, here-and-now assessment, including such areas of exploration as (1) job gratification, (2) level of investment, (3) emotional experience of the loss, and (4) the individual's attempts to cope. Assessment of gratification might consider basic survival, social interaction, role and role value, status, and prestige. Degree of investment is reflected by such factors as years of service, type of employment, and verbal affirmation, for example, "first good job I've had," and is usually a reliable indicator of the intensity and signficance of the loss. The employment risk can be experienced as a threat or bereavement, with resulting states of anxiety, depression, or a combination of both. Last, evaluation of coping skills includes that of current and past efforts particularly with job-related issues.

During this early phase of treatment, the second objective is to develop rapport with the client as quickly as possible. At this point two therapeutic concerns need to be emphasized. The first is that throughout a time of actual or threatened job loss, feelings of abandonment and mistrust run high. Thus, extra effort and attention should be directed toward developing and maintaining the therapeutic bond. Second, despite the here-and-now focus of this model, crises do reactivate old losses. Therefore, past disappointments, failures, and perceived injustices may be rekindled, making levels of anger or sadness appear excessive.

For the person experiencing job loss, long periods of anxiety and uncertainty may precipitate periods of passive helplessness and/or aggressiveness that in and of themselves can trigger even higher levels of emotional discomfort. Frequently the boss or parent figure who has "caused" the situation becomes the focus of the anger.[7] Because the employer is often too threatening a target, however, the anger may be turned inward or displaced onto co-workers, family, and/or friends.

In cases of imminent employment termination, the therapeutic task is to facilitate "worry work," which Caplan defines as anticipatory guidance, a technique used to help the person confront the threat in advance. Through encouragement, hope, and support, the individual is helped to face the scenario of leaving the job and planning for the future. Worry work of this kind can enhance coping, reduce anxiety, and relieve the burden when the loss actually occurs. Without it, motivation and hope may not be forthcoming, leaving helplessness and anger unchecked.[8]

The predominant affective response to actual job loss is characteristic of other bereavements. Shock and disbelief (even after warning and preparation) are followed by periods of emptiness, anger, and despondency.[9] People often describe these feelings as similar to those felt after "having lost their best friend" or "falling into a hole." Here the therapeutic task is helping the person mourn and do their "grief work." The professional encourages ventilation, sharing of feelings, and re-experiencing of pain and sadness from previous losses. Together, worker and client review the investment and attachment to the job. The goal is emancipation, closure, and substitution with other roles and activities.

No discussion of affective intervention is complete without mention of the possibility of suicide. For some individuals the loss of employment may result in so much depression and unexpressed anger that, combined with a sense of hopelessness and helplessness, the situation may present a real suicide risk. The worker needs to make a rapid and accurate assessment of this risk in order to take appropriate action.

Cognitive Distortions

A common characteristic of the state of crisis is that of cognitive confusion. Rapoport states that the individual "literally does not know how to think about the problem, how to evaluate reality and to formulate the outcome." In addition, cognitions become distorted and attention span is narrowly focused on the hazardous event. Typically, these distortions are self-incriminating and pessimistic in nature, for example, "I should have worked harder," "I'll never work again." Compounding this is the fact that the unemployed person spends a disproportionate amount of time at home, alone, and, perhaps for the first time, without schedule or routine. Loneliness and lack of stimulation can fuel obsessive rumination and self-doubt. Work for many is a bond, not just with the present, but with the past. Not to work is at odds with societal, familial, and religious values, and elicits strong feelings of wrongdoing and shame.[10]

The therapeutic task at the cognitive level is "mental work," that is, correcting misperceptions, cognitive restructuring, and rehearsing for reality.[11] The worker begins by encouraging the client to provide a perception of how the crisis came to be and how he or she anticipates the outcome. The role of the therapist is to refute faulty interpretations, for example, "I'm a failure," "No one can be trusted," and provide more empirically based explanations. The therapist also provides education, clarification, and reassurance to the client who fears, like many people in crisis, that he or she is "cracking up." Understanding that these feelings are normal serves an important restorative function.

Cognitive restructuring and generating problem-solving strategies is the second aspect of the "mental work" that must be done. It is essential that the worker maintain a flexible, optimistic approach that encourages consideration of alternatives.[12] If the problem has been revised from no job prospects to exploring new kinds of work possibilities, the means of accomplishing this should be broken down into workable steps, for example, (1) identifying job skills and interests; (2) listing jobs that require these skills; and (3) seeking out or identifying possible employers and companies where these jobs are found. Rehearsing for reality, the third aspect of cognitive work, involves emotional and behavioral preparation. Anticipating and planning for anxiety-producing situations, such as telephoning a prospective employer, applying for benefits, or telling family and friends about the job loss, can dispel tension, build coping skills, and increase feelings of mastery.

Environmental Supports

The environmental needs of the unemployed and their families are immense. Loss of income creates immediate threats to financial security and in some cases to basic survival. A sense of helplessness may be increased for those individuals facing unemployment for the first time, because of their total lack of sophistication about what benefits are available and how they may obtain them. Likewise, the maze of job information, training, and placement services may be incomprehensible. With a home mortgage, car loan, and other financial obligations in jeopardy, individuals may find that legal and consumer services can be essential in preventing further decompensation. Termination of paid health insurance creates a need for free or sliding-scale health services such as those provided by the public health department, Planned Parenthood, and neighborhood coalitions. Unemployed individuals, who are cut off from friends and colleagues with whom they may have interacted on a daily basis, can make use of alternative interpersonal opportunities such as support groups that can make a significant difference in their return to normal functioning. Encouraging community networking (among co-workers, neighbors, and relatives) may provide the person not only with a sense of shared concern about the situation, but hold promise of job possibilities as well.

Thus, the primary therapeutic task is that of linkage to interpersonal and institutional resources and to sources of compensation for the compounded losses of unemployment. Again, intervention begins with an assessment of immediate needs and survival techniques. Keeping in mind the hopeless, possibly numbed, and cognitively impaired state of the unemployed individual, the professional should use a directive, educational, and active approach. In order to connect people to necessary resources as quickly as possible, a thorough knowledge of community assets and how to best utilize them is crucial. Communication and collaboration among professionals is also a vital ingredient. It is further recommended that, during a time of widespread unemployment and shrinking resources, regular meetings between staffs of local agencies and organizations that work with recession casualties be conducted to facilitate feedback, identify voids in service, and generate mutual support.

Social workers must also become finders and developers of resources, while using the existent ones more creatively. Job banks and job skill training seminars do not require large funding sources, can be established quickly, and are of tremendous practical help. Support groups cost little and are a service sorely lacking for those at employment risk. Although some companies and governmental agencies have initiated this kind of service in anticipation of layoffs, it is generally not available for the out-of-work, isolated individual. Thus, family service agencies or departments of social services might develop support groups with the assistance of the local division of employment and department of vocational rehabilitation. Groups can offer emotional support, socialization opportunities, job-finding ideas, and an important substitute group-membership reference.[13] Better use of already existing programs, or use of them in combination, may provide the extra motivation or role replacement a person needs to compensate for a deflated ego or to approach a new alternative. For example, career counseling, coupled with an adult education course at a local high school, may give just the right amount of direction and confidence to help the individual feel functional and goal oriented again.

Any discussion of resources would be incomplete without mention of the family—in many cases the most important resource of all. Involving family members in the treatment process and educating them about what is happening can help to foster a spirit of teamwork at a time when it is needed most. It can serve to keep the individual connected to an important social system and ward off isolative tendencies. Family group sessions can be used to encourage sharing of feelings, generate reality-based thinking, and discuss adaptation to role and lifestyle changes. When problem-solving strategies are devised, tasks can be assigned to all family members to reinforce themes of cooperation and mutuality.

Advocacy

Advocacy, the fourth level of intervention, may be viewed as a synthesis or culmination of the other three target areas. At this level the therapeutic task is that of mobilization and motivation. The goal is to inspire and catalyze growth and change, all of which involve emotions, perceptions, and resources. The role of the social worker remains an active, dynamic one; he or she must advocate not just in behalf of the client but to the client as well.

To accomplish these objectives, several techniques must be utilized. Reshaping and feedback is used to help the client perceive the loss of employment as less of a tragedy and more as a challenge and opportunity to try something new—to take the chance that routine and security did not permit. Hope is continually emphasized as is self-expression and evaluation of personal and career goals. Unemployment can produce a period of self-reflection and reassessment of life priorities.

A second technique involves goal-setting and problem-solving strategizing. The social worker may need to help the client to develop a systematic job-hunting plan and assist him or her in carrying it out. In some instances it may be appropriate to contact prospective employers ahead of time to sensitize them to the client's circumstances. As an advocate, the social worker may need to assume a teaching role, not only concerning interviewing skills but basic job skills as well, that is, dress, speech, office conduct, and so on.[14] As the individual is mobilized to go on interviews, apply for benefits, and make job applications, further anticipatory guidance must take place to plan and prepare for possible rejections and disappointment.

A continuous effort will have to be made to structure and focus the problem-solving activities and to develop awareness of such tension-reducing exercises as procrastination, repetition, and rumination. At a time when the ego is still very fragile, the importance of positive reinforcement and focusing on strengths and accomplishments cannot be emphasized enough. The social worker needs to have an awareness of his or her own fears and feelings about job loss, particularly when the political times have threatened the profession as a whole. He or she must remain a catalyst, utilizing hope in an appropriate, realistic manner. Too little hope on the part of the social worker may further exacerbate the client's sense of crisis and may contribute to further immobilization, while unrealistic or unfounded hope may alienate the client's sense of trust.[15]

THE R FAMILY

Consisting of Mr. R, 44; Mrs. R, a homemaker, 38; Lilah, 14; and John, 11, the R family came to the agency when Mr. R was laid off from his

17-yearlong job as a steelworker. Because the company experienced a loss of business contracts, Mr. R was let go with no foreseeable resumption date. Because of the highly specialized nature of his work, the economic situation, and an abundance of co-workers in the same predicament, there was little likelihood that Mr. R would find another job easily.

Mr. R came in alone in crisis. He was deeply despondent and had just brought himself to the point of telling his wife what had happened. He had put off sharing the seriousness of the situation for about a week, telling her it was a two-week layoff. He recounted tearfully that he had broken down the day before, unable to hide the gravity of things any longer, needing support himself. He stated that while his wife attempted to comfort him, she had broken down herself, becoming extremely anxious about what they would do—how would they pay the mortgage, buy food, make the car payments? "These are questions I've been asking myself all week," Mr. R said. "I had no answers for her."

Mr. R initially had a great need to talk about his termination and demonstrated a wide range of emotional affect—disbelief that this could happen to someone who had worked as hard as himself, rage toward his company's and his country's indifference to him and his family, fear that he would lose everything he had worked for, self-doubt that he would be able to find another job, and depression, indicating his sense of hopelessness and shame. The worker recognized that Mr. R also had a great many cognitive distortions about his situation, some of which were impeding his ability to think clearly and make necessary decisions. These included his belief that he was a failure, that he had let his family down, that he might never find another job for which he was suited, and, the most severe, that his family might be better off if he were dead so that they could live off his life insurance. Before these cognitive distortions could be examined and altered, the worker allowed Mr. R sufficient time to ventilate his feelings. She sensitively treated the situation as a crisis, being available for short periods of time daily either by phone or in the office. Very soon after treatment began, Mrs. R was included and, while she needed to deal with her feelings too, she quickly rallied to support her husband, recognizing the severity of his needs. Once Mr. R's feelings were expressed, the worker focused on his immobilizing and self-destructive cognitive perceptions. Each one was examined in detail in an empathic, respectful manner, holding it up to rational scrutiny. The most severe, that is, Mr. R's suicidal thoughts, were dealt with first, and it was pointed out that his family needed him more than ever, and that for him to kill himself would validate his other distortions that he was a failure and had let his family down. Mrs. R was pivotal in helping her husband in this area.

The worker painstakingly raised with Mr. R life task issues that had been reactivated by this crisis—his shaken sense of trust, loss of autonomy, and inertia due to the reality of diminished opportunities and goals. She reviewed other life roles that had meaning to Mr. R—those of husband, father, coach of a community soccer team—to shore up his damaged identity. Issues of intimacy and generativity were focused on for the majority of the work, involving Mrs. R, encouraging and assisting her in providing nurturance and support. This segment of treatment proved exceptionally helpful for Mr. R—he seemed to derive a lot of comfort from "normalizing" issues of concern.

At this point the worker moved Mr. R into the problem-solving phase. Situational supports such as unemployment compensation and union benefits were explored. Mr. R had mixed feelings about utilizing such assistance, acknowledging that the money was rightfully his, yet ashamed that he had to ask for it. These feelings were accepted while keeping his focus on primary needs. The worker supported Mrs. R's desire to help out by returning to work. A former bookkeeper, she would have less trouble finding a position. Again, Mr. R did not handle this easily but was able to accept her decision. Both Mr. R and his wife were referred to the state employment service and other agencies that might help each of them to locate employment. Since Mrs. R's working would require some role changes in the family, the worker spent time with all members reviewing altered responsibilities. In addition, the worker recognized that Mr. R was having difficulty accepting the unjustness of what had happened and encouraged him to become an advocate for himself, by recruiting his fellow workers and the union to write to legislators and even to the president to protest the situation. This suggestion surprisingly brought a smile to Mr. R's face and the most enthusiastic response thus far. "That's a great idea! I'm going to get a petition." Throughout her contact with the Rs, the worker had the greatest difficulty with the issue of hope. While she wanted to convey a sense that things could be better, that Mr. R might be rehired or find alternate employment, she was also conscious of not wanting to raise his expectations unrealistically. She decided to take a forthright approach and found that Mr. R responded well to this. In fact he noted that he was glad she was "telling it to him straight and not trying to con him."

After ten sessions with the Rs, they were better able to cope with the crisis that had occurred and were less apprehensive about dealing with an uncertain future. The worker in this case was able to delineate those areas in which she could attempt to bring about change and those that neither she nor the Rs could control.

SUMMARY

Unemployment causes severe psychological and social problems among normally well-functioning individuals. Likewise, fear of unemployment creates a set of psychological circumstances that are not well recognized or addressed. Eriksonian and crisis theories provide a useful framework for conceptualizing the complexity of issues associated with unemployment and employment risk. Underlying the application of these theories is the assumption that work is an intrinsic part of an individual's identity. When an individual is abruptly deprived of work, the loss may precipitate a grief reaction as significant as that resulting from death or separation. Unlike death and separation, however, the reaction produced by actual or threatened loss of employment is not well recognized by professionals or by society as a whole.

The crisis intervention model described above has an obvious limitation as applied to unemployment—it is not geared toward, nor intended for, the marginally employed individual or chronically unemployed person who has never become integrated into the workforce. Rather, it represents an attempt to cushion the immediate and multiple effects of job loss, or feared job loss, and in doing so to prevent long-term maladaption.

NOTES AND REFERENCES

1. Bureau of Labor Statistics, *Baltimore Sun,* August 7, 1982, p. 1.

2. Abby Snay, "Career Counseling for the '80's: Providing Service in a Shrinking Job Market," *Journal of Jewish Communal Service,* 58 (Spring 1981), pp. 264–271.

3. Michael Waldholz, "Child Abuse Seems to Be Increasing in Areas with High Unemployment," *Wall Street Journal,* August 6, 1982, p. 17. See also Judith Gaines, "Children Feel Job Pinch, Too," *Baltimore Sun,* August 15, 1982, p. 1.

4. Erik H. Erikson, *Childhood and Society* (2d ed.; New York: W. W. Norton, 1963), pp. 249–250.

5. Lydia Rapoport, "The State of Crisis: Some Theoretical Considerations," in Howard J. Parad, ed., *Crisis Intervention: Selected Readings* (New York: Family Service Association of America, 1969), pp. 22–31.

6. Erik H. Erikson, *Insight and Responsibility* (New York: W. W. Norton, 1964), p. 115, as quoted in Angelo Smaldino, "The Importance of Hope in the Casework Relationship," *Social Casework,* 56 (June 1975), p. 328.

7. Gerald Caplan, *An Approach to Community Mental Health* (New York: Grune & Stratton, 1961), p. 55.

8. Ibid., pp. 56–57; and Irving L. Janis, "Emotional Innoculation: Theory and Research on Effects of Preparatory Communications," in Werner Muensterberger and Sidney Axelrod, eds., *Psychoanalysis and the Social Sciences* (New York: International Universities Press, 1958), pp. 141–142.

9. David Peretz, *Loss and Grief: Psychological Management in Medical Practice* (New York: Columbia University Press, 1970), pp. 22–24.

10. Rapoport, "The State of Crisis," p. 28; and Frederick Horzberg, *Work and the Nature of Man* (Cleveland, Ohio: World, 1966).

11. Rapoport, "The State of Crisis," pp. 28–29.

12. Norris Hansell, Mary Wodarczyk, and Britomar Handlon-Lathrop,

"Decision Counseling Method: Expanding Coping at Crisis in Transit," *Archives of General Psychiatry,* 22 (March 1970), p. 464.

13. Alfred H. Katz, "Self-Help Organizations and Volunteer Participation in Social Welfare," *Social Work,* 15 (January 1970), pp. 51–60.

14. Frederick Spencer, "Vocational Intervention: A Need for Social Work Training," *Social Work,* 25 (September 1980), p. 395.

15. Rapoport, "The State of Crisis"; and Smaldino, "The Importance of Hope in the Casework Relationship," p. 332.

Stepfathers, Stepmothers, and Stepchildren: A Perspective

Thomas Hlenski

T he higher incidence of divorce and remarriage indicates that the number of stepfamilies has increased dramatically over the past 15 years. As a result, social workers and others in the helping professions can expect to encounter more members of stepfamilies in their caseloads. Despite this increase, stepfamilies have received little attention in the current literature. Empirical research about this unique family living arrangement is almost nonexistent. There does exist a growing body of knowledge based on clinical and personal experiences; however, the information is often limited and does not emphasize the unique experience of individuals within a stepfamily system, such as the stepfather, stepmother, or biological parent not living with the children.

As a result of this paucity of information, social workers are making clinical assessments and formulating strategies of intervention that run the risk of being misguided in their attempts to mediate a change between the stepfamily, or stepfamily members, and the environment. Furthermore, legal, educational, medical, religious, and other systems affecting stepfamilies, uninformed by the social work community, remain archaic in their delivery of services to this population. Various myths and negative societal stereotypes continue to flourish unchecked by the facts.[1]

In the immediate environment, members of extended families, grandparents, relatives, and friends are unclear as to how to interpret the stepfamily situation. At risk are the stepfamilies themselves. Members of stepfamilies remain confused as to their respective roles and often feel the strain of being viewed as second-class citizens.[2] Stepfathers, stepmothers, and stepchildren have become, as it were, ecological refugees in an environment that tends to ignore their special culture and fosters instead a negative or indifferent view.

The importance of understanding transitions that a family experiences from before the separation and divorce through remarriage, and how these transitions have particular meaning for family members, have begun to receive attention in the literature. Messinger and Walker write:

> Problems that burden remarriage are frequently tied in with unresolved problems from the first marriage and with the transitional tasks from the marriage breakdown through the separated-divorced stages.[3]

Schulman, in her clinical article on stepfamilies, emphasizes the sequential stages of a family structure from separation to divorce and eventual remarriage and addresses the various characteristics and tasks created by each different structure.[4]

In this article, the author identifies some of the major clinical issues that social workers will need to consider in their practice with stepfamilies and stepfamily members. This framework regards the stepfamily both as a unique structure in and of itself, as well as having evolved from a prior family process that has particular meaning for the ongoing functioning of the stepfamily and its members. Special emphasis is given to the sequential stages of separation and divorce, reorganization and single-parenting, and remarriage, and how the stepfamily experiences and manages these transitions. A family therapy approach is discussed; however, this does not suggest that other modalities are inappropriate. Regardless of the treatment modality selected, workers need to expand their knowledge of stepfamilies in order to provide adequate delivery of services. Some of the issues discussed are illustrated with case material from the author's direct practice with stepfamilies.

SEPARATION AND DIVORCE

Despite the tendency to view the stepfamily as similar to the traditional nuclear family, significant differences exist that have particular meaning for the functioning of the stepfamily and the emotional and psychological development of its individual members. The stepfamily, unlike the traditional nuclear or intact family, is preceded by a prior family organization with its own specific history, culture, identity, and pattern of relationships that have endured over a period of time. Of greatest significance, however, is that the prior family structure has experienced a family dissolution either as a result of divorce or death of a spouse. This article concerns those families that have experienced family dissolution as a result of divorce.

Although separation and divorce may frequently be a healthy adaptational response to an unsatisfactory marital situation, this in no way diminishes the strong emotional upheaval that many families experience during this process. During separation and divorce, families are confronted with a variety of emotional and practical tasks that have to be managed in some way by their members. Identity crisis, role conflict, economic and vocational changes, a sense of failure, developing new relationships, and feelings of loss are just some of the issues divorcing families face.[5]

During this difficult period of readjustment, the marital couple with children is called on to begin to develop some type of coparental relationship. This is an extremely difficult task because it is hard for couples to separate the issues related to divorce from those of continued child care.

Involvement of the children in the marital struggle is a possibility at this stage. Unfortunately, there are at present few empirical studies of coparental relationships.[6]

In addition to the emotional and psychological upheaval experienced by the immediate family during the process of separation and divorce, relations with extended family members are altered and at times abruptly discontinued. Further complicating matters is the mixed and often negative view that is communicated to the family by the community.[7]

SINGLE-PARENT OR CARETAKER PARENT FAMILIES

In addition to the dramatic changes in most facets of family functioning inherent in the process of separation and divorce, many divorced families reorganize in a single-parent or caretaker parent structure. Typically, the single-parent family consists of the mother, who retains custody of the children. In addition, in cases of divorce, the single-parent family also includes the absent biological parent, usually the father, who maintains an emotional relationship of some type with the children, has predetermined visits with them, and provides some fixed financial support. These behaviors vary considerably from father to father and are often a continued source of strain for the entire family. Schulman underscores the importance of viewing the absent biological parent as part of the single-parent family system and the implications of this situation for the practitioner. She writes that to call a family in which the marital partners are divorced or separated a single-parent family is a misnomer, because both parents are living.[8]

The new sets of relations and transactions developed by the single-parent family system are in some ways determined by the impact of the divorce on the family and the degree to which the family mastered the numerous tasks involved in the process of separation and divorce. Of special importance is the nature of the continued parenting of the children by the divorced parents, because, for the absent parent, this represents a significant part of the family's ongoing relationships. Ironically, a good coparental relationship between divorced spouses may have a negative effect on the children, who may wrongly interpret it as a signal that their parents will reunite.[9]

In addition to the problems of continued parenting, the new family structures are often hampered by unclear role expectations or guidelines for behavior. Single-parent families are easily overburdened, because the mother is often placed in the position of being both mother and father. Also, these families tend to be plagued by extended legal battles involving custody of the children and financial support.

Another aspect of single-parent families that may have consequences for the ongoing functioning of stepfamilies is the phenomenon of the "parental child." Schulman writes that the parental child is usually the oldest child, who tries to assume the role of the absent parent. She adds that one of the inherent weaknesses of this phenomenon is that the parental child is accorded special power and recognition that is abruptly at risk if a stepparent enters the family. Competition, envy, and jealousy between the stepparent and stepchild could result.[10]

Divorce represents an end to a marriage and a significant structural change for the family. The effects of divorce on family members are considerable and long lasting.

REMARRIAGE OF PARENTS WITH CHILDREN

The caretaker parent's decision to remarry has implications for the entire single-parent structure, which includes the visiting or absent biological parent. When children from a prior marriage are involved, the choice of marriage between two adults becomes a whole-family affair. Remarriage, for these families, requires yet another shift, this time to include the spouse who will be a stepparent. The remarriage represents both an end to the prior family and a beginning for the newly emerging stepfamily. This may, of course, result in much ambivalence early in the stepfamily's development, because the marital couple is celebrating their union and the children are facing an end to any fantasy of their biological parents' reunion.

After remarriage, members of the stepfamily are placed in a position of creating, defining, and redefining their relationships and interactions, both among themselves and with the environment, with all the emotional and psychological obstacles and hurdles this involves. Complicating the transition to becoming a stepfamily is the lack of clear role definitions for family members and an uncertain societal response.[11] Stepfamilies are left, by and large, on their own to work out the intricacies of multifaceted relationships. In addition, there is some pressure on remarried families to operate in the same way as first-married families.[12]

Of particular importance for stepfamilies is the modification, to include the stepparent, in the existing coparental relationship between the divorced spouses. After remarriage, the children acquire another parent with whom they are required to negotiate a relationship. Furthermore, the relationships of the stepparent and of the absent biological parent to the children frequently overlap, and they can easily become competitors. For a variety of reasons, the relationship between the stepparent and the visiting biological parent varies considerably among stepfamilies, depending on such variables as the extent of the stepparent's involvement with the children, the nature of the postdivorce relationship between former spouses, the presence of a parental child, and the involvement between the children and the absent biological parent. It should be noted that in those cases in which the biological parent is deceased, the stepfamily must frequently deal with the ghost or fantasy of this parent.[13]

The inherent strain of stepfamily living is often reflected in the adjustment of the children. Frequently, the children's only role has been that of spectator throughout the process of divorce and remarriage. Many times the children are against the divorce, which is perceived as the loss of a parent. Furthermore, these same children are usually reluctant to see their parents remarry because it clearly marks an end to the fantasy of parental reunion. In addition, the children are asked to accept a new relationship with a stepparent who is often viewed as a replacement parent. It is common for these children to become noticed by the schools, as their academic performance frequently suffers.

In addition to the extreme complexities of developing new relationships among its members, the stepfamily is hampered more or less by the residual impact of the prior family life. Schulman writes:

> Issues and tasks which belong to an earlier period, and particularly those which were poorly resolved, tend to come up again at a time when the family enters into a new living arrangement. Old jealousies, loyalty struggles, competition and envy tend to re-emerge and affect both the new unit and the old split-off one. The reasons for this are the invisible threads which continue to link these families.[14]

Unfortunately, an overall lack of empirical research on these issues complicates matters for the social worker attempting to deal with the difficulties facing stepfamilies, especially in regard to the parental child and the stepparent/biological parent relationships.

CLINICAL WORK WITH STEPFAMILIES

Before attempting to work with this population, it is important that workers develop an understanding of stepfamilies' special needs that arise from their unique process of reorganization and their varying family structure. Differences among families in which either the father or the mother is a stepparent and those in which both parents are stepparents need to be understood. Workers must expand their knowledge of stepfamily functioning in order to assess dysfunction and provide the stepfamily with a sense of understanding and acceptance. In addition, the stepfamily's perception of societal responses and how these might trigger various nonadaptive behaviors should be investigated. Stepfamilies are often relieved when they discover that their perceptions of the environment are valid.

It is important that the worker develop an understanding of the transitions a family has experienced on the way to remarriage. These transitions impose new demands for these families and require new responses.

The worker should clarify how the family managed the many tasks involved in the divorce and remarriage process in order to rule out any residual impact on current family functioning. Careful attention should be given to the invisible threads that continue to link members of these families. Certain vulnerable areas, such as how the family managed the divorce, the modifications in the coparental relationship, the relationship between the children and their biological parent not living with them, the impact of remarriage on the prior family structure, the remote control exercised by the absent biological parent, and the relationship between the stepparent and visiting biological parent should be thoroughly explored by the worker.

Workers should also attempt to understand the meaning in terms of the entire family process of the presenting problem, especially when it involves singling out one particular family member. The presenting problem may actually be symptomatic of a whole-family problem. In addition, workers should be cognizant of the common problems that plague stepfamilies; these include lack of a clearly defined role for stepparents, problems with discipline of the children, and role ambiguity.[15]

THE C FAMILY

The C family illustrates how reorganization is affected by the past and how stepfamilies often pretend that the past did not occur or ignore its strong residual presence. The C family consisted of two adults each with an 11-year-old child by their former marriages. The reason for seeking social work assistance involved the father's 11-year-old son, who was described as not listening to his parents, as being manipulative, and as having caused an undue amount of tension for the entire family. Everyone, including the 11-year-old son, described the problem as such, and the parents predated the problem to the time of remarriage, two years earlier.

An examination of the family's past revealed that the son came to live with his father nine months prior to the remarriage because of his mother's hospitalization for alcohol abuse. During the boy's stay with the father, his mother died suddenly and the cause of her death was not fully disclosed to him. The son never attended any funeral service for his mother. During the time of remarriage, Mr. and Mrs. C apparently mistook the son's sadness as a statement of his displeasure about the remarriage. Part of their reaction was related to the heightened sense of anxiety about marital failure that remarrying couples place on themselves.

The tendency to forget the past was not limited to Mr. C, however. Mrs. C's prior marriage had ended because her husband was an alcoholic. This was another family secret, which had been kept from Mrs. C's 11-year-old daughter. Nonetheless, an examination of the present relationship between the 11-year-old daughter and her biological father revealed that a stomach disorder from which she suffered was related to her current relationship with her biological father.

The past had different meaning for each member of the C family and, in part, their reluctance to discuss it was related to their needs to move on with their lives. The result, however, was that this need to move ahead overrode the need of the 11-year-old son to mourn his mother's death. Furthermore, the son had no one to talk to about one of the most important people in his life and no one to share his memories of her.

The daughter reported having had a sense that her father had drinking problems. However, the family attempted to keep this as a secret from her, putting her in a position of "knowing and not knowing" at the same time. In addition to invalidating her own perceptions and reinforcing secretiveness, this covering up also caused the daughter to be uncertain about why her parents had divorced and may have fostered in her a sense of being partly responsible.

In working with this family, the author had to balance carefully between the family's need to move on and its need to go back into the past. The author needed to serve as a bridge for the family, linking the past with the present to undo problems created by unclear messages from the past. At the same time, the author had to be sensitive to the family's understandable hesitation to rehash old pains and old memories.

THE B FAMILY

The case of the B stepfamily underscores the importance of understanding the meaning of the presenting problem in terms of the larger family process. Mr. B was referred to the author after his psychiatrist, whom he had been seeing for 1½ years for individual psychotherapy, left the clinic where both he and the author worked. Mr. and Mrs. B attended the first session with the author and defined the problem in terms of Mr. B's depression and frequent outbursts of anger. They both presented a rather elaborate explanation of his symptoms in terms of childhood history and environmental factors not related to the family. Mr. B noted that there had been a small reduction in his symptoms, which he attributed to his individual therapy, but added that recently they were increasing.

During the assessment, the author discovered that the Bs were, in fact, a stepfamily. The stepfamily consisted of Mr. and Mrs. B and her two children, a son 19 and a daughter 16. Mr. and Mrs. B had both previously been married and had now been remarried for five years. Neither Mr. nor Mrs. B saw any connection between Mr. B's symptoms and the problems of reorganization that they had faced.

During a session that included the entire stepfamily and that was devoted to tracing the family's past, it was learned that Mr. B's anger and depression were very much related to his struggle with his wife and stepson over who was in charge of the house. In addition, the remote control maintained over the children by the absent biological father was such that the absent father continued to be a source of tension for Mrs. B and, as a result, for Mr. B to some extent.

In this family, the 19-year-old son was the parental child who saw his role as one of protecting and caring for his mother; he was having a great deal of difficulty separating from the family. The mother, on her part, had considerable ambivalence about releasing her son from the parental child role. As a result, Mr. B was feeling impotent as a husband and was playing second fiddle to a family process entrenched in the past.

The author focused treatment on helping the family redefine their interrelationships. At the same time, he helped them develop an understanding of the absent biological father's impact on the family system.

THE FUTURE

In this article, the author described a clinical perspective for work with stepfamilies. The importance, for the stepfamily, of understanding the transition from divorce to remarriage has been stressed. In addition, the author has emphasized the worker's role in tracing the family's past to determine its impact on the present level of family functioning.

The social work profession needs to conduct research to help differentiate among families in which the mother, the father, or both parents are stepparents. Unclear roles, especially those of stepfathers, need to be examined. Researchers and practitioners should explore family therapy as an efficacious approach to use with stepfamilies. Social workers who have expertise in treating this population need to develop programs to sensitize their fellow workers to the experiences of stepfamilies. Finally, the social work community needs to develop awareness of the special needs of stepfamilies. In the future, special cases will arise regarding financial obligations of stepparents, divorce and visitation rights of stepparents, as well as divorce and stepparents filing for custody of stepchildren. The legal community, as it attempts to resolve these problems, will need guidance from social workers.

NOTES AND REFERENCES

1. Gerda Schulman, "Myths that Intrude on the Adaptation of the Stepfamily," *Social Casework*, 53 (March 1972), pp. 131–139.

2. Doris S. Jacobson, "Stepfamilies: Myths and Realities," *Social Work*, 24 (May 1979), pp. 202–207.

3. Lillian Messinger and Kenneth N. Walker, "From Marriage Breakdown to Remarriage: Parental Tasks and Therapeutic Guidelines," *American Journal of Orthopsychiatry*, 51 (July 1981), p. 430.

4. Gerda Schulman, "Divorce, Single Parenthood and Stepfamilies: Structural Implications of these Transitions," *International Journal of Family Therapy*, 3 (Summer 1981), pp. 87–112.

5. Dory Krongelb Beatrice, "Divorce: Problems, Goals, and Growth Facilitation," *Social Casework*, 60 (March 1979), pp. 157–165.

6. Constance R. Ahrons, "The Continuing Coparental Relationship between Divorced Spouses," *American Journal of Orthopsychiatry*, 51 (July 1981), pp. 415–428.

7. Messinger and Walker, "From Marriage Breakdown to Remarriage," pp. 429–437.

8. Gerda L. Schulman, *Family Therapy: Teaching, Learning, Doing* (Lanham, Md.: University Press of America, 1982), p. 41.

9. Helen A. Mendes, "Single-Parent Families: A Typology of Life-Styles," *Social Work*, 24 (May 1979), pp. 193–200.

10. Schulman, "Divorce, Single Parenthood and Stepfamilies," pp. 87–112.

11. Emily B. Visher and John S. Visher, *Stepfamilies: A Guide to Working with Stepparents and Stepchildren* (New York: Brunner/Mazel, 1979).

12. Ann Goetting, "The Six Stations of Remarriage: Developmental Tasks of Remarriage after Divorce," *Family Relations*, 31 (April 1982), pp. 213–222.

13. Schulman, "Divorce, Single Parenthood and Stepfamilies," pp. 87–112.

14. Ibid., p. 103.

15. Harriette C. Johnson, "Working with Stepfamilies: Principles of Practice," *Social Work*, 25 (July 1980), pp. 304–308.

Counseling Married Gay Men, Married Lesbians, and Their Spouses

Arleen B. Nelson and
William S. Etnyre

Many lesbians and gay men are or have been heterosexually married. Some of these individuals and their spouses seek counseling to help them deal with many of the issues that they face as a result of their homosexuality. This article highlights these issues and discusses how social work intervention can be useful to them. Because the authors' observations are based only on individuals who sought treatment, we do not purport to generalize our findings to everyone who is, or has been, involved in a gay-straight marriage. In this article, *mixed marriage, mixed couple,* and *gay-straight couple or marriage* refer to a couple or marriage in which one spouse is lesbian or gay.

Gay men and lesbians comprise 8 to 12 percent of the adult population. Moreover, various studies show that 12 to 20 percent of all gay men have been married at least once. Studies of the percentage of lesbians who marry indicate that 18 to 35 percent have been married at least once.[1] Thus, we are dealing with a sizable number of people who are or have been involved in mixed marriages.

The authors initially began working with this client group when married gay men came for individual therapy to deal with disclosure and other issues. During the course of our work, it often became appropriate to include the wife in treatment following the husband's disclosure. Because of the difficulty and acute pain these clients felt, the lack of existing services for them, and our growing expertise, the authors identified Social Workers Northwest as an agency where people with such problems could be served.

LITERATURE REVIEW

A review of the professional literature indicates that previous efforts to assist homosexual people who are or have been involved in mixed marriages were minimal and were mostly directed at changing the homosexual orientation of the married gay male to heterosexual.

The authors found only two references in professional journals to therapeutic intervention that focused on helping the individual partner as well as the couple come to grips with their situation without attempting to change the sexual orientation of the male partner. Dulaney and Kelly, in an article about improving services to gay and lesbian clients, devote a few paragraphs to mixed marriages. Their emphasis is on the use of supportive therapy, education, and practical advice to assist the straight spouse following divorce. In an article on homosexual marriages, Gershman discusses gay-straight couples as well as gay male couples. He explores how individual and conjoint therapy can be used to help the mixed couple negotiate a successful relationship, without attempting to "convert" the gay man to a heterosexual orientation.[2]

Other references, though providing useful information about the relationship between gay men and straight women, do not discuss how these people might be served by mental health professionals. A few references discuss involving the wife in either conjoint or individual therapy in order to "cure" the husband's homosexuality.[3]

THEORETICAL UNDERPINNINGS

Our work with these clients is based on current theory as well as increasing professional opinion (1) that homosexuality is a normal variant of human sexual behavior, (2) that it is basic to one's core identity, (3) that efforts to change a gay or lesbian person to a straight orientation do not succeed, can be psychologically harmful, and offer false hope, and (4) that therapeutic efforts should be aimed at helping the married gay or lesbian individual and his or her spouse accept the fact of the homosexuality and deal with its impact in appropriate, realistic, and positive ways.[4] We recognize that married gays and lesbians can be helped to improve their sexual functioning with their straight spouses; we assert that this is a behavioral shift, not a change in basic sexual orientation.

Moreover, the therapists follow the basic values of social work: acceptance of the client and recognition of his or her right and ability to make choices.[5] To adhere to these values, therapists who work with this client group must come to terms with their own sexual orientation and homophobia.[6] Because of the deeply rooted homophobia in our culture, this is a process that includes ongoing self-reflection, therapeutic exploration, and consultation.

CLIENT POPULATION

The therapists saw approximately 50 clients involved in mixed marriages over a four-year period. Fourteen couples were involved in at least one conjoint session. More than 20 individuals sought counseling without the other partner's participation.

Clients ranged in age from the early 20s to the early 60s, with most of them between 30 and 45. There were about the same number of straight clients as gays and lesbians. Clients came from socioeconomic backgrounds ranging from working class to upper middle class. All clients were white except once, who was black.

ISSUES

Societal and intrapersonal homophobia persists despite increased public awareness and purported changing of values and attitudes about gays and lesbians. Thus, the homosexual orientation of one spouse was the implicit underlying issue as mixed couples grappled with a complexity of other issues. These issues included disclosure, isolation, loss, assault on self-worth, decisions regarding the marriage, child custody, the impact of religious beliefs, and intense emotional reactions.

Disclosure. As gays and lesbians began to be honest with themselves about their sexual orientation, they considered whether or not to tell their spouses and confronted the possibility of devastating consequences. Several gay men chose to bear the discomfort of "living a lie" and did not disclose. The remaining gay men and all the lesbians did tell their spouses, because they wanted to establish an honest relationship and were willing to face the consequences that would ensue. Their spouses initially reacted with intense feelings of shock, disbelief, anger, betrayal, and confusion.

Once the straight spouse knew, both partners were faced with deciding whether or not to tell others—children, parents, relatives, work associates, and others. The decision to tell parents and children was particularly hard. Clients often had to deal with unrelated issues in their relationship with parents as well as their own homophobia and fear of the parents' reaction. Clients often struggled with the possibility of adverse effects on their children should they know. When considering disclosing to other relatives, business associates, and others, the clients showed more concern about the possibility of rejection, discrimination, and harassment. Although a few clients told nearly everyone they knew, most were very selective about whom they told. Many clients told only two or three other people.

Isolation. Because they decided to tell so few people, gays, lesbians, and straight spouses felt isolated; they had shut themselves off from those to whom they usually turned for emotional support. They also felt that the few they had told did not really understand their situation. One client reported, "My friend told me I can become straight," and another said, "She told me my husband is just going through a phase." Isolation was more intense for straight spouses and lesbians than for most gay men, who quickly developed support in the gay community.

Loss. The loss of their idealized view of marriage was a focus of therapy for all clients. Whether they came for one session or many, they verbalized their pain as this view was shattered.

The gay men and lesbians experienced loss of their image of themselves as heterosexual persons; this loss was usually accompanied by an assault on their self-worth. They saw themselves as bad, disgusting, and perverted in terms of long-held views of homosexuality. They berated themselves for ignoring what they had been feeling and felt guilty for lying to themselves.

As the straight men and women faced what it meant to have married and unknowingly lived with a homosexual spouse, they experienced loss of their self-image. Husbands experienced an assault on their manhood and were insulted when they were rejected by their lesbian wives. Wives experienced an assault on their femininity and questioned their ability to attract and please any man. They felt inadequate, guilty, self-blaming, and helpless—"If I had been a better sexual partner. . ."; "I could compete with another woman. . ." They experienced an assault on their self-worth as they bargained to stay in the marriage even at the expense of their own sexual needs.

For clients who divorced, the actual loss of the marriage was added to the other losses. For those who had completed grieving the loss of their idealized view of marriage and loss of self-image and had worked through the assault on their self-esteem, the grief over the loss of the marriage itself was of less intensity and shorter duration compared to those who had not.

Decisions. Clients decided whether or not to stay married. Those who chose to stay married faced decisions on how to accommodate the gay or lesbian spouse's sexual orientation into their marriage. The clients who chose to separate worked on decisions about division of property, child support, custody of children, and a future nonmarital relationship with each other.

Religious Beliefs. Many clients were influenced by their religious beliefs. Some clients who had religious beliefs that supported homophobic attitudes were unable to accept homosexuality as a normal sexual orientation. Other clients questioned the discrepancy between homophobic religious viewpoints and other religious beliefs that affirm the intrinsic worth of all humans. Often they were able to use those affirming beliefs to come to accept homosexuality as normal.

Emotional Reactions. Clients experienced many intense emotions, the most frequent being depression, anger, guilt, and fear. Many clients reported mild to life-threatening depression. They reported inability to cope with ordinary daily routine, changes in eating and sleeping patterns, and suicidal thoughts. One woman made an overt attempt at suicide.

Most clients felt anger. Gays and lesbians were angry that they were homosexual; straight spouses were angry that their spouses were homosexual. As individuals learned that homosexuality is an orientation, they became angry that they could not understand or change it. "What causes it?" "Why does this have to happen to me?" As they began to accept homosexuality as an orientation, they became angry at those they held responsible for teaching damaging myths and lies about homosexuality: mental health professionals, educators, church leaders, parents, and childhood peers. Some used many sessions to vent their anger, and others acted out their anger. For example, straight spouses told others about their spouses' sexual orientation to hurt them. Spouses fought over possessions and money. Even children became targets of anger. One man, on numerous occasions, chased all over town looking for his wife and her lesbian lover and once broke down the door of the motel where they were staying and battered them.

Gay, lesbian, and straight clients felt guilty. The gays and lesbians felt guilty for marrying instead of facing half-buried feelings and for rationalizing, denying, or repressing them. They felt guilty for living a lie and for the pain they were causing their spouses. Straight wives felt guilty for failing to be able to meet all of their husbands' needs, even after they intellectually accepted that their husbands were gay.

Several wives felt guilty and blamed themselves for not having paid more attention to signs of their spouses' sexual orientation prior to or early in the marriage. "By marrying him, I condemned each of us to half a life."

Clients were afraid of being alone, of losing the emotional support of their spouses, of creating adverse consequences for children. Also, they were afraid of being ostracized and of losing financial security. They were afraid that the gay or lesbian person would encounter physical or emotional abuse, harassment, and discrimination. All these diverse issues were the focus of treatment for this group of clients.

TREATMENT

Treatment modalities included crisis intervention, conjoint couples therapy, individual therapy with one spouse, individual therapy combined with conjoint sessions, and group therapy. The therapists' role was both supportive and educational. We assisted clients in understanding the various aspects of their dilemma and in improving their capacity for decision making; we provided information as needed.

For example, we helped straight spouses to understand their partner's homosexual orientation through the use of clarification and education. When a straight wife voiced the opinion that "My husband's just going through a phase," the therapists acknowledged the client's hope that her husband's homosexuality would go away and her deep caring and love for him. We also reminded her of her husband's assertion that he is gay and talked about the view that sexual orientation is basic to one's identity.

In another example, we assisted parents to make decisions about child custody. We recognized the clients' fears and shared with them our knowledge that gays and lesbians do successfully parent their children and that the sexual orientation of the parent will not influence the child's sexual orientation.[7]

As part of the support and education, the therapists offered clients the options to use readings and support groups in connection with the counseling. The therapists maintained up-to-date lists of readings and community resources.

OUTCOMES OF TREATMENT

Social work intervention, based on the theoretical stance that homosexuality is a normal sexual orientation, is of service to individuals who are or have been part of a mixed marriage. Approximately 10 percent of the clients seen left therapy after one to three sessions when they were unable to get past homophobic views and feelings.

Approximately 10 to 15 percent of the clients used the therapy as crisis intervention; they expressed satisfaction that it had helped them to reduce anxiety, depression, anger, guilt, and fear. Most of these clients denied their own or their spouse's homosexuality, saying "It's only a stage," or "He'll be back when this man dumps him." Two couples weathered the gay man's affair with another man, terminated therapy at the end of the affair, and resumed their marriages. For one couple, this has evidence of becoming a pattern. Therapy was resumed when the man fell in love a second time and terminated when his love cooled. A straight wife came into therapy in crisis and remained until the initial shock, confusion, depression, anger, and fear subsided. At that point, she mobilized her defenses against acknowledging that her husband was gay, planned an elaborate program for keeping her marriage intact, and terminated therapy.

Approximately 10 percent of the clients, all couples, sought short-term therapy to clarify specific issues. By using the therapist as educator and supporter, they were able to increase their understanding of sexual orientation and their thoughts and feelings about it. This process supported them in making appropriate decisions. One couple, who traveled several hundred miles for a two-hour consultation, clarified their understanding of the husband's homosexual orientation. They left knowing that he was gay and that this was not a phase. The wife wrote a few weeks later stating that the session had mobilized them to make important and satisfying decisions about divorce and custody matters.

The remaining 65 to 70 percent of the clients used longer-term therapy to work through losses and emotional reactions, to accept their own homosexual orientation or that of their spouses, to explore and accept homophobic views and feelings, and to assist them in making decisions. Some examples highlight how couples and individuals used longer-term counseling to resolve a variety of issues and feelings and to make appropriate and satisfying decisions.

Four couples remained in their marriages by accepting the reality of the man's gay orientation and accommodating their marriage to include it. One of those couples spent six months reaching their decision. During that time they considered divorce; looked at financial matters; explored ways they each could achieve sexual satisfaction; verbalized anger, fear, and guilt; and discovered what each partner wanted from the other. The therapists supported them in learning to experience their feelings and encouraged them to take time to clarify their needs so that their decisions were appropriate, satisfying, and not precipitous.

Another couple, who had earlier agreed to an open marriage, used therapy to examine the feasibility of continuing this arrangement. Both fully accepted the husband's strong need for same-sex relationships. The wife experienced being left out when her husband had a long-term affair with a man, asserted that she needed the continuity of a monogamous relationship, and initiated divorce.

Several individuals were faced with a unilateral decision on the part of the other spouse to leave. These clients were able to complete their grief process and then to move on with a sense of restored self-image and self-worth.

IMPLICATIONS FOR PRACTICE AND POLICY DEVELOPMENT

As indicated by the practice described here, we are dealing with a neglected yet a sizable client group. As an increasing number of people in mixed marriages "come out of the closet" and ask for social work services in the 1980s, workers will be challenged to educate themselves on current knowledge about this field and to examine their own attitudes and feelings about homosexuality and this client group. Schools of social work, continuing-education programs, and in-service training programs in agencies must take an active role in providing social workers with adequate knowledge and skills relevant to these issues. Social workers need to know

> that exclusive homosexuality probably is so deeply ingrained that one should not attempt nor expect to change it. Rather, it would probably make more sense to simply recognize it as a basic component of a person's core identity and to help the client develop more positive feelings about and respect for his or her sexual proclivities.[8]

Also, social workers should know that, although many mixed couples choose to divorce, others can negotiate a satisfying marriage. The social worker who does not have adequate knowledge of this area or is uncomfortable working with these clients must know resources in the community from which to seek consultation or make appropriate referrals.

Any actions the social worker takes to eliminate societal homophobia will benefit these clients. Such actions may include (1) working through one's own homophobia and assisting colleagues to do the same, (2) educating other professional and community groups about homosexuality, and (3) supporting political action aimed at protecting the civil rights of gays and lesbians.[9]

The profession of social work must expand its knowledge base through further study and research of this client group in order to improve services to them. Study of a much larger number of mixed couples and persons who have been in a mixed marriage would be invaluable. Such studies should include individuals who do not seek treatment as well as those who do.

Some specific questions and areas for further study are

1. What factors contribute to a satisfying marriage for those mixed couples who choose this option? How do they work it out?
2. For couples who choose to divorce, what contributes to constructive dissolution? How then do these couples relate to each other following the divorce and how can they be helped to make this transition constructive?
3. How can social work intervention serve people who are considering entering into a mixed marriage?
4. Follow-up study of the effectiveness with this client group of social work intervention that is based on current knowledge about homosexuality and mixed couples is important. What is the long-range impact of social work intervention on the successful resolution of the many issues these individuals bring to treatment?

CONCLUSION

The authors' work with mixed couples and people who have been in a mixed marriage indicates that social work intervention based on current knowledge of homosexuality and the needs of these clients is invaluable in assisting clients resolve a variety of difficult issues. This sizable client group has been virtually ignored by the social work profession. To provide adequate and sensitive services to these individuals, social workers must prepare themselves through education and through examination of their own views and feelings about homosexuality. The latter is a particularly important issue because of the persistent nature of homophobia within our culture.

68 *Nelson and Etnyre*

NOTES AND REFERENCES

. Figures for percentage of gays and lesbians in the adult population from Raymond M. Berger, "The Unseen Minority: Older Gays and Lesbians," *Social Work*, 27 (May 1982), pp. 236–242; Diana D. Dulaney and James Kelly, "Improving Services to Gay and Lesbian Clients," *Social Work*, 27 (March 1982), pp. 178–183; and Sandra J. Potter and Trudy E. Darty, "Social Work and the Invisible Minority: An Exploration of Lesbianism," *Social Work*, 26 (May 1981), pp. 187–192. Figures for the percentage of gay men and lesbians who marry from Alan P. Bell and Martin S. Weinberg, *Homosexualities* (New York: Simon & Schuster, 1978), pp. 162, 166.

2. Dulaney and Kelly, "Improving Services to Gay and Lesbian Clients"; and Harry Gershman, "Homosexual Marriages," *The American Journal of Psychoanalysis*, 41, No. 2 (1981), pp. 149–159.

3. John Malone, *Straight Women/Gay Men* (New York: Dial Press, 1980); Rebecca Nahas and Myra Turley, *The New Couple: Women and Gay Men* (New York: Seaview Books, 1979); Michael W. Ross, "Heterosexual Marriage of Homosexual Males," *Journal of Sex and Marital Therapy*, 5 (Summer 1979), pp. 142–151; Myra S. Hatterer, "The Problems of Women Married to Homosexual Men," *American Journal of Psychiatry*, 131 (March 1974), pp. 275–277; and Aaron L. Rutledge, "Treatment of Male Homosexuality Through Marriage Counseling: A Case Presentation," *Journal of Marriage and Family Counseling*, 1 (January 1975), pp. 51–62.

4. Alan Bell, Martin S. Weinberg, and Sue Kiefer Hammersmith, *Sexual Preference* (Bloomington: Indiana University Press, 1981), pp. 210–211; Sophie Freud Lowenstein, "Understanding Lesbian Women," *Social Casework*, 61 (January 1980), pp. 29–38; Marny Hall, "Lesbian Families: Cultural and Clinical Issues," *Social Work*, 23 (September 1978), pp. 380–385; Potter and Darty, "Social Work and the Invisible Minority"; Raymond M. Berger and James J. Kelly, "Do Social Work Agencies Discriminate Against Homosexual Job Applicants?" *Social Work*, 26 (May 1981), pp. 193–198; Berger, "The Unseen Minority"; and Dulaney and Kelly, "Improving Services to Gay and Lesbian Clients."

5. Florence Hollis, *Casework: A Psychosocial Therapy* (2d ed.; New York: Random House, 1972), pp. 14–15.

6. Dulaney and Kelly, "Improving Services to Gay and Lesbian Clients."

7. Ibid.

8. Bell, Weinberg, and Hammersmith, *Sexual Preference*, p. 211.

9. See Hilda Hidalgo, Travis L. Peterson, and Natalie Jane Woodman, eds., *Lesbian and Gay Issues: A Resource Manual for Social Workers* (Silver Spring, Md.: National Association of Social Workers, 1985).

Group Therapy with Adolescent Female Victims of Incest

Robert P. Dunleavy and
Mary Lou Misci

In July 1980, the Children's Bureau of Delaware instituted a program that was to use a comprehensive approach to working with all members of incestuous families. It was called the Intra-Family Sexual Abuse Treatment Program (IFSATP) and was funded by Title XX through the Delaware State Division of Social Services. The original contract, which ran from July 1, 1980 through July 30, 1981, called for, in addition to individual, family, and couple counseling, the establishment of group therapy sessions for the female adolescent victims.

In 1981, the agency looked for additional funding to focus on and ensure the continuation of this Adolescent Victims' Group. The agency's increasing commitment to working with this population came from what had been learned, from the parent program as well as from the initial adolescent group, of the psychological, emotional, and social needs of these young women. Additional funds were obtained from the Law Enforcement Assistance Agency (LEAA) through a grant from the Delaware Criminal Justice Commission.

In this article, we focus solely on the Adolescent Victims' Group component of the program. Group I began in January 1981, and was funded under the original contract with the Division of Social Services. Groups II and III were funded by the Delaware Criminal Justice Commission and began in June and September 1981, respectively.[1]

It was decided that a group co-led by male and female cotherapists was the modality that could best serve this young population by providing them with (1) a safe environment to talk about the incestuous experience, (2) the knowledge that others have had a similar experience, and (3) the skills necessary to get in touch with their feelings about themselves, their mothers, and the perpetrators.[2]

THEORETICAL STANCE

The focus of the Adolescent Victims' Group was the adolescent and her needs. We found the adolescents with whom we worked to be angry, depressed, confused, frightened, and in many cases, socially isolated.

They experienced these powerful feelings in addition to having to work on the normal adolescent developmental issues of identity, independence, authority, and emergent sexuality. It was clear that any mode of intervention that was to be accepted and effective would have to be carefully tailored to our clients' needs.

We chose to run a group in conjunction with individual treatment because (1) group activity is part of an adolescent's normal development, (2) peer contact is so necessary at this stage in adolescent development, and (3) we wanted to attempt to lessen the effects of isolation and perceived stigmatization. We incorporated into our group process what Yalom described as "curative factors." He identified 11 of these curative factors that the authors believe were present and addressed in our adolescent groups. They are: (1) instillation of hope, (2) universality, (3) imparting of information, (4) altruism, (5) corrective recapitulation of the primary family group, (6) development of socializing techniques, (7) imitative behavior, (8) interpersonal behavior, (9) group cohesiveness, (10) catharsis, and (11) existential factors.[3]

We believe that Yalom's concepts are understood by our colleagues and feel the need to expand only on those in which our use and understanding may differ from his interpretation. Instillation of hope has been interpreted by us as acknowledging the adolescent's victimization while instilling the belief that she need not portray the victim role throughout her life. Imitative behavior we see not only as being able to learn from the therapy of another person in the group,[4] but as learning from the role models presented to the group by the cotherapists. The members of our groups had not experienced men and women as equals. Nor had they experienced a man and woman who could be both strong and sensitive as circumstances demanded.

The existential factors are perhaps the most difficult to convey in our work with these young women. To many of our young clients, the notion that they could make choices that could change the direction of their lives was initially met with disbelief. They appeared to be basically fatalists. However, as we continued to enforce such ideas as "I must take ultimate responsibility for the way I live my life no matter how much guidance and support I get from others," we saw change.[5]

Our use of group therapy is by no means unique. What we believe to be the unique nature of our experience is that we see ourselves as social workers weaving feminist theory throughout our therapy sessions. Using this philosophy we acknowledged that the socialization of women into subordinate roles in this society begins in early childhood, as our client population clearly shows. We believe it is destructive to blame women/female children for those problems that have their roots in a sexist social order.[6]

We tried to help our group members see the connection between their personal troubles and social issues, for example, to identify those conditions that have been oppressive for them and women in general, including their mothers.[7] We acknowledged that sometimes their behavior, for example, running away, drugs, promiscuity, and so on, is an understandable reaction to oppressive and unbearable conditions. In addition, throughout the group experience, we use ourselves as examples by rejecting rigid sex-role stereotypes and by being strong, sensitive, caring, or authoritative regardless of our sex. We encouraged our members to act assertively in their own behalf, and we feel we are working toward empowerment when we give them as much control as possible over their environment and activities in the group.

GROUP COMPOSITION

Our group members were all adolescent females who were victims of some form of intrafamily sexual abuse. They ranged in age from 12 to 17 with a median age of 15 years. The girls were referred for therapy by their state child protective worker soon after the incest disclosure. In most cases, one of the cotherapists from the Children's Bureau would accompany the child protective worker to meet with victims as soon as possible. On the initial visit, the group program was introduced to the girls; they were told when and where the group met, its reason for being, and its goals. It was made clear that attendance at the group would be voluntary, but they were strongly encouraged to attend at least one meeting. The girls were visited at least twice so that a relationship existed before they entered a group.

Group I began with 9 members and was designed to be a closed group run for 20 sessions. Group II differed from Group I in that it was developed as an open group to allow immediate access by a victim after an incestuous disclosure. The number of sessions were left open. Though this group had an overall membership of 10, attendance by the members was not consistent. Group III, also an open group, began with a core membership of 7 girls, 4 of whom had been in Group I and felt the need for "more help." The overall membership of this group reached 11. All three groups were biracial and the members came from working-class families or from families on AFDC.

Group I met weekly on Monday evenings for an hour and a half. Groups II and III met weekly on Tuesday evenings in the lounge at the Children's Bureau for an hour and a half. This provided an informal setting and easy access to the soda machine. However, in Group III, the members' smoking became an issue for the nonsmokers and a decision was made to move to a room with better ventilation. The group members chose the Board Room, where sitting around the table seemed to facilitate working on heretofore untouched issues, such as confrontation.

METHODOLOGY

The group process, intertwined with feminist theory, and using male and female cotherapists, was our primary method of practice. We found several benefits to this model: (1) it forced the group members to recognize their feelings about men in general and the perpetrator, in particular, (2) it encouraged them to assess their stereotypical views of men and women, and (3) it provided an approximation of a primary family group. In contrast to what others have hypothesized, our members used the experience with a male therapist constructively to work out their fears and hostilities.[8]

We believe that it was more than just the use of both sexes that allowed the members to work through many issues in the group; it was also the manner in which we used ourselves, not only as therapists, but in the way we expressed our own masculinity or femininity. It was essential to be caring and empathic and, we felt, particularly important to be genuine if we were to be accepted by the adolescents. We often disagreed in the group, a point addressed by Shulman:

> Finally, we had an understanding that we would feel free to disagree in the group. In many ways, the co-worker and I were a model of a male/female relationship in action. It would be a mockery of our effort if we supported honesty and willingness to confront while maintaining professional "courtesy" towards each other in the group. Observing co-leaders disagree, even argue in a group and still respect and care for each other can be a powerful object lesson for group members.[9]

This was especially relevant for group members whose experience with male/female confrontations has generally involved some form of violence.

Each group, while guided by the same theoretical perspectives, took on a slightly different form and utilized different techniques. Included were peer leadership, role playing, Gestalt "empty chair," Toka Bats (large soft bats used to strike objects in anger), video- and audiotaping, written and filmed communication with imprisoned sex abusers, art and music therapies, films, educational and recreational outings, relaxation therapy, and body language interpretations. An educational component was added to Group III by supplying various topics, such as values clarification, to be discussed, while still allowing time for the members to bring their own agendas to be worked on in the group.

One experience that we feel was of great value to our members was the all-day (six hours) group sessions. We began Group III in this way and found that this session quickly allowed the members to get to know each other and us and to understand what a "group" is supposed to be. These sessions also facilitated group cohesiveness. Another such session was held several months after the group began, at the members' request.

PROBLEMS

We experienced a number of problems while conducting our groups, but the most significant were with transportation and with structure versus nonstructure in Group III.

Transportation was a problem in all three groups when the responsibility was left to the members' caretaker. Members were not brought to sessions because, according to the caretakers, the sessions (1) were inconvenient or inaccessible; (2) caused the members to become upset, angry, and hostile; or (3) were valued by the members and therefore were withheld as punishment for some transgression. In order to eliminate these problems, the cotherapists began transporting the members themselves. Although this assured a more consistent attendance, it created other problems. We found that we no longer had time immediately after the group for debriefing, which we believed to be essential for understanding what had happened in the group. Second, the members began withholding information, preferring to talk to the therapists privately while traveling to or from the meetings. Our unwillingness to discuss these issues except in group evoked feelings of rejection and hostility. Finally, there were instances when members tried to put us in the caretaker role, which would have changed the character of our relationship. These problems were solved when our funding source and sponsoring agency agreed to alter the contract specifications and allow us to use an agency car and to hire a driver to transport the members as necessary.

The structure versus nonstructure problem in Group III became a significant barrier to treatment. The therapist's attempt to include discussion of such things as values clarification and alternatives to acting out behaviors, in addition to feelings about the incest, brought a subtle rebellion from the members. We saw this as a challenge to our authority and tried to regain control by enforcing the few rules the group had accepted and by being more directive than reflective. We began to act out the age-old problem of adolescence versus authority and it escalated over several sessions. At times, it seemed as if we were locked in mortal combat and that we would all be casualties. We spent hours examining this problem with each other and with the program coordinator. It became apparent that the leaders of the revolt were the members who had also been in Group I. They sensed a difference in this group and were responding to it. The problem was finally identified as the introduction of issues and structures without adequate preparation for those who "remembered what the group was supposed to be." Our method and the timing of this change as well as our response to their rebellion ensured the ensuing power struggle.

The resolution of this problem was simple, yet effective. We devoted one session to identifying what we felt was happening in the group and

asked the members to do the same. We believed their perception of being led instead of guided was valid. We acknowledged this and apologized
for not being clear with our method and intention. This incident not only
supported the quality of genuineness that we espoused but also became
a powerful example for the group members of how adults can admit that
they have made an error. The experience also provided an opportunity
for a discussion of authority, and its use and abuse, which proved both
enlightening and beneficial. This experience did not negatively affect our
relationship; in fact, it appears to have deepened the members' respect
for us as persons and helpers.

DISCUSSION

The techniques we used in working with our groups were many and
varied. We learned through trial, error, and frequent evaluation which
techniques were acceptable to our members. Early in Group I, it was
learned that any technique that included displays of violence was devastating and therefore unacceptable. In this group, Toka Bats were introduced,
and it was suggested that they be used to displace some anger onto the
male therapist as the "father figure." The members, at first, were reluctant to do this, but then several agreed. The exercise came to a halt when
one young woman cried out, as she ran to hide in a corner, "When I hit
you, you didn't flinch. You are just like my father. You can't be hurt."
All the members were deeply affected by what they perceived as
violence—reminiscent of episodes in their own lives. While the group
voted not to use the bats again, the incident did afford an opportunity
to acknowledge and discuss their sense of their own helplessness and the
perceived invulnerability of the perpetrators.

Another technique that pointed up the groups' reaction to violence was
the showing of a film on rape by an acquaintance.[10] The therapists had
previewed the film and believed it could lead to some valuable discussion about differences between male and female perceptions. Further they
believed that it could be used to initiate a discussion of the adolescent's
right not to have her body violated. Aware of the violence at the end of
the film, the group was told that the final minutes would not be shown.
The group objected, wanting to "see it all." The therapists agreed—much
to their later dismay. One young woman, whose own experience closely
paralleled the violence in the film, developed body tremors and could not
stop sobbing. The female therapist held the girl for awhile and tried to
calm her by talking but was unable to alleviate either the tremors or the
sobbing. Then with the girl's permission, relaxation therapy was used.
In less than 20 minutes, she had quieted, the tremors cleared, and she
returned to the group to answer the questionnaire on the film. We have
since used this method on the entire group during our all-day sessions

or when meetings become too emotionally stimulating for the participants. The members liked this method because in their words, "it's a high."

Another technique that seemed to cause great discomfort was confrontation either between group therapists and members or between members. Several of the girls had the "peacemaker" role in their own families and would immediately step in to divert the discussion or to try to have everyone "kiss and make up"; failing this, they would try to flee the group. Confrontation that did not lead to violence but to a working out of issues was a difficult process for them to trust. We spent much time identifying and working on their willingness to do anything (including having sex with their fathers) to avoid confrontation.

We found, also during the first group, that using the Gestalt "empty chair" (a method requiring the client to speak to an empty chair while visualizing the object of the conversation occupying the chair) was a method too emotionally laden for our members; consequently, we did not introduce it in the other groups. We used role playing instead. The members in all three groups seemed to prefer this method and used it willingly and frequently. We found that simulation was most helpful (1) in freeing members' long-suppressed feelings; (2) in preparing members for court appearances and meetings with parents; and (3) in showing what kind of image we presented to others. No one who participated was immune from this—and we include ourselves here, as we were continually made aware of how the group perceived us by the way they played our roles. Our own words coming back to us were sometimes difficult to hear but always enlightening.

During Group III, the agency obtained videotaping equipment, which was offered to the group as another tool. After struggling for several weeks with the idea of taping their role playing and then self-critiquing, the members agreed. They showed good insight in reading their body language and in hearing what was and what was not being said. The method of videotaping allowed for much peer feedback and more trust in confrontation.

Although we used many techniques in our groups, some extensively and some just for diversion, we believe that it was our direction and the way that we allowed ourselves to be used as helping persons that were most important in providing a successful group experience for many of our clients. Our availability and openness; our willingness to be questioned, rebuked, and mimicked; and our positive and confrontative use of authority allowed honest, therapeutic relationships—both collectively and individually—to develop and work.[11] We found in Group III that our willingness to risk acknowledging our humanness and our mistakes, and engaging the group to work on their issues with us made for a stronger group, and certainly for more sensitive therapists.

IMPLICATIONS FOR PRACTICE

Almost every article or proposal on child sexual abuse makes what may be called "the tip of the iceberg" statement. Though it sounds like a cliche, its meaning is grave. Sexual abuse may not be increasing but its reporting certainly is. As state child protective laws and child protective investigating teams become more sophisticated, it is certain that social service agencies will be seeing sexually abused adolescents in increasing numbers during the coming decade.

We believe some of our findings can be helpful to individuals and agencies that plan to work with this needy client population. We have described what we have found to be helpful in the treatment of these adolescents. But we remind the reader, as does Sgroi, that

> the field [of child sexual abuse] is too new and the body of accumulated knowledge and skills is too small and inadequately tested for anyone to claim that he or she has *the* answers.[12]

We do not claim to have all the answers. We describe only what we have found to work with our group members. In reporting our findings, we offer areas for research and evaluation.

An area that we believe merits research is the correlation between non-supportive mothers and the need for long-term treatment of the victim. We have found in our practice that adolescents living with a strong, supportive mother, where the perpetrator and not the victim has been removed from the home, appeared to require little more than a safe environment for ventilation and validation of feelings and not to require long-term therapy. Those adolescents placed in foster care, while the perpetrator remained in the home, seemed to experience significant behavior problems, to have greater emotional needs, and to require more intensive treatment. We hypothesize that there is a strong relationship between the lack of maternal support and the need for long-term therapeutic intervention.

In evaluating the groups' effectiveness, we asked the members in an eight-item questionnaire to design a program they thought could be helpful to adolescents like themselves. They designed one very similar to the one they had experienced, including the use of a male therapist. Their unanimous suggestion was that they wanted the group to be held twice a week with more all-day sessions. One member seemed to reflect the feeling of many when she stated: "This group has helped me feel better about myself. I'm not afraid of my father anymore."

The members' evaluation and our observations of change in the group leads us to believe that group therapy utilizing a male and female co-therapy team is an effective treatment model for working with adolescent female victims of incest. We believe that it can be incorporated into existing programs with little difficulty if agencies are willing to be flexible in the use of their resources and facilities.

NOTES AND REFERENCES

1. Group I was co-led by R. B. Morris, Jr., and Mary Lou Misci; Groups II and III were planned and co-led by both authors of this article.

2. See Lawrence Shulman, *The Skills of Helping Individuals and Groups* (Itasca, Ill.: F. E. Peacock, 1979); and Irving H. Berkovitz, "On Growing a Group: Some Thoughts on Structure, Process and Setting," in Berkovitz, ed., *Adolescents Grow in Groups* (New York: Brunner/Mazel, 1972).

3. See John C. Colman, "Friendship and the Peer Group in Adolescence," in Joseph Adelson, ed., *Handbook of Adolescent Psychology* (New York: John Wiley & Sons, 1980); and Irvin D. Yalom, *The Theory and Practice of Group Psychotherapy* (2d ed.; New York: Basic Books, 1975).

4. Yalom, *The Theory and Practice of Group Psychotherapy.*

5. Ibid.

6. B. Beigleiter et al., "Feminist Theory and Social Work Practice." Unpublished paper, University of Pennsylvania, School of Social Work, May 1980.

7. Kevin McIntyre, "Role of Mothers in Father-Daughter Incest: A Feminist Analysis," *Social Work,* 26 (November 1981), pp. 462–466.

8. Linda Canfield Blick and Frances Sarnacki Porter, "Group Therapy with Female Adolescent Incest Victims," in Suzanne M. Sgroi and others, *Handbook of Clinical Intervention in Child Sexual Abuse* (Lexington, Mass.: Lexington Books, 1982), pp. 147–175.

9. Shulman, *The Skills of Helping Individuals and Groups,* p. 276.

10. *The Date* (San Francisco: ODN Productions, 1978).

11. Merle M. Ohlsen, *Group Counseling* (New York: Holt, Rinehart & Winston, 1977).

12. Sgroi, *Handbook of Clinical Intervention in Child Sexual Abuse,* pp. 5–6.

PART II

Advances in
Service Provision

Editor's Comments

Part I considered advances in clinical social work practice. Part II examines advances in program development and service provision (with many of the articles providing case examples as well). These programmatic advances, lead to and/or support greater practice effectiveness, broaden the range of people served, extend the scope of services offered, and often enhance the value to host settings of social work services.

In the first article, Gerard reports on the development, design, and content of a primary prevention program for U.S. Naval personnel and their families. A group approach using a psychoeducational format was adopted, and content was based on the stressful demands made on each family member by the deployment of the submariner for sea duty of five to six months' duration, as well as by his or her return to the family.

The program exemplifies the primary preventive principles of (1) identifying the potential stressor facing a population in an at-risk situation, (2) seeking to reduce the impact if the stressor cannot be eliminated, and (3) strengthening the personal and environmental resources for coping with the stressor. It broadens the scope of services provided by social work; it enhances social work's value to the institution—in this instance the U.S. Navy—by reducing the untoward consequences of long deployment, such as family disruption, emergency leaves, and the like; and it extends the range of people served inasmuch as group members are not defined as clients or as inadequate in any way. Instead, the people served are regarded as a population facing exceptional life tasks because of their military status. Not only are negative outcomes prevented by such an approach, but positive outcomes of continued growth, health, and adaptive functioning are supported.

In the next article, Wheeler examines the development and achievements of a community-based mental health service for cancer patients and their families. The program is distinguished by the successful collaboration of the local Cancer Council, the county department of mental health, three mental health clinics, and a medical center. The clinical social workers draw on a variety of social work roles and therapeutic approaches, including work with the environment, to aid patients and families in managing the emotional and social consequences of the disease.

The overall conception is a view of grave chronic disease or of terminal illness as a life transition that presents stressful adaptive tasks for the patient, the family, and the practitioner. The clinician's activity is directed to sustaining or strengthening the patient's and family's internal and external resources for mastering the demands to the greatest degree possible. Such an objective also requires the provision by the agency and by staff peers of adequate personal and environmental supports for the practitioner. Clearly, there are primary and secondary preventive aspects to this program. Not only does the author describe and evaluate how negative outcomes are obviated, but it appears reasonable to assume that some patients and family members may experience positive growth and improved functioning over premorbid levels.

Next, Olmstead, Hamilton, and Fein introduce a creative use of the child welfare concept of "permanency planning" in outpatient services. Children receiving child guidance services, for example, may not be in the child protective system. Yet they may be at risk of, or already subject to, neglect and abuse. Or, they may be in substitute care, but the child guidance worker is not aware of permanency planning issues and does not consider them.

The authors provide suggestions for identifying such children and/or their parents in outpatient services and for assigning families to workers with expertise in permanency planning. The authors also analyze the clinical roles and skills needed for effective work in behalf of this population. Such a program, based on a concept that is fundamental to one service and transferred across service boundaries for application to another service, enhances the effectiveness of practice in behalf of many children and their families. It also broadens the range of people served in outpatient programs and increases the scope of agency services. In this respect, the program manifests at least a secondary preventive aspect. It also provides the means for implementing the profession's value commitment to meeting the needs of children and their families.

In the next article, Lurie, Rich, and Shulman describe a program for the frail elderly, provided by a large medical center treating medical and psychiatric patients. The program is innovative because clinical social work staff developed a simulated environment for independent living through the use of a congregate living arrangement, with protective aspects, for this emotionally, socially, and physically frail group of elderly individuals. The authors identify the clinical issues involved in developing and implementing the program, and specify the clinical knowledge and skills required for effective practice in this setting.

Notably, the program emphasizes not only the vulnerability but the strengths and the potential for growth and improved functioning of this population. Greater practice effectiveness is reached through broadening the range of people served and increasing the scope of services. The program also is likely to enhance social work's value to the medical center's administration because inappropriate use of the emergency room by the elderly and their readmission to the hospital are reduced. Patients and families report greater satisfaction with the center's quality of care.

The next two articles demonstrate how to introduce an innovative feature into ongoing programs and existing treatment modalities. Fuller and Russell describe a public child welfare program to which family team conferences were added to enable family members, members of their support systems, and social work staff to reach decisions together. Despite the difficulties in implementing the family team conferences, the feature has proved to be productive and has led to greater practice effectiveness. It has strengthened the adaptive capacities of parents, expanded the skills of the clinical social work staff (both supervisory and line), and increased the accountability of the agency to its clientele and to its legislative, fiscal, and professional sources of sanction and support. The programmatic change permitted the real implementation of social work vaues, which are sometimes forfeited in services that are mandated.

Thomas and his colleagues introduced an innovative element—that of working exclusively with a cooperative family member as a mediator of positive change with the noncooperative alcohol abuser—into the existing treatment modality of family therapy. Generated in the process of the authors' developmental research, the approach, called unilateral family therapy, is characterized by particular foci and methods. The reader's attention is directed also to its design for the evaluation of effectiveness.

The authors report their initial clinical impressions derived from the first evaluative study. Further study is expected to lead to criteria for selection of this approach as the treatment of choice for a resistant alcohol abuser, to guidelines for setting appropriate objectives to use in treatment, and to further specification of effective clinical skills. The work, although in an early stage, holds promise of increasing practice effectiveness with families. It may be appropriate not only for uncooperative clients who abuse alcohol, but also for others with seemingly intractable behaviors. Hence, unilateral family therapy has the potential to broaden the range of people served and to extend the scope of clinical services.

The final article in Part II, by King and Mayers, reviews self-help or mutual-aid groups by analyzing the characteristics and developmental stages of these groups, as well as the clinical social worker's prescribed roles, functions, and requisite skills in working effectively with them. Next, the authors link each clinical role to the group's developmental stages. They also suggest directions for the continued development of these groups as natural support systems.

Most self-help groups are "freestanding," that is, they are not institutionally based. As such they are additional environmental resources for the clinician and client to consider in treatment planning. These important programmatic aids have already extended the scope of services in many agencies, and can be expected to continue to do so. They also broaden the range of people served to the degree that the clinician provides specified functions for the group itself, and as requested by the membership. Clearly, self-help groups have the potential for increasing the effectiveness of services.

Clinical Social Workers as Primary Prevention Agents

Dianne Gerard

Clinical social workers have long been expected to provide casework services after the fact, although they know that prevention efforts would be more effective and less costly socially, financially, and emotionally. There has been some programming and much lip service given to the concept of prevention, but little has emerged over the years to switch the service provision emphasis in social work to one of preventive programs and techniques. Wittman observed that "in spite of an implicit and indirect commitment to prevention, the concept of preventive social work has not become explicit and the implications for practice methodologies have not been confronted." Several explanations are available, namely that preventive efforts rarely receive top funding, that professional training of social work clinicians focuses on identification and treatment, that maintenance of the status quo rather than social change is typically the rule, and that results are difficult to assess.[1]

Primary prevention requires that situations be identified as probable stressors before they have an effect on, and create a problem for, people and that intervention be devised to either neutralize that effect or to enable the affected people to grow and learn from it. The most popular prevention vehicle is education. Thus, if clinical social work concepts are used in educational settings, there is good possibility of preventive impact.

The Navy Family Service Center at Pearl Harbor, Hawaii has devised and implemented an educational program for families who are experiencing deployment: sea duty assignment that separates families for five to six months. Aimed at informing husbands and wives of the emotional, practical, and social role changes that frequently occur during deployments, the program, which is taught by clinical social workers, covers all phases of the separation experience from predeployment, through the months of sea duty, and the reunion process. Although the program consists largely of lectures, it provides opportunities for discussion between husbands and wives, informal meetings and talk between wives to decrease social isolation, and availability of social workers for personal questions during the seminar and later in casework sessions, if desired by attendees.

With this program, the clinical social worker steps out of the consultation room and into the realm of education. The clinician uses traditional skills of empathy, assessment, and problem solving, as well as community referrals to inform, to translate psychosocial concepts into understandable and useful information, and to make the private experiences of anxiety, loss, family friction, and stress feel normal and bearable rather than unexpected and pathological. Furthermore, the social worker presents as an understanding, competent, and knowledgeable mental health professional; he or she can challenge fantasies or stereotypes about clinicians by appearing in public and working openly with the community while also being available for private consultation.

Identification of social, environmental, and emotional stressors is the first task in preventive social work. It is necessary then to understand the lifestyle and demands of the Navy in order to create effective programming. Like all military members and their families, Navy families encounter frequent moves, low income, separation from extended family and friends, and threat of loss of life; however, they also experience frequent and prolonged separations from closest family members. At any given time, 80,000 people are deployed, leaving thousands of single parents. Such separations due to sea deployments can affect families as often as every three months when submarines operate on a three months in and three months out rotation, or they may occur less frequently but for longer periods, such as six months at sea every 12 to 18 months. These separations require emotional flexibility to cope with reactions to loss and reunion, sex-role adaptations within the family to deal with one parent's absence and the other's increased work load, effective communication to handle the myriad of details necessary for family functioning and emotional closeness, and parental understanding to facilitate children's expressions of feelings and to devise innovative strategies to maintain ties with the absent parent.

These repeated separations may tax even the most flexible and psychologically healthy individuals and families; for those who are less well adjusted, their experiences with deployments may completely disrupt functioning. Such disruption undermines not only adult self-concept and the healthy growth of children but also job functioning and mission effectiveness. On the other hand, successful coping satisfies needs for competence and mastery within the individual, bolsters interdependence among family members, and results in greater satisfaction with Navy life. The retention of military personnel fostered by this satisfaction strengthens the concept and practice of a volunteer military in this country.

Phase two in prevention is the creation of programming or strategies to reach people affected by stressors before they define themselves as suffering from those stressors. Maintenance or improvement of emotional health is the goal.[2] The predeployment seminar was devised to help prepare Navy couples for their upcoming separation. Seminars are arranged for the crews and families of individual ships and submarines approximately one month prior to deployment. Reunion seminars are provided for Navy wives one month prior to homecoming. In addition, a videotape pilot program is being developed to inform husbands of the special stresses and situations that occur at reunion; this media program will provide a cost-effective alternative to sending social workers to sea. A pilot program in which social workers rode Navy ships back to home port was instituted in Norfolk, Virginia; information about family reunion, small-group discussions, and individual casework were included in this innovative project.[3]

Meetings of those serving on individual ships rather than of squadrons or of groupings of unrelated individuals are deemed essential to capitalize on a natural community of people who share the same experience, to build a social network among wives, and to facilitate understanding at the command level of the impact of deployment on the family.

PREDEPLOYMENT SEMINAR

A two-hour program is planned usually in the evening so that both husbands and wives are able to attend. Child care is often available. All married personnel are invited by the commanding officer. Involvement by supervising officers is vital given the authority and influence they possess; therefore, upper-ranking officers and enlisted personnel are introduced and are incorporated into the program. For example, the commanding officer discusses why this deployment is necessary; the anticipated schedule of departure, itinerary, and return; and often the work that occurs at sea. This latter point serves to more accurately inform spouses about their partners' work, thus eliminating incorrect fantasies. Chaplains, legal officers, and the ombudsman (the person appointed by the commanding officer to serve as the official liaison between the ship and the families) briefly inform the audience about their roles and services.

Clinical social workers conduct the remainder of the program, using both lectures and audience participation. Clinical skills are challenged, in that style of presentation is vitally important for establishment of trust and rapport as well as for effective conveyance of information. Informality, eliciting of audience feedback, empathy, and limited self-disclosure create a relationship between the social worker and the couples.

The emotional aspects of separation and ways to communicate those effectively comprise the bulk of the program. In a study of the effects of shorter-term deployments, Dunks devised a flowchart of emotional changes during sea-shore rotations.[4] While these pertain especially to wives, they also describe the emotional lability and adjustment that husbands and children experience. Two to four weeks prior to deployment there is an increase in either dependence or withdrawal behavior. "Clingers" tend to feel frightened and anxious and attempt to elicit frequent reassurances from the spouse. On the other hand, those who withdraw do so prior to deployment in order to spare themselves the emotional pain of parting. Not infrequently "clingers" and "withdrawers" marry each other. This results in misunderstanding plus feelings of anger and rejection. The social worker explains this cycle, looks for recognition responses within the audience, and asks for hints from participants (usually the more experienced Navy families) on how to cope with this. Primarily, information is used to forewarn couples, and coping strategies, such as talking about feelings, spending "dating" time together, and reassuring the spouse of continued love, are discussed to increase individuals' sense of control. Concrete suggestions such as financial planning, automobile maintenance, legal matters, and emergency precautions are offered to bolster security: forearmed is forewarned.

Because children are especially vulnerable, special consideration is given to their needs. Boys suffer more stress than girls do because their primary role model has left. Children who are at transition points, such as entering school for the first time, and those in their early teens are at risk in that these are times of normal separation and strengthening of sex-role identification.[5] Their increased need for reassurance plus the inadvisability of delegating one child as "man of the house" are stressed. Taking the family to see the ship leave presents a concrete explanation to children about where father is. It also serves to facilitate the expression of emotions rather than denial of them, and as such, discharges them.

The early weeks after deployment are typically characterized by loss, numbness, and depression; these feelings may be expressed in lethargy or in frenetic activity. Sailors are likely very busy with shipboard work, so they may suppress their loneliness until the middle of the cruise when the newness of the deployment has subsided. Children take their cues from the at home parent, usually the mother. She now has the responsibility of expanding her role to become both mother and father. If she presents competence as well as empathy, she increases the children's security and eases them through their loss of father. Alternatively, if she is severely depressed, she serves to undermine the children's trust that there is security and increases fears of abandonment and loss.

Women especially need support from other adults during deployment. Unfortunately they may be perceived as "third wheels" at parties or as threats to other women. Furthermore, husbands may try to isolate their wives in attempts to alleviate their fears of being cuckolded. Yet without adult social contact at work or at home, women are unable to decrease loneliness. Deployment presents opportunities for independent decision making, socializing, and managing; these can strengthen individuals' feelings of competence and enhance the relationship, if the increased autonomy is not perceived as a step out of the marriage. This topic is dealt with briefly during the predeployment seminar and serves mainly to inform couples that the reunion process may be difficult as well as joyful.

REUNION WORKSHOP

Approximately one month prior to homecoming, wives meet again with the social workers who taught the predeployment seminar. How to open the family circle to welcome the husband home is the focus. Typically, wives and children have settled into a comfortable routine and wives are proud of the competence they experience in themselves. They are also excited about reunion and desire recognition for the good job they have done during the cruise. Husbands, on the other hand, are frequently worried about whether their wives and families have any need or love for them. This is expressed by a changing of family rules, irritation and arguing, and often criticism of changes that occurred while they were away. Despite excellent communication, the couple is at risk: the husband missed the daily changes of his children's growth and his wife's life. She must inform him and let him back into the family with reassurance. Dysfunctional marriages may crack under the strain. Here counseling is suggested. Even people with healthy marriages may expect four to six weeks of tension as all family members grope to establish roles and functions. If both adults are aware of this process and if they express their affection as well as irritation, they reunite with a honeymoon and an affirmation of their marriage. This is ideal, obviously.

The reunion workshop and the shipboard video program aim to inform, so that the feelings experienced seem familiar rather than frightening; the arguments or tension seem normal and tolerable rather than indicators of marital dissolution. Social workers, too, are perceived in perhaps a different light: as understanding, accessible people who have in some ways "lived through" the deployment with the couple. Clinicians helped prepare them for the separation, were there near the end to help with reunion, and are available for private consultation if needed. Certainly this would facilitate a couple's consideration of counseling for problems associated with deployment.

EVALUATION

As with all prevention programs, evaluation of preventive effects are difficult to measure. However, fewer family breakups, incidents of financial crisis, and visits to physicians for stress-related symptoms, as well as improved mission effectiveness due to decreased family stress and emergency returns home for military personnel, and greater subjective appraisal of family solidarity are used as indicators of program success. Accurate baseline data do not exist, so command personnel, the ombudsman, and health facilities must be surveyed for subjective impressions of program success. Preliminary evidence shows increased use of Family Service Center (FSC) programs and clinical consultation and referral by the command and the ombudsman. Increasingly, clients for marital or family counseling state at intake that they became aware of Family Service Center services at predeployment or reunion seminars. Thus, these programs are effective at the least for publicity. Most often one of the social workers who taught the seminar will be called or requested by the client, proof, perhaps, of the program's impact in increasing perceived helpfulness and accessibility of the clinician. Lastly, the fact that more commanding officers are requesting these programs for their personnel attests to program success. Ship staff and families are permitted to meet, learn, and support each other through this normally stressful time with the knowledge that those in charge, the command, understand the difficulties of family separation and are available for support.

NOTES AND REFERENCES

1. See Milton Wittman, "Preventive Social Work," *Encyclopedia of Social Work,* Vol. 2 (17th issue; Washington, D.C.: National Association of Social Workers, 1977), p. 1050; and Michael Roskin, "Integration of Primary Prevention into Social Work Practice," *Social Work,* 25 (May 1980), pp. 192–196.

2. Donald C. Klein and Stephen Goldsten, *Primary Prevention: An Idea Whose Time Has Come* (Rockville, Md.: National Institute of Mental Health, 1977).

3. Jon Parry, "Reentry for Sailors: An Account of the Norfolk Family Service Center On-Board Program for Crews Returning from the Indian Ocean." Paper presented at the Navy Family Service Center Conference, Annapolis, Md., March 10, 1982.

4. Max E. Dunks, "Military Enforced Separations: Ministering to the Marital and Family Readjustment Needs of Dependents of Deployed Navy and Marine Corps Men Returning Home." Unpublished Ph.D. dissertation, San Francisco Theological Seminary, 1981.

5. Eli Breger, "On Navy Families: Separations," *Wifeline* (Spring 1981), pp. 12–13.

A Psychosocial Program for Cancer Patients and Their Families

Joan Wheeler

The Nassau County Department of Mental Health, in response to unmet psychological needs of cancer patients and their families, received a grant to provide counseling and supportive mental health services to members of the community affected by this illness. At the time, many cancer patients and their families were unable to find resources in the community to help with their cancer-related problems. Even now, powerful resistances operate against the recognition and treatment of the emotional needs of the physically ill. This new approach to practice began in 1977 as part of a community-based cancer-control demonstration project supported by Long Island Cancer Council (LICC), a nonprofit voluntary agency funded by the National Cancer Institute for a period of five years. Similar projects were begun concurrently in New Mexico, California, Rhode Island, Detroit, and Hawaii. This demonstration project was established to test the hypothesis that the coordinated use of all interventions (educational, medical, and psychosocial) in dealing with the cancer patient with certain types of cancer (breast cancer, cancer of colon or rectum, or cancer of the uterus or cervix) could have a greater impact than a fragmented or single approach to intervention.

The LICC through a coordinated program of interventions planned to provide

1. public, patient, and professional education, and information and referral;
2. screening and detection;
3. pretreatment evaluation and treatment; and
4. rehabilitation and continuing care.

To reflect the true community-based nature of the LICC, a diverse group of 11 subcontractors were selected to conduct intervention projects together with the LICC. The subcontractors included four hospitals, two universities, the American Cancer Society, Cancer Care, Inc., Visiting Homemakers Service, Inc., and the Nassau County Departments of Health and Mental Health.

The Cancer Support Program began with a request for a counseling group from a number of postmastectomy patients. Recognizing the emotional and psychosocial stress of cancer, the Nassau County Department of Mental Health contracted with LICC and placed this special counseling service in three mental health clinics and a medical center so that it would be available to a wide range of people. An emphasis was put on reaching minority populations with information on risk factors, symptoms, and the availability of screening, detection, and counseling services. Throughout the first two years of the program, a very effective referral network was organized and integrated under the coordination and supervision of the LICC. Due to policy changes at the National Cancer Institute, grant contributions to the program became sporadic and completely terminated on May 31, 1981. When funding was withdrawn, the Cancer Support Program, renamed the Psychotherapeutic Program for Cancer Patients and Their Families, continued to provide specialized counseling services through the Department of Mental Health and its contract agencies. This was the only psychosocial intervention project out of the original six in the United States to continue.

Nassau County, one of the most densely populated counties in New York State, has a population of 1,321,582 with an annual recorded death rate from cancer of 3,000 and an estimated incidence of 5,000 cases per year. An estimated 1,500 patients per year, along with an equal number of family members, will experience significant despondence. According to a recent survey of mental health clinics, approximately 300 clients or only 2 to 6 percent of total admissions apply for help for cancer-related emotional problems. This indicates that an estimated 1,200 cancer patients with a corresponding or greater number of family members do not seek treatment through conventional means but do respond to an identified Cancer Support Program. It should be pointed out that a good percentage of cancer patients would not have sought intervention prior to their illness as many had excellent coping skills. With the added stress of this disease, cancer patients frequently appear more comfortable in not viewing their experience as a mental health problem but as a crisis in their lives needing supportive intervention.

Currently, four clinical social workers with a specific interest in, and experience in, working with cancer patients and their families work out of three strategically located mental health clinics and one hospital. The staff has an orientation that is specifically directed to the therapeutic management of the emotional impact of cancer and the specific ways of coping with that impact upon the cancer patient and his or her family. Briefly, the three main interventions include catharsis and validation of feelings, restoring communications, and understanding the meaning of the illness. These approaches are not mutually exclusive, nor should they be relied upon as rigid formulas for intervention. Rather they are recommended as ways to organize one's thinking during the process of evaluation and as general guidelines suitable for the majority of cancer patients around which the novice cancer therapist may develop his or her individual style.[1]

Special competencies for intervention required of the clinical social workers include the abilities to assume a variety of roles, from therapist to advocate, and to use the client's environment as a resource for, and instrument of, change. One example of the range of services and flexibility of the program concerns a 40-year-old man, married and the father of two children, who was diagnosed as having lymphoma. While bravely fighting the illness, he was seen individually for 1½ years and worked on conflictual areas of his life, including identity issues and employment discrimination. As the prognosis worsened, he was helped to deal with his loss of functioning and the ego devaluation that accompanied that change. He had been estranged from his family of origin for a number of years and was able to come to terms with that decision. Feelings of loss and separation were important areas of concentration, as were preparing his family for his death and their future life without him. During the final stage of his illness, sessions took place in the hospital where the worker met his wife and children, and was able to establish a relationship with them. Three hours before he lapsed into a coma and died, he telephoned the worker to say farewell and to express appreciation. His wife and children are now rebuilding their lives and are involved in bereavement counseling with the same worker.

It appears that the clinical social workers' knowledge of psychosocial dynamics, family interaction, and community resources, and their expertise in mental health services make them uniquely qualified to work effectively with this target population.

In order to be eligible for the program, a patient must have a debilitating illness that has a profound emotional impact as well as the possibility of resulting family disorganization. The procedure for those interested in service is to call or come to the closest listed agency to discuss the individual or family situation with a staff member. In this manner, a mutual decision can be made as to whether individual, family, or group assistance, or some combination of these services, will be most helpful. Services can include crisis intervention, information and referral, and short-term or in-depth therapy. Most clients come to the agencies but home or hospital appointments are provided for those who are too ill to travel or who have transportation difficulties.

The group program has been a primary focus. Types of groups that appear to be most beneficial and successful are the mastectomy group, the mixed patient and relative group, the relatives group, the family bereavement groups, and groups consisting of the spouses of mastectomy patients. Originally, groups were scheduled to be time-limited to a period of eight weeks. However, experience shows that once begun, groups are strongly cohesive and at the end of an eight-week period, the request is usually made for a contract to continue for an additional eight weeks or longer. This arrangement works well, allowing those who find eight weeks a sufficient period, to leave the group, permitting a new person to enter the group, and yet allowing those who need ongoing support to continue. Sharing concerns and feelings in a small group can be of benefit even to those who are coping well with the concrete, as well as the emotional, stresses of cancer. Group members cite as particularly supportive the feeling of no longer being alone and the validation of their many emotions. A decrease in anxiety, in depression, and in feelings of isolation are gains that are most often mentioned by group participants.

Emotional support to the whole family at a time of crisis is critical to total family well-being. This pertains not only to a better quality of life in the present, but to the functioning of the family in the future. Marital conflicts, school and work difficulties, and substance abuse are examples of what may appear as a reaction to the stresses of cancer when adequate support is lacking.

The Cancer Support Program is similar to the Life Model, or Ecological Approach, which has been defined as a model of service to individuals, families, and groups dealing with stresses that arise from problems in living. It uses individual, family, or group approaches differentially in response to client's needs and objectives. Together the worker and client seek to understand the meaning and impact of the pertinent forces on the person and the presenting problem or need in order to set objectives and to devise action that will engage positive forces in the person and in the environment, remove environmental obstacles, and change negative transactions. The social worker helps to build self-esteem and strengthen defenses against disabling anxiety and depression so that the client can better cope with the problems. The focus of practice is on the area where the coping patterns and adaptive potential of the person and the qualities of the impinging environment come together.[2]

PROGRAM MODIFICATION

The abrupt withdrawal of funds and the cessation of a vital alliance with LICC in 1981 created a difficult period of transition for the Psychotherapeutic Program for Cancer Patients and Their Families. In order to take on responsibilities previously assumed by LICC, it was necessary to utilize four basic approaches to the continuing development of the program. These included

1. reestablishment of the links with subcontractors and other agencies in the county on a countywide level;
2. making the program and its continuance known to the population of Nassau County;

3. integration of the program within those clinics and the hospital in which it is based; and
4. development of a program of education and support for the clinical social workers.

Reestablishing Links

To reestablish a referral network, it was necessary to inform people of the program's continuing existence, albeit in a modified form. All mental health clinics, hospitals, former subcontractors, libraries, schools, business and industry groups, senior citizen centers, volunteer agencies, clergy, self-help groups, physicians, nurses, social workers, and allied health professionals were contacted. Literature describing the program was distributed. The modifications of the program included a broadening of the eligibility to a patient with any type of cancer and to family members. There was also the implementation of a sliding-scale fee instead of the free service that had been available when the program was federally funded. A centralized telephone information and referral service was established to direct the cancer patient and family members to the appropriate agency. Outreach by the project coordinator and social workers as well as lectures and collaboration with other professionals at professional conferences all facilitated the rebuilding of a referral network.

Publicity

Media coverage (newspaper articles, community service announcements, spot radio announcements, display of brochures in public places like libraries and shopping centers) has been helpful in reaching and informing the target population, which includes the person who is first being suspected of having cancer, to the person who has been living with the disease for some time, to the individual at the terminal stage of the illness. Publicity, outreach, and liaison efforts must be ongoing to reach the many people still receiving inadequate support in coping with the impact of cancer.

Integration of the Program within the Host Agency

An important objective has been to integrate the program within those agencies in which it is based. There is an impression that mental health workers specializing in the treatment of cancer-related problems provide a disproportionate share of the treatment to this population, while general mental health practitioners by and large shun the field. In addition to the usual anxieties provoked in psychotherapists by patients with physical disease or overwhelming reality problems, the cancer patient evokes powerful resistances around fears of mutilation, contagion, death, and dying and may stimulate feelings of therapeutic impotence.[3] In an attempt to overcome resistances within the staff of clinics working with cancer patients, educational seminars were presented by our staff to heighten awareness of the psychological and emotional needs of cancer patients and their families.

Not only have our clinical social workers had to deal with counter-transferential feelings about their clients, they have been further stressed by the manner in which they have been treated by friends, relatives, and especially by colleagues, who may often request that they not discuss their "depressing work." One worker in the program was even referred to by her colleagues as "the cancer lady." This deprives workers of an important source of peer support. In several cases, room assignments were in the basement or other remote areas of the agency or hospital. When the hardship of the location for physically ill people was pointed out, for example their difficulty in navigating steep stairs or in walking long distances, the pattern was continued in another form, by not having the worker's office in too visible an area. Whether the erratic funding problems present since the inception of the program reflect broader counter-transferential feelings in government and the community is an interesting question.

Professional Frame of Reference

The cancer patient, in particular, tends to arouse anxieties even in the experienced and analyzed social worker. This program, recognizing the difficulties inherent in treating the cancer patient population, has provided an effective and stable professional frame of reference to organize the worker's approach and to provide clinical intervention. The program is structured to provide support for the staff in addition to whatever the respective agencies provide. This includes formal and informal supervision with the project coordinator, peer support, and group supervision provided by a psychiatric and group consultant with whom the entire staff meets weekly for a period of three hours. The goals of the professional support network are as follows:

1. To foster greater understanding of the cancer patient and family.
2. To provide a mutual-aid system for the exchange of resources and information and the teaching of coping skills.
3. To create a peer-support network so that staff members may express their feelings freely and be less prone to experience negative psychological or physical reactions. The unique stress placed on the staff requires a setting conducive to catharsis and ventilation of intense feelings.
4. To develop greater self-awareness and to enhance understanding of one's reactions ot the cancer patient and family member. If a situation is too disturbing for one worker, a referral can be made.
5. To increase one's ability to experience painful feelings, without

panic. It is believed that dealing with and accepting feelings such as aggression, anger, sadness, disgust, anxiety, or fear in working with the cancer population promotes general growth of staff.

It is impossible to work with cancer patients without periodically experiencing disturbing emotional reactions to the malignancy and also to the client. Intense countertransferential reactions are usually generated by the more severely disturbed client or one like the cancer patient who threatens one's own sense of security. One worker had to deal with the deaths of five cancer patients within a three-month interval. Another worker, herself the parent of adolescent sons, began to feel a heightened sense of anxiety and vulnerability when her community experienced a cluster outbreak of leukemia in local high school students. A third worker, one with chronic cystic mastitis, became unduly focused and fearful that the condition could lead to a malignancy. In the weekly meeting, one frequently hears "I have felt the same way." All fears, aversions, repressions, and dislikes aroused by certain clients are ventilated in the belief that recognition of these feelings leads to effective use of them.

As a result of this program, a cohesive staff of therapists has emerged. The turnover rate is low, given the high concentration of work with a specific population and the fiscal uncertainties of the program. The general level of commitment is reflected by the behavior of one worker who was let go for four months when the federal funding was initially withdrawn, but who decided not to seek other employment and returned when funding was restored. It is very possible that without the program's internal support features, staff turnover would have been much higher. Until resistances in the agencies are resolved, the availability of support in the central program is crucial.

To further ease stress and reduce burnout, it has been helpful for the clinical social workers to do some outreach and to also work with a percentage of clients who do not have cancer.

RESULTS

The Cancer Support Program, which began service in 1978, grew steadily, providing services for cancer patients and their families. In the first two years of the program, 932 new admissions were noted—404 patients and 528 family members. In 1980 the first major disruption occurred, with funding and staff reductions, and this was reflected in a decrease in referrals. In 1981 and 1982, with the hiring of new staff, the program resumed its productivity. A total of 6,383 individual sessions, 2,946 conjoint and family sessions, and 786 group sessions took place through 1981.

While the program was under the auspices of LICC, there was the following breakdown indicating referral source: 20 percent physicians,

20 percent American Cancer Society (ACS), 28 percent media, and 32 percent other professionals, including social workers and nurses. Once the referral network was disbanded, physician referrals dropped to 0 percent and ACS to 5 percent. What occurred was that the majority of referrals came from the media (39 percent), or patients, friends, and/or family members (22 percent), while referrals from allied professionals stayed at a moderate level of 25 percent.

Patient and family testimony indicates that the program has been very effective in ameliorating the emotional consequences of cancer. In a sample of 91 patients, 94.8 percent felt positively about their group experience —60.4 percent believed it to be a very worthwhile experience, 30 percent believed it useful to some degree, and 4.4 percent felt neutral about the experience. The contribution of others in the groups (advice, sharing of confidences and feelings) was found very helpful by 62.5 percent and moderately helpful by 37.5 percent of the population sampled. Bereavement, mastectomy, and patient-relative groups were found the most helpful.

An exciting extension of the program has been the formation of a postmastectomy group. The goal of this group is the compilation of a list of questions to help other women facing surgery deal more effectively and assertively with their physicians.

CONCLUSION

Because of the significant resistances that have retarded the entry of general mental health professionals into clinical work with cancer patients and because many cancer patients simply could not find resources in the community to help them with their cancer-related emotional problems, a model psychosocial rehabilitation program was begun. The original objective to develop a community-based model treatment program has been realized, as has the broadening of the utilization of the existing mental health system to the needs of individuals and families in severe emotional crisis. With the expertise gained in the last four years, it is now possible to effectively utilize the mental health system of Nassau County by training therapists and then placing them in strategic locations throughout the county.

The professional frame of reference, including the support features and techniques, could be decentralized from the Department of Mental Health and incorporated directly within the agencies, but it would first be necessary to overcome prejudice and resistance to treating cancer patients and their families. In an encouraging move, one of the clinics has recently implemented a new procedure. In addition to the clinical social worker, three other professionals (one female and two male psychologists) have expressed an interest in working with this population. This interdisciplinary team effort, with the clinical social worker providing supervision, has been effective in facilitating a better matching between therapist and client. One student social worker has had a field placement in the program, and several others are scheduled for the near future. The professional frame of reference, so integral to this program, could be easily duplicated for other at-risk populations and contribute to increased effectiveness on the part of other treatment workers. This author is aware that support groups have been formed for oncology staff of hospitals, but has been unable to locate similar professional frames of reference for professionals working on an outpatient basis.

The strength of this program and its service to an underserved population is reflected in its survival in altered form. The Psychotherapeutic Program for Cancer Patients and Their Families has made a significant contribution by providing a model of clinical services to persons under severe medical and emotional stress. It is through innovative programs such as this that a growing professional awareness of the psychosocial needs of families facing cancer can be more clearly elucidated, defined, and met.

NOTES AND REFERENCES

1. Stephen M. Saravay et al., "Psychotherapy of the Cancer Patient." Unpublished paper, December 1981.

2. Carel B. Germain and Alex Gitterman, "The Life Model of Social Work Practice," in Francis J. Turner, ed., *Social Work Treatment: Interlocking Theoretical Approaches* (2d ed.; New York: Free Press, 1979), pp. 361–384.

3. R. Renneker, "Cancer and Psychotherapy," in Jane G. Goldberg, ed., *Psychotherapeutic Treatment of Cancer Patients* (New York: Free Press, 1981), pp. 131–166; M. M. Cohen and D. K. Wellisch, "Living in Limbo: Psychosocial Intervention in Families with a Cancer Patient," *American Journal of Psychotherapy,* 32 (1978), pp. 561–571; and Renneker, "Counter-Transference Reaction to Cancer," *Psychosomatic Medicine,* 19 (1957), pp. 409–418.

Permanency Planning for Children in Outpatient Psychiatric Services

Kathleen A. Olmstead, Joyce Hamilton-Collins, and Edith Fein

The right of all children to a secure home was formally noted in the Children's Bill of Rights that came out of the 1930 White House Conference on Children. Yet many children—over half a million in 1978—are still in foster care.[1] In response to the problems that placement out of the home engenders, permanency planning as a philosophy and as a technique for providing child welfare services has emerged.

> Permanency planning is the systematic process of carrying out, within a brief, time-limited period, a set of goal-directed activities designed to help children live in families that offer continuity of relationships with nurturing parents or caretakers and the opportunity to establish lifetime relationships.[2]

Permanency planning encompasses the belief that all children are entitled to continuity of care in a nurturing environment, preferably with their biological parents, but when it is impossible to prevent placement and a return to the biological parents is not feasible, children have a right to the least-restrictive alternative placement. In order of preference, this means permanent placement with a responsible relative, adoption, specified long-term foster care, or residential care.

Children in foster care typically come from families with multiple needs in health, education, housing, family relationships, and social supports.[3] In a study of foster care, 76 percent of the reasons given for placement included school behavior, home behavior, community behavior, mental problems, family conflicts, and similar categories that indicated the predominance of mental health needs in this group.[4]

Although families receiving child welfare services are increasingly being affected by the permanency planning philosophy, this is not true for those not yet in the protective services system. Parents at risk for having their children taken from them who seek professional assistance report receiving little help with child-caring concerns. A study by Coltoff and Lucks recommended that a training program be established for agency staffs to assist them in intervening in behalf of the child.[5]

Because permanency planning characteristically is not integrated into outpatient work, those cases that can use such planning are often inadequately served. The worker may not understand permanency planning issues and may treat children only in the context of their present environments instead of using appropriate techniques to plan for future stability. In this article we attempt to describe how permanency planning can be reconciled with outpatient practice, especially in child-guidance clinics.

IDENTIFYING A PERMANENCY PLANNING CASE

Most child-guidance clinics have formal or informal systems for classifying clients at the point of referral. Common categories include refusal to attend school, suicidal potential, delinquency, and learning disability. Refusal to attend school, for example, brings a quick reaction: waiting list priority; immediate efforts to return the child to school; school conferences; and an examination of the parent-child relationship. Classifying clients at referral permits a clinic to assign particular categories of clients to workers who have demonstrated a special interest or skill in those areas.

A "permanency planning" classification is suggested as an addition to the more familiar categories. Such a classification would trigger responses assuring that adequate service is offered. The classification would designate any child referred for outpatient therapy who is already placed out of his or her own home; any pregnant woman in conflict about keeping or giving up her unborn child; any child currently at home but with a history of one or more previous placements; any child referred for a trial of outpatient care prior to consideration of residential care; any parents referred for help as a prerequisite for resuming care of children in placement; any families referred by protective services for prevention services in cases in which children are at risk of being placed; and any parents who are seriously questioning their ability to keep a child at home. Once a case is thus identified, it would be assigned to staff members who have expertise in permanency planning, or assigned with the promise of permanency planning consultation.

UNIQUE ROLE OF THE SOCIAL WORKER

Permanency planning requires that the social worker assume the role of case manager. In an outpatient clinic, the worker must be certain that this role is being filled so that important permanency planning steps, which will be discussed later, can proceed. A second important role for the worker is that of ally with the parents, based on mutual concern that a child have permanence. This is important in cases in which children are already in placement as well as in cases in which there is a risk of placement. Prior to a child being considered for placement, a parent must understand that the goal of such a placement is permanency for the child.

When a parent knows that multiple or frequent placements or long-term nonpermanent placements are not realistic considerations, the parent may have a greater investment in making the progress necessary to prevent placement.

A third role, which is familiar to those involved in inpatient work, but also applies to those working in outpatient permanency planning, is a dual role in which the social worker is both a supporter and an evaluator. This dual role must be clear to parents at the beginning. Although parents come to know that the worker is committed to assisting them to achieve the goals necessary for a child to return or remain home, they also must realize that the worker is committed to evaluating progress, and may need to report to the case manager or to the court. In evaluating progress, the worker must tell parents that records will be kept to document what is occurring. For example, if a treatment goal is keeping regular appointments, the worker will keep an accurate record. If there are goals that include participation in groups such as Alcoholics Anonymous or in those that teach parenting skills, the worker will keep an attendance record. Similarly, the worker may note observations of interactions between parents and child if improving the quality of that relationship is a goal. An honesty about this dual role and regularly scheduled evaluation conferences provide a framework that parents can accept because it eliminates vagueness and invites participation in self-evaluation.

Finally, the worker's role is to support the parents regardless of the outcome for the child. If a child is removed permanently from the home, the parents need to be aware of the worker's commitment to them as well as to the child. This provides support for a feeling of self-worth even when circumstances dictate that parental rights must be relinquished. It is important for parents to know that such support will be available if they need to adjust to a life separate from their child.

IMPORTANCE OF THOROUGH COLLABORATION

The various roles of the social worker are complicated by the requirements for full collaboration that permanency planning imposes. When a child is in placement, the host agency is compelled to bring all parties together. In a specialized foster care program, for example, the admission procedure includes a meeting in which all parties participate: the foster care worker, the state worker, the biological parents, and the foster parents. After placement, collaboration is ongoing and includes periodic progress and planning conferences. As new persons become involved, they too are included in the collaborative effort: Parent aides may meet with the biological parents and the foster care worker; foster parents and biological parents may meet on a regular basis; foster parents, the foster care worker, and the biological parents may meet with school personnel; or adoption resource people may be involved in relevant cases.

When a child is in placement, the worker of the host agency usually assumes the case manager role. As case manager, the worker ensures that all team members are clear about responsibilities, and that all activities that facilitate a permanent plan for the child within a specified time frame are taking place. Because the host agency "owns," that is, has physical care of the child, it seems natural that its worker is the case manager.

In outpatient permanency planning cases, on the other hand, the outpatient clinic does not "own" the child. Consequently, the pressure for case management is not felt keenly. It is common for a troubled foster child to be worked with individually, with occasional conversations with foster parents about child management. When a child shows improvement in adjustment to the foster placement, it is not unusual for the case to be closed as "improved." Permanency planning issues typically are not addressed, because they are not presented by the clients. In light of the current understanding of a child's right to permanence, such an approach can contribute to a prolonged stay in limbo for a child.

To deal with permanency planning issues, outpatient clinic workers must be attentive to collaborative work. Although they may not necessarily assume the role of case manager as described for the worker from a host setting, outpatient workers must determine who does have that role and provide outpatient care on condition that case managers are addressing the issues important to achievement of permanent plans for each child. An outpatient clinic worker can ask to be included in progress and planning meetings. The worker should obtain from the case manager such information as the time frame for a permanent plan; the involvement of biological parents; the opportunities afforded biological parents to improve their situations to the point at which they can resume permanent care of their children (i.e., parent-aide services, role-model sessions with foster parents, clear statements of what must happen for the child to return home, and so on); the visiting schedule for child and biological parents; and the termination of parental rights or court date for a termination petition if the biological parents are not involved.

If the case worker is not taking appropriate steps toward achievement of a permanent plan for the child, the outpatient worker must make this a prerequisite for individual work with the child or parent. Until this occurs, the outpatient worker might offer consultation to the worker of the host setting and delay work with the individual child or family until permanency planning issues are being appropriately addressed.

TIME FRAMES AND SERVICE AGREEMENTS

An important element in permanency planning is the use of time frames and service agreements. These techniques are not new to outpatient work;

they are commonly used in brief treatment for setting specific time limits and identifiable, measurable goals. In permanency planning cases, time frames and service agreements should be in writing and must have the specific goal of a child having a permanent home in a reasonable time.

Although additional, less formal time frames and service agreements can be made between a client and an outpatient worker, the case manager should be responsible for the permanency goal in a permanency planning case. The service agreement should include the roles of all members of the team. The outpatient worker should obtain a copy of the service agreement from the case manager and make more specific agreements with the client concerning the outpatient work. For example, the case manager and biological parent may have concurred, in the service agreement, to outpatient counseling. The outpatient worker and biological parent may in turn agree on specific goals and time frames for the outpatient counseling, perhaps deciding to work on more consistent discipline of children, more ability to enjoy activities with children, more sensitivity to feelings of children, and so on. The child's right to permanence should always be the guiding principle in setting any goals.

Service agreements should be in writing for two reasons. First, because a time frame is essential, it is important to set times for periodic review of progress. The written service agreement serves as a basis for such evaluation. Second, if progress is not made and the court is petitioned to terminate parental rights, a written service agreement offers assurance that there was clarity of goals for both the worker and the parent.

PARENT-AIDE SERVICES

Permanency planning is often enhanced by access to parent aides. Aides work with parents in their own homes using time-limited, goal-oriented contracts negotiated by the social worker, the aide, and the parent, to improve parenting skills, manage the environment, and otherwise enhance the probability of permanency for the child. In providing service, a parent aide may make two home visits per week in a 12-week contract period, with such specific goals as assisting a family with budgeting; modeling appropriate child-management techniques; and helping an isolated parent find appropriate supportive resources. Progress is noted in weekly meetings between the parent aide and the social worker. The assumption in these goals is that the aide's ability to support and nurture the parents will enable them to better meet the needs of their children.

IMPORTANCE OF CONSULTATION

In a large, multiservice agency, consultation in permanency planning can be available when trained placement staff share their experience and expertise with outpatient staff. When this is not possible, an alternative is for outpatient child guidance clinics to include on their staffs at least one worker who has permanency planning skills so that consultation can be available to other staff members. Administrative support and time for team activity are important elements in strengthening the consultation effort. Without such consultation, many children in placement, or unidentified as at risk for placement, will be denied the service required to assure permanency.

CASE EXAMPLES

Case 1

Mrs. S was referred for outpatient services because her 3-year-old son, John, had been burned while in her care. John had been temporarily placed with his maternal grandmother, after a brief time in a foster home. The parents, who were separated, each visited John for one and a half hours per week. All the adults were in conflict and presented discrepant information about how, and with whom, the burn occurred.

The protective services worker referred the case with the request that a recommendation be made as to the mother's ability to resume care of the child. A court date regarding this issue was scheduled for three months later.

Without knowledge of permanency planning, the intervention in this case would have been primarily with the mother, with the other family members included only in the assessment phase. The focus would have been on gathering information about the mother's parenting skills, on assessing conflicts between the families, and on attempting to determine if the mother was capable of parenting. The mother in all probability would have succumbed to the stress of her life situation and to the interrogation and would have dropped out of therapy. The decision would have been quickly, or eventually, made to terminate her parental rights.

Instead, the following occurred. An initial interview was scheduled with the protective services worker and the mother to clarify the reason for the referral, and explain what was expected of the mother and the agency. Individual roles and responsibilities were clarified, and the need for the protective services worker to remain involved, and the appropriateness of parent-aide services, were emphasized. At this time, the mother indicated a wish to resume custody of her child. Weekly parent-aide visits and weekly therapy sessions with the mother followed; these focused on developing parenting and child-management skills, alternate ways of handling stress, the ability to ask for help and utilize appropriate community resources, confidence in being able to understand the needs of the child, and better communication among family members. Monthly

Figure 1
Service Agreement between Mrs. S and Child and Family Services
Regarding a Plan for John

Mrs. S agrees to work with Child and Family Services toward resuming permanent care of her child, John, before the end of 1981. Child and Family Services agrees to work with Mrs. S toward that goal. Mrs. S knows that Child and Family Services will assist her in achieving permanent care of John but also must evaluate progress and, if necessary, recommend that another permanent plan be sought for John.

JH, agency social worker, agrees to

1. See Mrs. S weekly to work on goals necessary to John's return.
2. Assign a parent aide to Mrs. S.
3. Have a family session once per month.
4. Communicate with the state worker, maternal grandmother, and parent aide.
5. Arrange visiting schedules for John.
6. Keep records about scheduled and kept appointments and visits and notes indicating progress.

Mrs. S agrees to

1. Keep weekly appointments to work on marital relationship, child-care skills, communication with relatives, appropriate handling of stress.
2. Adhere to visitation schedule (see attached).
3. Work with parent aide toward developing parenting skills (see attached).
4. Secure reliable babysitting resource for John.

Mrs. S and JH agree to review this agreement on a monthly basis.

Signed,

Mrs. S   JH

_____   _____

Date: June 19, 1981
_____

family sessions were held with both parents, maternal and paternal grandmothers, the child, the protective services worker, and the parent aide to discuss issues and to facilitate communication among family members. Visitation progressed from one and a half hours per week to two overnight visits with the mother and weekend visits with the father. A service agreement was used, which clearly listed what the mother had to do to resume care of her child, and what the worker's responsibility was in keeping records of scheduled appointments and notes indicating progress (see Fig. 1). There was weekly contact with the maternal grandmother regarding the child and the visitation schedule. The mother was aided in obtaining needed furniture for her apartment.

The worker's role as case manager involved advocacy; working in collaboration with a court monitor, the protective services worker, and a parent aide assigned to the case; and utilizing community resources to assist the mother in developing the skills and confidence she needed to resume care of her child.

Within eight months, the mother resumed care of her child. The outcome was dependent on several factors: an awareness of permanency planning, effective consultation, appropriate use of collateral resources, timely intervention, and sensitivity to the needs of the client.

Case 2

Mrs. M, age 35, was referred to the Child Guidance Clinic to assess her ability to learn and apply parenting skills before the state would consider a return of her two children, Mark, 9, and Jim, 8, from foster care. She had voluntarily placed them after a suicide attempt. The children had been in placement for eight months, and the case was scheduled to appear in court in seven months.

Mrs. M had been reared in residential settings because of abusive and neglectful parents. She had limited ability to parent her children, being unable to separate their needs from her own. Because of the financial difficulties and the distance between her home and the foster home, Mrs. M was not able to maintain the prearranged visits with her children.

Without a permanency planning focus, Mrs. M would have been seen individually by the therapist, and contact with the foster mother, children, and other agencies, would have been by phone or mail. With the permanency planning focus, the state worker was involved from the beginning. The initial interview with Mrs. M and the state worker clarified the purpose of the referral and the expectations and responsibilities of the state worker, Mrs. M, and the clinic. A parent aide was immediately assigned to work with Mrs. M twice a week, to provide assistance with housing, financial aid, budgeting, appropriate use of medication, nutrition, parenting, and child management. The parent aide accompanied Mrs. M biweekly to visit with her children, and children's worker, and the foster mother. This assured continuity of visits, and permitted the aide to observe the quality of interaction between mother and children and to address problem areas through modeling.

A service agreement was used to outline what was required of Mrs. M and the worker regarding a permanent plan for Mrs. M's children (see Fig. 2). Adoption was mentioned as an alternative to returning the children home. Weekly sessions with Mrs. M were planned to focus on helping her to care for herself, develop child-management skills, learn to deal with crises and stress in a less self-destructive way, and function on her own.

Figure 2
Service Agreement between Mrs. M and Child and Family Services
Regarding a Permanent Plan for Mark and Jim

Mrs. M agrees to work with Child and Family Services toward resuming permanent care of her children Mark and Jim. Child and Family Services agrees to work with Mrs. M toward that goal; to evaluate her progress; and, if necessary, to help her to consider other permanent plans such as releasing the children for adoption.

JH, agency social worker, agrees to

1. Meet with Mrs. M once a week to talk about Mrs. M's progress in her ability to care for herself, to handle crises in constructive ways, to provide a safe environment for her children, and to develop effective child-management skills, while also considering other possible plans for the children.

2. Assign a parent aide to work with Mrs. M on ways of handling crises, developing of parenting skills, increasing self-confidence, and learning budgeting skills.

3. Refer Mrs. M to a parenting group.

4. Explore the possibility of a vocational rehabilitation program for Mrs. M.

5. Keep records about scheduled and kept appointments and visits and notes indicating progress.

Mrs. M agrees to

1. Keep weekly appointments to work on parenting skills, child management, dealing with crises, problem solving, increasing self-confidence, ability to parent herself as well as ability to function on her own.

2. Agree to work with parent aide for 12 weeks, toward developing parenting skills, child management, ability to parent herself, budgeting, and handling finances.

3. Keep weekly appointments with Dr. H (local hospital).

4. Visit with her children at the agreed-upon scheduled time.

Mrs. M and JH agree to evaluate progress every six weeks so that a decision can be made within six months time.

Signed,

Mrs. M   JH

Date: _____

The worker's reponsibility included keeping a record of attendance at appointments and assessing and monitoring progress.

As work proceeded it became clear that Mrs. M was not ready to resume responsibility for the care of her children. She understandably found it difficult to be confronted with her limitations and required extensive support for her decision to release the children for adoption. An agency adoption worker was brought in as an outside collaborator to explain the adoption process more fully to Mrs. M; the state worker postponed filing for termination of parental rights to give Mrs. M more time to make a decision. The permanency planning perspective—using a parent aide, becoming involved with the visitation, collaborating with the state worker and foster parents, and use of a time-limited service agreement—provided sufficient demonstration to Mrs. M and to others of Mrs. M's inability to parent.

Termination of parental rights seemed the most viable course. Although Mrs. M could not bring herself to surrender the children voluntarily, she was able to understand their need for permanence; the clinic worker continued to offer support to help Mrs. M to accept the evidence of the past few months. It was hoped that this would help her to live with the court decision and allow her to emotionally free the children so that they can attach themselves to a new family.

CONCLUSION

Permanency planning is defined both by its philosophic stance and by its specific techniques. These include the carrying out, within a brief, time-limited period, of a set of goal-directed activities designed to help children live in families that offer continuity of relationships with nurturing parents; the involvement of the parents and the social worker in a joint commitment to permanence for the child; the use of service agreements; the use of time frames; the delineation of clearly defined roles among professionals in helping the family and child; the necessity for collaboration with other professionals; and the dual role of the worker as supporter and evaluator. Case examples were presented to document the practical value of this approach in an outpatient setting and to illustrate the positive outcomes for families that permanency planning can achieve.

NOTES AND REFERENCES

The work on which this article is based was supported in part by Grant No. MH 15971-03 from the Mental Health Social Work Education Program of the National Institute of Mental Health.

1. Ann W. Shyne and Anita G. Schroeder, *National Study of Social Services to Children and Their Families,* Publication No. [OHDS] 78-30150 (Washington, D.C.: U.S. Government Printing Office, 1978).

2. Anthony Maluccio and Edith Fein, "Permanency Planning Revisited," in Martha Cox and Roger Cox, eds., *Foster Care: Current Issues and Practices* (Norwood, N.J.: Ablex Publishing Corp., 1984).

3. David Fanshel and Eugene Shinn, *Children in Foster Care: A Longitudinal Investigation* (New York: Columbia University Press, 1978); Jane V. Hamilton et al., "After Foster Care: Outcomes of Permanency Planning in Foster Care" (Hartford, Conn.: Child & Family Services, 1982) (mimeographed); and Shirley Jenkins, Anita G. Schroeder, and Kenneth Burgdorf, *Beyond Intake: The First Ninety Days,* Publication No. OHDS 81-30313 (Washington, D.C.: U.S. Government Printing Office, Department of Health & Human Services, 1981).

4. Trudi Lash and Heidi Sigal, *State of the Child: New York City* (New York: Foundation for Child Development, April 1976).

5. P. Coltoff and A. Lucks, "Preventing Child Maltreatment: Begin with the Parent—An Early Warning System" (New York: National Council on Alcoholism, 1978).

Focusing on Emotional Vulnerability and Developing Strengths in the Frail Elderly

Abraham Lurie, Joy C. Rich, and Lawrence Shulman

In the last decade, the study of aging has come into its own. Today there are more than 22,000,000 elderly people in our society; approximately 11 percent of our population, compared to 3 percent in 1900. Projections are that by the year 2000, this group will comprise more than 13 percent of our total population.[1] It is important to remember that many people remain quite healthy and active long into their old age. In fact, statistics indicate that only about 5 percent of the elderly population are ever institutionalized for significant periods of time, and that, in addition, only another 20 percent of the elderly suffer from disabling conditions at any particular time. The great majority of the elderly, therefore, while needing supports and programs designed to their special and particular needs, may never come into sustained contact with social agencies, hospitals, and health facilities.

However, for the growing number of elderly people included in the above percentages, it is clear that social workers and the agencies in which they work need to have an in-depth understanding of the interplay and close relationships between the social, the economic, and the physical—in effect the total psychosocial/psychological—aspects of the makeup of the elderly in considering service design and program implementation. Although the purpose of this article is not to explore the overall issues, these issues do exacerbate emotional vulnerability in the frail elderly and also have an effect upon the ability of clinical social work services to deliver effective programs to meet these people's needs and help them develop strengths to live out their lives with a sense of dignity and self-esteem.

In order to properly serve the elderly, an effective health provider/community interaction must be established in the planning, development, and implementation phases of services. Our experience over the last decade has shown that when institutions provide supportive living, socialization, and medical care programs, patient/client functioning is enhanced and the avoidable deteriorations of old age are significantly delayed or, indeed, put off indefinitely.

Recent statistics published in the *Journal of Gerontology* indicate that 11 percent of the population who are over age 65 utilize 30 percent of the health care dollar and account for 36 percent of all hospital days.[2] Thus, a small proportion of the population, the institutionalized and the frail elderly, account for a disproportionate share of health care expenditures.

MYTHS

The negative view of aging that has existed is a problem of Western civilization. At our present level of biological sophistication, there is no practical way to "stop aging." Age by itself is not the determinant in the problems of old age. In our society old age is associated with loss of self-esteem and effectiveness. The elderly are perceived as confused, repetitive, frail, and unproductive. For many, aging is synonymous with a pathological condition, and society's view becomes a self-fulfilling prophecy. The elderly, and frequently those involved with them, introject society's view. No other portion of the life span is viewed in this way. Butler uses the term *ageism*, which he defines as a "system of stereotyping, discriminating against people because they are old; just as racism, sexism, can accomplish this with skin color and gender."[3]

Myths exist because of unconscious wishes. We tend to be "phobic" about the elderly. These thoughts and feelings affect the social work clinician as well. Because we fear our own feelings, we may have a tendency to talk at and not with older adults. It is important to continually focus on the person and not just the problem, or crisis, at hand. New outlooks on aging can dispel these stereotypes, and we should not expect that old age must be pathological. Successful aging is very individual and more common than assumed.

In the program for the frail elderly described later, many planning and operational issues emerged. After three years of experience, we have found that with an early and immediate awareness of the various social, physical, and, particularly, emotional vulnerabilities of the aged, the trained social work staff can work effectively with this population in a congregate living arrangement that allows them to reverse a regressive and pessimistic lifestyle in the last stage of life and to live community-based, active, more effective, and personally more satisfying lives.

Among the most evident vulnerabilities facing the aged are socially related issues such as the loss of a spouse; loss of peers who seem all too rapidly to die, move away, or enter institutions; and loss of family supports because of either physical or emotional distancing.[4] Added to these is the loss of economic productivity as a result of moving out of the active job market. There are few opportunities for the elderly to engage in productive, remunerative employment—one gauge for determining adequate functioning. This loss of economic productivity brings with it a concomitant change in the lifestyle that had been supported by a higher economic level for the individual and family. In addition, in recent years the inflationary erosion of planned-for income has significantly added to the deterioration of possible retirement lifestyles.

An elderly person viewed as nonproductive and no longer useful or needed by society, senses his or her own value and prestige as diminished, and suffers a significant loss of self-esteem. There is a narrowing of social outlets and social roles that leads to increased isolation, loneliness, and aloneness. Prescribed "retirement" roles are often seen as meaningless by the elderly and this accelerates the introjection of a negative societal view about the aged as a caste.

Many of the elderly are increasingly fearful about going into the streets, even for the most simple tasks, such as shopping and visiting. They feel themselves, because of rising urban and suburban crime rates, to be particularly vulnerable targets and restrict their activity based on this both real and perceived vulnerability.

Other major problems for the aged are the physical changes that take place. Diminished energy levels, decreases or even significant losses in hearing and vision, indeed of the "social senses," lead to decreasing capacities in handling the activities of daily living. These particular losses significantly affect the ability to carry on relationships through conversation, reading, and traveling. There are a number of health changes and an increase in health risks for the elderly population as a whole. For elderly women, who outlive men as age increases, there are several physical and psychological losses that occur or are perceived: the loss of physical attractiveness; significant change in physical shape; loss of the ability to procreate; and, because of postmenopausal syndrome, diminished opportunities for sexual involvement. Rubin refers to myths about sexuality in the elderly, namely, that desire and ability will no longer be present at a particular age.[5] This too, becomes a self-fulfilling prophecy, although surveys of the elderly usually indicate that at least two-thirds still have significant interest in, and engage in various levels of, sexual activity.

These physical changes and others that could be added, tend to produce in many elderly people a psychological trauma and heightened anxiety. They become reminders of getting old and of being less effective. This trauma can lead to significant disengagement, both socially and psychologically, when individuals become fearful that they will become unable to function and to be independent and care for themselves—in effect, incapable of meeting their total life needs.

The many external realities and changes the elderly must face frequently manifest themselves as depression and sadness. According to many researchers and workers in the field of the aging, depression is the major psychological symptom.[6] The impetus for the retreat into oneself and into a more isolated stage may be gradual or traumatically induced, as for example by the death of a close relation or spouse, or by a serious physical trauma. Depression, however, when treated, has a good prognosis. The problem is that health and mental health professionals are quick to label such behaviors "organic brain syndrome" and to relegate such patients to "untreatable" status.

For the greater majority of the elderly, these are not golden years; the current economic state of the United States has seriously eroded and tarnished that vision. Funds put aside 10 to 20 years ago have little effective purchasing power today. With the current attacks on the economic support systems of the elderly, that is, Social Security, Social Security Disability, and Supplemental Security Income, day-to-day survival issues and fears add to the already growing load of anxiety and depression and fear of living alone. Public policy issues clearly effect the well-being of the elderly.

Because the elderly are a particularly vulnerable group, the amount of psychological and physical energy involved in seeking help deters many of them from doing so. When they do ask for assistance it is usually not as a result of emotional stress, but rather because of external factors such as a change in lifestyle, the death of a spouse, a change in environment caused by neighborhood deterioration, or a housing crisis.[7]

To help an elderly client appropriately, it is necessary to assess the person's need and to judge his or her capacity for change. Such judgment involves the balance of psychosocial and biological forces. Often families seem to make changes without regard for the wishes of the elderly person, or the elderly make changes out of deference to other members of their families. But, beneath this is the pressing desire, sometimes very consciously articulated, and sometimes unconsciously present, to remain as independent as possible. To do this, however, the elderly must be able to care for themselves and to be economically viable. The social work clinician has to view a lifetime of experience, not just an existential condition.

A trauma caused by a problem that requires immediate help must be dealt with at once. But, this should not dim the view of the social workers to the reservoir of coping mechanisms that many elderly people have and have used well in their lifetime. Their survival mechanisms are often quite strong, stronger than might appear on the surface. Some of these mechanisms are successful, others marginal, and some dysfunctional.[8]

A SUPPORT PROGRAM

Housing was seen by the social work department at Long Island Jewish/ Hillside Medical Center as one of the most pressing needs for the elderly. Many of the elderly did not require a hospital bed, and yet there were not and still are not adequate resources in the community to help them live independently, despite all of the rhetoric by governmental agencies about their cost-containment policies. These policies did not and have not produced enough housing resources for the frail elderly living in these circumstances.

Long Island Jewish/Hillside Medical Center, therefore, decided to develop the concept of enriched housing for frail elderly for a number of reasons. The first is that the number of inpatients older than 65 was increasing at a fairly rapid rate. It had increased from about 20 to 35 percent during a two-year period, and included the frail elderly who require some monitoring for a physical illness and may become unable to reside in the community without support.

It was projected that an enriched housing program for this target population would result in a diminished use of emergency rooms, inpatient services, and other services that many of the frail elderly require. In some instances the hospitals, particularly emergency rooms, have been used to provide functions traditionally performed by social agencies that are now feeling the effects of budgetary constraints. It was hoped that a congregate living arrangement that provided the elderly with needed supports could be developed, and in this way, the extensive use of the emergency room for psychological reassurance would lessen and the expensive hospital facility could be put to more appropriate use.[9]

Another objective was to help some of the frail elderly to remain out of institutions, particularly when institutionalization is against their wishes. A housing arrangement that would offer the elderly a viable living arrangement in the community at a low cost could indeed improve their functional capabilities and retard physical and emotional decline. Some of the elderly who are transferred from home to a permanent institutional arrangement give up the will to live and, in many instances, they begin to decline emotionally and physically. There is a need for institutions for some of the elderly, but for others institutionalization is an unnecessary end of the road. The congregate living arrangements that we developed from the concept of enriched housing met these objectives.[10]

Intake Process

With the planning and inception of our enriched housing program for the frail elderly, the social work staff had the opportunity to view the dynamics of the elderly—and their adaptive capacities—from different vantage points. In the initial screening phases, a number of perceptions emerged that clearly delineated the psychological bind in which many of the elderly found themselves and the ambivalence the elderly felt toward these living arrangements. On the one hand, there was the intense desire the elderly had to remain as self-sufficient and functionally independent human beings. On the other hand there was their considerable fear of living alone; of being unable to handle their day-to-day needs; of being forgotten about, unneeded, uncared for; and perhaps underlying all of this, the unstated fear of dying alone. The manifest expressions of why the elderly we interviewed wished to change their living arrangements fell into a number of groupings:

1. They no longer wanted to live alone, but rather to live in a companionship arrangement with peers, which many felt would magically change their situation.
2. They wanted to take the responsibility for their care from their families. This desire resulted, in many instances, from pressure from adult children in the family to have the person living in a more "protected" environment, although many of the elderly children gave both realistic and psychologically based reasons for not wanting the elderly parent to live with them.
3. They needed help with home management and responsibilities.

What quickly became clear was that a more complex, latent set of dynamics were at work with these elderly applicants to the enriched housing program. These dynamics could be broadly categorized and included the fears of loss of control and autonomy and of being psychologically submerged, resulting in a loss of personality in an alien environment. At the beginning, the enriched housing program was indeed viewed as an alien environment. Typical of this viewpoint was the comment of one potential resident who stated, "I never expected to end up my golden older years in a place like this." This statement reflected her anger, feelings of rejection, and her sense of being thrown out by her family of seven children upon whom she had relied for care. Her attitude is reflected in the often-heard comment that "one mother can take care of seven kids, but seven kids can't take care of one mother."

Because of our awareness that so many complex dynamics were operating, the intake procedure was developed as a "leisurely" assessment and review process. This enabled patient, family, and clinician to effectively deal with the realities and capabilities of a plan for success with that particular individual. At least one interview with each of two social workers was held with each applicant and family to give additional viewpoints in the review and evaluation process. From the patient and family point of view, the process would give family members time to react, to work through ambivalences, and to raise as many questions as could be anticipated before their acceptance into the program and their actual move into a congregate apartment. When the clinical staff assessed an applicant as "a good prospect," and when the applicant felt ready to make a commitment to entering the enriched housing program, a luncheon visit was arranged to the potential apartment. The applicant then had an oppor-

tunity to interact with staff and the other residents within the environment in which they would be living.

The leisurely admission process allowed sufficient time for the staff to
obtain medical reports, work with the family on legal issues, obtain
"social references" from individuals who had known the applicant, and
develop an extensive psychosocial data base on every patient. It also
enabled the staff to work out, with the patient and the family, the financial arrangements that would permit the person to enter, and handle the
costs of, the program.

Assessing Ability

It may seem from our array of services that residents' autonomy and
independence are difficult to maintain. It is true that because of the
nature of this protective environment and support system, some dependence is fostered. Many of our residents who were growing up in the
early part of the century, some native born, some as immigrants, experienced emotional and physical deprivation. Many struggled to establish
themselves, worked, married, had families, and watched children grow
and leave the nest. Now they are alone again and struggling to maintain
themselves. Many state explicitly the wish to reverse the role from care
giver to care receiver, others express the wish through their behavioral
reactions.

All residents have some degree of frailty. Some are capable of functioning on different levels of daily living; some are more demanding,
wanting total care. As the social work clinicians began to establish relationships with individual residents, we became aware of the different ways
some coped with feelings of emotional vulnerability. For example,

> Rosa, a frail 77-year-old woman with losses of hearing and sight and a de-
> teriorating arthritic condition, was once a community leader and a fine
> pianist, and was accustomed to many cultural experiences. She became so
> demanding of assistance from staff and her peers that she eventually "turned
> off" everyone in the apartment. It was soon clear to the social worker that
> Rosa was defending herself against a deep sense of humiliation at the
> decrease in her daily living activities and against the need for assistance from
> staff and residents. Her feelings of humiliation at her dependence produced
> anger and hostility that was acted out on an interpersonal level.
>
>   The social work clinician was able to utilize the understanding of depen-
> dence and the feelings it stirs up to help Rosa accept the need for help in
> certain areas and to foster independence in areas she could manage. Even-
> tually Rosa's experience became the basis for other residents to learn that to
> be independent and to develop interdependent relationships, one must also
> be able to be dependent.

It also became clear that the more capable people wanted to differentiate themselves from the more frail because of their own fears of similar losses, as well as fears of being seduced into caretaker roles, since they were on the scene. It was more possible for the "well" frail elderly to give support and assistance to another resident once they had established some bonds and were on a more equal footing. If the degree of need was too divergent, resentment and anger were often expressed.

Depending on their prior adaptation and their current levels of functioning, the residents in our enriched housing program exhibited a wide range of differences regarding their self-esteem, their tendency to be either aggressive or passive in their adaptation, and the degree to which jealousy and envy played a part in their ability to involve themselves in the mutual support concept of the apartment. There seemed to be a fairly direct relationship between deprivation or a sense of deprivation in childhood and the capacity for creative and effective adaptation in the older years. If during childhood—a period of curiosity, gathering information, and generally expanding and learning from one's experiences—there had been successful behavioral growth, in the later years there was a continuing opportunity to clarify, deepen, and find use for those experiences.

Those who suffered childhood deprivation, however, despite a total lifetime of learning and adapting, still had significant maladaptive patterns that reemerged and were brought to the experience of the new setting. Once again they were in a family setting with siblings that re-created earlier childhood dissatisfaction and rivalries. These, however, were a group of siblings, with conflicting needs, from diverse ethnic, socioeconomic, and religious backgrounds. We learned that to adjust to the losses and changes, older adults need positive reinforcement and gratification. These can be developed slowly and carefully in each resident through interpersonal relationships within the congregate care setting, through recreational activities, and through small but substantial achievements.[11]

Growth-Producing Experiences

The clinical social workers in this program have to be creative in relating to the group situations in order to keep the situations from turning into gripe sessions and reinforcing negative adaptations. Our experience has shown that using such adjunct techniques and materials as photography, poetry, and creative reminiscences helped to create a commonality and opened up arenas for examining past history and adaptation. Much has been written about the therapeutic value of reminiscence.[12] It helps to link the elderly to each other as well as to the positive aspects of their past and also to concretize emotions. This method permits an easier flow of emotional material in a more comfortable kind of environment. We are now beginning to experiment with art therapy, using watercolors and finger paints to add a more expressive environment for the residents of the apartments.

A stated emphasis of the clinical approach by the social work staff was to involve the residents of the apartment in greater decision making concerning their lives, their futures, and their day-to-day environment. As an example, in one apartment where six women of very mixed backgrounds live, the residents were encouraged to view themselves as women in the mainstream of the ERA movement. When a decision needed to be made about changing a homemaker in that particular apartment, the residents met several times to discuss the qualities and the requirements they had for a homemaker for themselves. As a result of these discussions, the hiring of a new homemaker was significantly influenced by the wishes, concerns, and interests of the residents of that apartment. This was a significant growth-producing experience for them and the social work staff. Although three unsuccessful homemakers had previously worked in that apartment, the homemaker who was chosen on the basis of these discussions has stayed and become involved in the apartment and in the living situation of these women. Moreover, she has successfully added to the functioning of the program. The women, in turn, have found less need to project underlying hostilities, jealousy, and envy onto the homemaker and problems of food. As they felt safer in the environment of their group, they began to develop more successful coping mechanisms to deal with their frustrations and dissatisfactions. Working with the resident group also permitted both the clients and the clinician to address the issues of their "expectations" and provided an opportunity to help the clients in their adaptation to group living.

SUMMARY

It has been fascinating to have the opportunity to study a small group of frail elderly living in a re-created family setting that simulates as closely as possible independent living in the community. The aging organism is bombarded by many internal and external stimuli. The function of the ego is to mediate stimuli to effect action and produce change. It is essential to understand what is going on for the older person, and to study the defenses that have been built up over a lifetime to deal with the array of stresses they are experiencing. The staff of the enriched housing program do not want to break down defenses of the elderly involved in the program but instead, through the client/social worker relationship, want to develop a therapeutic relationship that can become an agent for change to help clients build and utilize ego strengths.

Understanding all these issues has enabled staff members to work with residents on a multilevel basis that includes the individual, the group, and the family. We have slowly effected behavioral changes in the elderly through focusing on emotional vulnerability and strengthening the reintegration of social, emotional, and environmental adaptive capabilities.

NOTES AND REFERENCES

1. Census Bureau estimate reported by Associated Press, November 9, 1982.

2. Lawrence Z. Rubenstein, Lois Rhee, and Robert K. Lane, "The Role of Geriatric Assessment Units in Caring for the Elderly: An Analytic Review," *Journal of Gerontology*, 37, no. 5 (1982), pp. 513–521.

3. Robert N. Butler and Myrna I. Lewis, *Aging in Mental Health* (St. Louis, Mo.: C. V. Mosby, 1973).

4. Arthur Peck, "Psychiatric Aspects of the Geriatric Problem," in Minna Field, ed., *Depth and Extent of the Geriatric Problem: Authoritative Original Contributions* (Springfield, Ill.: Charles C Thomas, 1970), pp. 137–146.

5. I. Rubin, *Sexual Life After Sixty* (New York: Basic Books, 1965).

6. N. E. Zinberg and I. Kaufman, eds., *Normal Psychology of the Aging Process* (New York: International Universities Press, 1964).

7. M. Powell Lawton, "The Impact of the Environment on Aging and Behavior," in James E. Birren and K. Warner Schaie, eds., *Handbook of the Psychology of Aging* (New York: Van Nostrand Reinhold, 1977).

8. Jack Botwinick, *We Are Aging* (New York: Springer, 1981).

9. Robert Snow and Lawrence Crapo, "Emotional Bondedness, Subjective Well-Being, and Health in Elderly Medical Patients," *Journal of Gerontology*, 37, no. 5 (1982), pp. 609–616.

10. This program was initiated with support from the Nassau County Department of Senior Citizens Affairs, New York State Department of Social Services, Office of Enriched Housing Programs, and additional developmental funds were provided by the Federation of Jewish Philanthropies.

11. Eric H. Erikson, *Childhood and Society* (2d ed.; New York: W. W. Norton, 1963).

12. See, for example, Allen Pincus, "Reminiscence in Aging and Its Implications for Social Work Practice," *Social Work*, 15 (July 1970), pp. 46–53.

Problem Resolution through Team Decision Making in Family Team Conferences

Don R. Fuller and
Janette B. Russell

Practice excellence in clinical social work may be observed in Louisiana's approach to problem resolution through team decision making, which is facilitated by regularly scheduled family team conferences. This process, named the Louisiana Plan, is being implemented throughout the state in the public family service and foster care programs of the Louisiana Office of Human Development. It was developed by a committee from the Monroe Region and ran as a pilot program from September 1, 1980, for one year. The program allows optimal opportunities for families to resolve their problems without removing children from their homes. When foster care is necessary, it assists parents in taking corrective action so as to facilitate an early return of the children. When parents do not work toward correcting their problems or cannot achieve resolutions, alternate planning becomes possible for children.

Team decision making in family team conferences represented the most difficult task undertaken by the entire staff; it was also the most rewarding. The committee was charged with designing a program similar to the Kentucky Plan,[1] which was used as a guide. After careful evaluation of each step, the Louisiana Plan for foster care was devised, and this was followed by a similar system for the child protection program.

Examination of this agency's past practices revealed that a consistent support system for the family or the social worker did not exist. The structure of team decision making provides a support system and sets a standard of expectations for each team member. Each person is held accountable for his or her portion of the responsibilities. Woven into this supportive structure are the key elements of the group process—leadership, worker skills, and client motivation—that mesh together to create a total system. This blend culminates in shared decision making and brings each component into communication with one another. The process begins with the first contact with the family and continues until the end of treatment.

An evaluation of the agency's responsibility to the public and its ability to meet the mandates required by law was necessary before the program could be implemented. The emphasis of services for the agency changed. One specific, clear goal evolved: to protect children in their own home; when foster care becomes necessary, to rehabilitate the family so the child may be returned early. Services to families with children in their own home and to parents of children in foster care became the priority. The agency's new commitment places in motion effective permanent planning.

Prior to the project, meeting the child's most basic need, to be with his or her birth parents, or to have the stability of a permanent family, was not consistently addressed. Our efforts had been in the wrong direction. With the new commitment came the removal of the global, trivial, and vague services, which have bogged down public service agencies for 20 years.

PROGRAM DESCRIPTION

A family team conference may be defined as a conference led by an objective leader, in which the family service worker, all significant family members, and any other person who can be helpful in solving the problems come together as a team to make decisions. The conference has definite tasks to be achieved but allows for open, honest communication in a relaxed atmosphere. The family service worker's supervisor serves as the team leader. The crisis intervention worker attends the first conference to confirm the findings of the investigation. The conference participants may include the child, foster parents, the foster care worker, relatives, or anyone the parents feel may be helpful in resolving the problems. Often these members include mothers, boyfriends, siblings, grown children, or attorneys. The agency has invited physicians, psychologists, a child's therapist, or a court-appointed attorney. A clerical person records a summary of the conference. Team members vary according to the needs and capabilities of the child's parents and the severity of the problem.

Conferences are scheduled at regular intervals. The first family team conference in family service cases is scheduled within 20 working days following referral for services and every 90 days thereafter, or more often if needed. The initial team conference for foster care is required within five working days for children who come into the program through the regular court process and within 20 working days for children placed by a temporary court order. Ongoing conferences are scheduled every 90 days with the direction of permanency planning for the foster child being addressed at the six-month conference. Every effort is made to schedule the conference so the parent can attend, but the conference is held, whether or not he or she comes. After the initial team conference has occurred and parents receive their copy of the confirmation containing the decisions reached and the proposed treatment plan, they often request another conference to be scheduled.

At each family team conference, specific tasks should be achieved. The first task is to explain the agency's responsibilities and goals, so that the team can concert their efforts toward maintaining the family unit and allowing the children to remain at home, or to return home. The second task is for each team member to have a clear understanding of the problems to be resolved. When the parents are able to state the problems, this task becomes easier. The ultimate goal that will be achieved when the problems are resolved, such as "my children will remain in my home," or "my children will be returned to my home," needs to be clarified. The objectives that must be obtained to reach that goal are defined, and this is followed by a discussion of each alternative and the consequences of the alternatives. The idea is for the parents and workers to reach an agreement on the explicit tasks that each person will complete to resolve the problems. When other members of the team agree to accept specific responsibilities, these are included. The date by which each task should be completed is stated in the agreement that is signed by the agency staff and the parents.

Treatment Plan

The treatment plan becomes a commitment between the parents and the agency, not a plan between the worker and the parent. When caseworkers change, the new worker assumes the responsibilities already agreed on. This process maintains case continuity. For children in foster care, a visitation contract with their parents is completed.

Developing an individual service plan for each foster child is another duty required to assure that each child's needs are being met to the greatest degree possible while he or she is separated from parents. Setting the date for the next team conference is mandatory and provides for progress, or the lack of it, to be evaluated on a regular basis. At the succeeding conferences, the plan is reviewed to determine the progress each person has made toward fulfilling his or her agreements or the need to make changes in the plan.

In protective service cases in which progress is not occurring, the parents are encouraged to help the agency locate relatives for placement. The workers are required to interview each relative who might be able to provide a home for a child before foster care placement is considered. The goal toward which the parent will strive while the children are in placement is clarified, as is the court process and the information to be presented in the courtroom. Surprises should not occur with the parent this closely involved.

The safeguards provided in the structural design of achieving problem resolution in family team conferences account for much of the program's success. The first safeguard is the assignment of case responsibilities. Workers are divided into three units: crisis intervention (for which 14 new referrals per month are the caseload standard); family services for child protection in the family's home and service to parents of children in foster care (with 25 families as the caseload); and foster care (in which 45 children per caseload are the standard). This division of responsibility places primary emphasis on working with the family to keep the family functioning and to return children who are removed as early as possible.

The crisis intervention worker is charged with investigating each complaint completely. However, it becomes his or her responsibility to establish the agency's goal with the parents so that the parents become ready and willing to participate in the family team conferences. The crisis intervention worker provides immediate services while he or she is completing the investigation. The family is then transferred to the family service worker, who assumes responsibility for providing intensive services. Immediate and intensive services are vital at the point of crisis while the parents are highly motivated. Within this framework the family service worker is not involved in investigating new neglect and abuse complaints, nor is he or she responsible for maintaining a child's foster care placement in a particular foster home. The only crises to which the family service worker must respond are those that occur in his or her caseload. This division allows the family service worker time for careful planning.

Another essential element in the plan is to allow the parents in a valid protective service situation the option of participating in the treatment program. The agency accepts the parent's decision, unless the situation is so severe that it necessitates recommending court action for removal or supervision. Thus, the parents assume responsibility for the need to effect change and work toward that goal. Maximum motivation and the surfacing of inner strengths within the parents, coupled with immediate services and the scheduling of early conferences, assist in problem solving.

The parents of children who have been placed in foster care choose to work toward problem resolution and to have their children returned, or, by not working toward resolution, choose to relinquish their rights to plan for their child. Louisiana's termination laws have only recently been improved to facilitate termination so that alternative permanent plans may be developed for children in foster care who will never be able to return home.

Family Team Conference

Prior to the initial family team conference, the worker and the parents analyze problems that must be resolved and begin the treatment plan. The parents are prepared for participation in the conference by being helped to state their problems, to express their feelings and opinions freely, and then to decide upon the action necessary for them to meet the desired objective. The agency staff prepares by obtaining sufficient information, holding case planning conferences, and obtaining professional evaluations and consultations when necessary.

The foster care worker is responsible for assisting the child and the foster parents to understand the team approach and each team member's role. Maintaining the parent-child relationship is of foremost importance. Each child placed must have a visit with his or her parents within the first five days of placement. For treatment plans and goals to be meaningful, the foster care worker must have complete knowledge about each child and his or her problems and adjustment. Every foster care worker must be able to communicate with children of all ages. The feelings of hurt, anger, and despair experienced by children separated from their families must be managed constructively. For this, the team function of the foster care worker and the foster parents is vital. Without the sincere support and assistance of the foster parents, the goals may not be achieved.

The team leader must maintain objectivity in the conference and assure that each person's opinions and feelings are addressed. This task alone requires courage and the willingness to take risks. The leader must be honest and open and willing to model roles. The conferences are emotionally draining, especially when many children are involved and achieving solutions is difficult. The leaders have developed a unique personal power so that they do not dominate or manipulate. Stamina and a sense of humor have become recognized qualities of this ongoing job in leadership. During the pilot study, supervisors who were giving but felt uncomfortable in dealing with a person's "negatives" grew to become forceful and straightforward in their roles, and their effectiveness and self-confidence increased.

The significance each member plays is illustrated in a foster child's comment to his parent, "You did not do anything you agreed to do in the contract! I cannot come home until things are different!" The impact of such statements cannot be ignored by the team. Such understanding by the child clarifies for the group the reason this child is in foster care. No longer can the agency be held responsible for the lack of change when the social worker has fulfilled his or her agreements. We all recognize that some parents cannot change.

Documentation of each decision, commitment, and goal attainment is another feature of the plan that assures the child an opportunity for permanency. The facts are used to make recommendations to the court regarding a child's return to his or her parents or for termination of the parents' rights.

Professionals' Responsibility

Many professionals' first reaction to this plan is skepticism. They find it hard to believe that the parents will come to family team conferences.

But they do. In many cases, this is the first time they have been invited to attend a conference in which they and their children are the subject. Agency conferences have traditionally been held without the parents' knowledge or participation. If we as professionals want a plan to succeed, it is wise to include the parents from the beginning, rather than to seek their participation after all the decisions about the expected outcome have been reached. We have seen that parents do participate; they do understand. They understand the abuse and/or neglect that occurred, the need for it not to recur, the need for change, and the fact that the agency will assist. They learn to express their opinions and share their differences. The parents appreciate family team conferences. Some of their responses have been: "This is the first time I knew you cared about me!" "When I do these things, will you recommend to the court that my children be returned?" "I never knew what was needed to have my children returned."

It is always difficult to return children to parents who can provide only a marginal standard of living for themselves and their children. Those who have marginal standards of living include parents who receive Aid to Families with Dependent Children or whose income is low but above the qualifying standards to be eligible for many free services such as medical and dental care. In these situations, everyone involved recognizes that pretty new clothes, regular church attendance, and opportunities for the development of a child's talents are often bypassed. Providing all the necessities for a child and directing and motivating the child to develop to his or her fullest potential are important to all concerned child care personnel. In most instances, it seems that the birth parents would be unlikely to provide as many opportunities as the foster parents and the agency might do. It is with difficulty that we accept that a child has a right to grow and develop normally with his or her parents regardless of their financial status (as long as the child's basic needs are met).

The standard of living also includes the lifestyle of a family and the presence or absence of regular, consistent parenting. Effective parenting skills—even when they are known and usually practiced—are not always operational when the parents are physically or emotionally ill.

Case Example

One mother who received medical attention and mental health care functioned well while the children were in foster care. She received the close direction and support of the social worker. It could be predicted that following the children's return and stress on her increased, the mother's needs would go unattended and her functioning would diminish. In years past, social workers, agencies, and the courts would not have taken the risk of returning the children. Today we do.

A crisis in the family did occur after the children were returned, but the woman's husband and family members learned the necessity of monitoring her physical and mental health needs. Respect for the mother's health is gaining the rightful place necessary to keep this family together.

RESULTS AND REWARDS

The need for parents to become upper middle class, to improve their intellectual functioning, or to have money in the bank has probably been the "implied expectation" communicated by many workers. With these unspoken requirements, it is little wonder the parents became passive or out of touch with the agency. "Minimum acceptable level of child care" became a new concept requiring definition and interpretation at the beginning of each conference. The results for parents and children alike are remarkable. Parents have been able to achieve "minimum acceptable standards" and have the children returned. Others have surrendered their children for adoption, thus accepting the responsibility for making a permanent plan.

The reaction of the workers has been exhilarating. Although the caseloads continue to be high, the workers enjoy helping parents achieve success. They no longer feel totally responsible for any lack of progress. Line supervisors, who carry the weight of this program, become exhausted, yet these individuals praise team decision making as the ultimate in effecting change.

Respect for Parents

The group process in team decision making has several immediate rewards. Foremost, it serves as an avenue for practicing and experiencing each of the social work values. Respect for parents and their problems as well as their efforts and difficulties in problem resolution is gained by each team member. Foster parents have gained a greater respect and compassion for the parents and are able to assist the children in understanding their parents' problems. The parents gain more respect for the foster parents, especially because the goal of returning the child to the parents' home is the goal of each member.

The entire stage of the conference flows with empathic understanding, respect for individuality, and interest in the parent, child, and foster parent. The opportunity to be genuine and authentic exists because a nonjudgmental attitude prevails. Solving the problems becomes everyone's concern, creating true unity of purpose. The right to self-determination has brought about significant dividends for the children and their parents. Once parents realize that they are not being "ordered" to do explicit things, they assume the responsibility for the action needed.

Team leaders practice the skills every group leader strives to learn and use effectively, although they may not be able to name these skills. In most conferences, the following skills are probably used: active listening, reflecting, clarifying, interpreting, questioning, confronting, supporting, diagnosing, evaluating, facilitating, empathizing, summarizing (a routine at the close of each conference), and terminating. The correct use of authority is vital to the total process. The agency's responsibility for child protection and the necessity for protecting each child are expressed as representing the community's standards.

Yalom refers to studies that conclude that

> Group therapy draws its unique potency from its interpersonal and group properties. The agent of change appears to be the group intermember influence network. The effective group therapist must direct his efforts toward maximal development of these resources.[2]

Team decision making adds further credence to those conclusions.

Empowerment of Workers

Team decision making itself empowers the worker, regardless of his or her level of skill, to become "an enabler" while working with the family. As in most public agencies, the number of professionally trained staff is limited. Because team leaders set the pace for a therapeutic atmosphere, workers can easily follow their example. Traditionally, the workers have practiced supportive casework techniques. Confrontation in a nonthreatening manner is the most difficult skill workers and supervisors have had to learn. We have dubbed this technique "cool, calm, confrontation." Becoming proficient in this technique has enabled the workers to use authority more honestly and to assure parents that they want to help.

At the same time, each worker has had the opportunity to learn new skills. Visiting parents twice monthly, as required, demands that the workers become comfortable with the intervention skills of empathic responses, focused responses, clarification, and interpretation. The interaction observed in the team conference allows the worker an opportunity to confirm with the supervisor his or her observation of the parents' behavior. Workers of all skill levels, from the new ones without professional training to the highly skilled ones with master's degrees in social work, have an opportunity to experience success. For the first time, family service workers in the public sector may engage clients in specific strategies and plan their time as clinicians in the private sector would. As workers have opportunities for learning new techniques and skills, they also have opportunities to practice these skills. Task-centered casework and the development of treatment plans keep the workers and the parents focused on the objectives to be attained. Thus the family benefits from the caseworker's skills, as well as from the total efforts of the team decision-making process, which include the parents' desire to succeed, the leader's skill, and the group process.

PROBLEMS AND SOLUTIONS

Problems in implementing this program occurred with regularity. The number one problem has been, and continues to be, staff utilization. The rule that a family service worker cannot be assigned crisis intervention or foster care cases is the factor that ensures the effectiveness of the family service worker. Crisis intervention and foster care workers may share assignments when necessary. The Monroe Region covers 11 parishes (counties). Initially the caseloads and numbers of workers in each parish rarely met the guidelines for caseload assignments. Workers and supervisors had to be reassigned to cover adjacent parishes. As caseloads change, reassigning staff for effective coverage became necessary.

Prior to implementation, the number of protective service cases in the region was close to 1,000. Recognizing our inability to hold family team conferences on each of these cases, we closed every case that had not had worker-client contact during the past 60 days. Exisiting family service cases would have a team conference held within one year from the implementation date of the program. Closing these cases brought about immediate relief of a heavy burden.

Skepticism and doubt were expressed by the entire staff. The supervisors and workers questioned their ability to learn the new skills required. They questioned the wisdom of utilizing the vast amount of time demanded for the team conferences. They feared, as foster parents did, that children would be hurt if we risked allowing them to return home. We have not only learned to take risks, but also to evaluate progress more accurately. Developing treatment plans, while seemingly simple, has proved to be difficult. Many times the agreements decided on were not relevant to the goals that were set. Experience in developing treatment plans and critiquing by the supervisory and line staff have increased skills in this area. Supervisors and workers are planning their time on a monthly basis for six months to a year in advance. Careful planning is necessary so that commitments are realistic. Purposeful use of time and energy thus developed. Workers and supervisors continued to seek other methods to help in carrying out individual tasks and case planning conferences.

In filling vacancies, the agency has a firm policy of employing social workers with a master's degree in social work before hiring workers with a bachelor's degree. The Social Worker Supervisor I position requires a master's degree in social work. Because the agency experienced difficulty in recruiting supervisors on this level, the Louisiana Department of Civil Service did a study of the program, while the staff was implementing the Louisiana Plan, to validate the need for an MSW degree. If validation was not achieved, the MSW requirement was to be removed from the requirements for a supervisor's position, followed by the removal of the MSW requirement from the social worker's position.

The study showed that job tasks performed by the non-MSW and MSW supervisors did not differ. What did differ was the quality of job performance. In the Louisiana Department of Civil Service unpublished report, "Job Analysis Report for Social Worker Supervisor I," investigators stated:

> We were consistently impressed with the dedication of both MSW and non-MSW supervisors. They are working under heavy caseloads and in difficult circumstances. All are concerned about the welfare of their clients and the treatment they are providing. We were impressed with certain MSW supervisors who have taken inexperienced human service worker staffs and developed their analytical and counseling skills so that they could better serve their clients. We were impressed with other MSW supervisors who utilize their personal time and money to attend additional training sessions and pass information on to their workers. And, we were most impressed with those offices, who with the guidance of their Social Worker Supervisor II, have restructured their internal staff to facilitate the types of treatment that the MSW social worker has been trained to provide. It is in these offices that the "ideal" was found not only on paper but in reality as well.[3]

Social programs must be accountable. The system described here provides that each team member be accountable for his or her responsibilities. It demands that a permanent plan be developed for each child in foster care. The Louisiana Plan has been instrumental in helping the state to meet the standards set forth in P.L. 96-272. This quality was recently confirmed through a monitoring review by the Dallas regional office of the U.S. Department of Health and Human Services. The program's effectiveness was also indicated by a decrease of 11 percent the first year and an additional 3½ percent the second year in the foster care population. The number of children entering foster care decreased 14 percent the first year and 8 percent the second year, while the number of children leaving foster care increased 132 percent the first year over the previous year and 168 percent the second year over fiscal year 1979–80.

OUTCOMES

In summary, problem resolution through team decision making in family team conferences allows for a standard of expectations to be set, based on an environment in which each social work value and therapeutic process may be practiced. Decisions agreed on become commitments for those involved, generating motivation for each team member. The program has changed the direction of Louisiana's child protection and foster care programs, providing maximum opportunity for children to remain with their parents or relatives or return to their own home after foster care placement has been utilized. It provides accountability by setting forth the agency's responsibility to assist parents to maintain their families as a unit. The required scheduling of family team conferences to achieve problem resolution through team decision making assures assistance to the family in accomplishing a permanent plan for each child in foster care. When parents relinquish responsibility for permanency, the agency must assume it.

NOTES AND REFERENCES

1. *Manual for Foster Care Program* (Frankfort, Ky.: Bureau of Social Services, Department of Human Resources, February 1978).

2. Irvin D. Yalom, *The Theory and Practice of Group Psychotherapy* (New York: Basic Books, 1975), p. 103.

3. Lenard E. Servat and Ellen Montegudo, "Job Analysis Report for Social Work Supervisor I, Office of Human Development, Department of Health and Human Resources." Unpublished report, Louisiana Department of Civil Service, Baton Rouge, August 23, 1982, p. 15.

Unilateral Family Therapy for Alcohol Abuse: Early Clinical Impressions

Edwin J. Thomas, Cathleen Santa, Denise Bronson, and Joanne Yaffe

By consuming alcohol in excess, the alcohol abuser harms his or her health and incurs large costs for society through loss of work, loss of efficiency, and the greater likelihood of being in traffic accidents. In addition, the alcohol abuser increases the likelihood of distressed family relationships, violence in the family, reduced family stability, and marital dissolution. These are among the ways the abuser may inflict great discomfort, stress, and hardship upon those in his or her family. These effects of excessive drinking are well known and have been amply documented.[1] Clearly, alcohol abuse is a difficult problem, but refusal of the abuser to enter treatment makes an already difficult problem worse. Such refusal removes the abuser from direct access to remedial effort, allows the harm caused by the alcohol abuse to continue unabated, and restricts therapeutic options that may be exercised with the cooperative spouses or others. The alcohol abuser who refuses treatment poses troublesome and as yet unsolved problems concerning what the appropriate mode of treatment should be, considering the needs of everyone involved.

Unilateral family therapy is a new mode of family therapy particularly applicable to the problem of reaching and trying to change the uncooperative alcohol abuser. A central feature of the unilateral approach is that intervention is directed toward changing the behavior of the uncooperative family member by working exclusively with a cooperative family member who serves as a mediator. Emphasis in this approach is placed on helping the nonabusing spouse to strengthen his or her coping capabilities, to enhance family functioning, and, when appropriate, to facilitate greater sobriety on the part of the alcohol abusing partner.

Although the importance of the problem of reaching the uncooperative alcohol abuser is widely recognized, the need to develop a new mode of therapy appropriate to this problem may not be that evident. However, a good case can be made for the need for a unilateral family therapy for alcohol abuse. Consider the following:

1. There is a large population in need. Including those family members

who could be adversely affected by an alcohol abuser not receiving treatment and the number of such abusers in the United States, there are at least an estimated 40 million Americans (or 20 percent of the population) who could potentially benefit from methods of assistance that could reach them.[2]

2. Motivation to enter treatment, although highly desirable, is not a necessary condition for success. There is an element of constraint, coercion, and lack of voluntarism involved in many existing programs that have some record of success. Even in those cases of apparently voluntary entry into treatment, there is often strong pressure from the abuser's family, friends, physician, or pastor. In addition, the threatened or actual aversiveness of alcohol-caused illness, loss of social position, loss of friends, economic adversity, demotion, or loss of employment may also pressure the abuser into seeking treatment. Summarizing the research of Emrick, in which industrial alcohol treatment programs that constrain treatment have a reported success rate above that of most programs that involve purely voluntary entry, Paolino and McCrady concluded as follows: "Sadly, the belief that treatment outcome for alcoholics is poor because of their poor motivation has impeded the overall progress and interest in alcoholism treatment among many professionals."[3]

3. As a critical point of leverage, the nonalcoholic family member may be the only, or most significant, individual who has access to the uncooperative alcoholic.[4] In addition to recognizing that there is a drinking problem, the spouse is often cooperative and capable of functioning as a positive rehabilitative influence in the family.

4. Although Al-Anon may benefit many spouses of abusers and is a valuable adjunctive resource for alcohol counselors, it represents a self-help alternative that by its nature cannot be adopted directly by alcohol counselors. Patterned after Alcoholics Anonymous, Al-Anon is essentially a loosely organized network of relatively autonomous groups conducted for and by lay persons with strong emphasis on self-determination and anonymity.[5]

5. In general, research has shown that the involvement of spouses in treatment of alcohol-abusing spouses has been associated with at least some positive outcomes for the partners and, in some cases, for the abusers. In addition, several treatment efforts involving the spouse alone suggest that working with the spouse of an unmotivated alcohol abuser has therapeutic promise. The most appropriate role of the spouse, however, has not yet been determined.[6]

6. There is at present no developed, systematic methodology of unilateral family intervention applicable to alcohol abuse.

7. Sufficient work has been done in the area of alcohol abuse and in related areas of intervention to make it feasible to focus research on the development and evaluation of a unilateral family therapy.

OVERVIEW OF THE APPROACH

Drawing on the work of others in related areas and on the authors' current research on the unilateral approach, a conception of unilateral family therapy has been proposed.[7] This conception is a working framework that may help guide the further research and development on intervention methods needed in this area.

What is this approach called unilateral family therapy? At the outset, it should be recognized that the unilateral approach is a type of family therapy that shares objectives with family therapy in general. These are the goals of altering individual difficulties that arise from family dynamics, improving interpersonal relationships in the family, and, in general, of enhancing family functioning. However, in the unilateral mode it is not possible to work with all or most members of the family as is usually the case in family therapy. Unilateral treatment is carried out with one or more cooperative family members without the direct involvement of one or more others who refuse to participate. This refusal to participate in treatment may be due to the family member's failure to recognize that a problem exists or a lack of motivation to change. Those family members who do participate may themselves be clients in therapy as well as the mediators of change for the nonparticipating parties.

A major feature of the unilateral approach to family therapy involves a conception of the role of the cooperative family member as client as well as a mediator of change for others in the family, particularly for an uncooperative family member. This cooperative family member is usually a spouse but may be an older child or other relative. As the mediator, emphasis is placed on the cooperative family member as a positive resource in treatment who functions with the assistance of the practitioner to try to change the uncooperative member. This emphasis does not assume that the cooperative member is to blame for the difficulties but rather that this person is a crucial point of leverage whose strengths and influences may be productively employed by the practitioner to achieve change when other avenues of influence are limited or foreclosed. Thus, in contrast to the view held of family members in some treatment modalities and in Al-Anon, the spouse is viewed in the unilateral approach as a vital and potentially active agent of positive change who may be the main or only rehabilitative influence accessible to the practitioner.

More specifically, there are three main focuses of intervention in the unilateral approach. The first is the *individual focus* with emphasis on coping for the cooperative family member. When working with the spouse, such individual difficulties as stress, anxiety, lack of assertiveness, depression, anger, emotional overinvolvement, and failure to realize personal or career objectives could be the focus of intervention. The second is the *interactional focus* with emphasis predominantly upon family functioning.

Among the areas of intervention for this focus are marital and family communication, decision making and conflict resolution, parent-child relationships, and sexual and affectional enhancement for the marital partners. The last is the *third-party focus*, which involves work with the spouse or other family member to facilitate sobriety of the abuser. Among the methods here would be (1) inducing the abuser to seek treatment or other assistance for the excessive drinking, (2) removing spouse or family conditions that serve to promote the abuser's drinking, and (3) providing support for sobriety through strengthening nondrinking alternatives, neutralizing situational and other antecedents to drinking, altering drinking behavior of the abuser, and giving relapse and recovery training.

Considering the individual, interactional and third-party focuses, it is possible to rely mainly on one focus of intervention in a given case but, more commonly, two or three would be employed. All three focuses of intervention might be required in many cases. In any event, practitioners must be prepared to employ each focus of intervention as appropriate in any given case. It is this combination of interventional focuses, along with working only with one or a few cooperative family members in a rehabilitative capacity, that makes the unilateral approach a distinctive mode of therapy. Although considered here only in terms of alcohol abuse, the unilateral approach clearly has potential applicability to many other types of clientele not now accessible. Further details concerning the unilateral approach are to be found in the working conception reported elsewhere.[8]

OVERVIEW OF THE RESEARCH

Development and evaluation of the unilateral family therapy approach are currently being conducted at the Marital Treatment Project at the University of Michigan.[9] Among the objectives of the current research are (1) to identify further the treatment needs and relevant assessment and intervention procedures applicable to providing assistance in the areas of spouse coping, family functioning, and sobriety facilitating, and (2) to determine some of the conditions under which the unilateral approach is feasible and suitable as the intervention of choice. In examination of outcomes of the unilateral approach, attention is being given to the potential benefits to the cooperating family members as well as for the alcohol abuser.

In keeping with the developmental objectives of the project, a research design was adopted that allows for clinical and developmental flexibility while also providing a basis for evaluation. The basic unit in the design is a pair of comparable, cooperative spouses treated as a "yoked dyad." One spouse in each such dyad is assigned at random to receive unilateral family therapy for up to six months, and the other spouse is assigned to a condition of delayed treatment. Following this, when therapy is terminated for the spouse originally receiving unilateral therapy, the other spouse crosses over to receive the unilateral therapy. Individual therapy is provided by one of a team of practitioner-researchers. A battery of some 20 assessment instruments is administered five times for the spouses and those abusers who have elected to participate in the assessments. The research assessments occur before treatment, three months after beginning treatment, immediately following treatment, and at six and 12 months following treatment. Clinical assessment and monitoring are also carried out throughout treatment.

Each pair of spouses in the crossover dyad represents a self-contained experiment in which there are comparisons that may be made for each spouse before and after treatment as well as comparisons that may be made between spouses. In the clinical series being conducted, there are several sets of crossover dyads, each of which has a distinctive focus for assessment and intervention consistent with the design and development objectives pursued at that time. Although we have worked with many more, a total of some 16 subjects have received experimental intervention to date. Each case is analyzed in detail with the focus first on needs for design and development of the therapy and then on evaluation of outcomes. Although clinical practice continues, some of the series have been completed, and analyses of these cases are being carried out and reports prepared.

EARLY CLINICAL IMPRESSIONS

In developmentally oriented practice, clinical problems are addressed, potential solutions applied, and early evaluation of the results obtained as a basis for subsequent interventional design and development. Innovations systematically evolved through trial use may result in the step-by-step development of the various elements of an intervention strategy.[10] Much that is learned in this process is necessarily qualitative and based on professional experience and judgment. Complementing the quantitative results, such qualitative observations are essential in developmental research. The clinical impressions summarized here are based upon some two years of practice research using the unilateral approach.

1. It was apparent very early in the research that the unilateral approach is not suitable for every spouse who has an alcohol-abusing partner. The research required that criteria for inclusion be evolved to help ensure that the unilateral approach was feasible and appropriate. First, there are the basic criteria for the abuser. Thus the abuser has to have a drinking problem and be unwilling to receive treatment and to stop drinking. There are also basic criteria for the spouse. There are the absence of a drinking problem in him- or herself, recognition that the part-

ner has a drinking problem, and willingness to receive help to try to moderate the partner's drinking. Then there are additional criteria that in principle are optional but that were regarded at this point as essential. These other criteria are that neither spouse has a history of domestic violence, other drug abuse, or history of severe emotional disturbance, and that there are no immediate plans for marital dissolution. These additional criteria were imposed to facilitate focused development of interventions relating particularly to the alcohol area and to help avert potentially adverse effects. Even so, such additional criteria may turn out to be equally relevant in routine practice with spouses of unmotivated alcohol abusers. If so, including criteria such as these will necessarily restrict the field of eligible clientele and necessitate careful client screening.

2. Although the spouses of the abusers are those who have recognized that there is a drinking problem about which something must be done, most of these partners still underestimate the seriousness of the drinking problem. Some spouses recoil at the thought that their spouses are alcoholics, thinking that one has to be down and out and on skid row to be an alcoholic. Rather than preferring abstinence, most spouses would like the abuser to reduce his drinking and become a social drinker. Most spouses are poorly informed about the nature and effects of alcohol abuse. It has therefore been necessary in almost all cases to provide spouses with early, selective education concerning aspects of alcohol abuse.

3. Most of the abusers, of course, underestimate the seriousness of the drinking problem even more than their spouses do. Indeed, most abusers do not think that they have an alcohol problem in spite of the fact that they report drinking at levels that would definitely be considered problematic. For example, at the time of entering the project, the abusers who participated in assessment reported drinking the equivalent of 39 to 139 ounces of 86 proof alcohol per week, with a mean of 83 ounces. Despite consumption at these levels, many abusers typically hold to the illusion that they can exercise control over the drinking and can stop when they want to. There is the usual denial and resistance so amply documented in the literature. It would appear that most of the abusers underestimate the amount of alcohol consumed. To obtain fresh data for monitoring and evaluation, we have the spouse monitor the abuser's alcohol consumption using direct observation and systematic recording whenever possible. In a few cases we have also been able to have the drinking amounts monitored by the abuser as well, at the spouse's instigation.

4. Relationships in the marriages are frequently strained and discordant, as one might expect. We have had ample occasion to observe the conflict, anger, mistrust, resentment, and poor communication and decision making so frequently described in the literature on the alcoholic marriage and family. Such discordant relationships provide a poor basis for spouse mediation. To improve the working relationships between the

marital partners and to increase the ability of the spouse to influence the abuser, we have therefore developed relationship enhancement as one component of the unilateral approach. Based upon particular behaviors that the spouse is willing to carry out to improve the attractiveness of the relationship between the spouses, the relationship-enhancement module is introduced early in the treatment in most cases. Client reports to date indicate that such enhancement may indeed provide for more pleasant and harmonious interactions and facilitate the later mediational efforts of the spouse.

5. Most spouses, as is well recognized in the field of alcohol treatment, help to make the abuser's drinking possible (i.e., "enable" it), and, in this sense, are part of the problem. For example, it is not uncommon at all to find that the spouse drinks with the abuser, buys alcohol for the abuser, delays meals while the abuser drinks, and hosts cocktail parties and other social engagements where the abuser characteristically drinks too much. While thus making the drinking possible, however, it would be incorrect to conclude that the spouse can be held responsible for the abuser's drinking problem. We find that there are typically many factors that may plausibly relate to the abuser's drinking and that the actions of the spouse are only one possible contributing condition. However, even though rarely a major factor, such behavior by the spouse cannot be overlooked. Consequently, to begin to counter the enabling, an early focus of intervention with the spouse is to initiate a tailor-made program to deal with this problem—a program of "disenabling."

6. Most spouses have tried to encourage the abuser to stop drinking by several means, and generally feel discouraged about their ability to do very much about it. Nagging and complaining about the spouse's drinking are common. The spouses' previous efforts to bring about change have typically been carried out on an occasional, brief, and nonsystematic basis and have involved strongly ingrained responses that are generally ineffective or even counterproductive. Such customary ways of handling the drinking generally need to be neutralized. At the same time, it is important to provide realistic encouragement and appropriate direction, based upon an empirical assessment, of how the spouse may be helpful in the moderation of the abuser's drinking. For example, if the spouse nags the abuser when he or she drinks without this changing the abuser's drinking and fails to commend the abuser on those occasions when the abuser drinks less, the practitioner could encourage the spouse to stop the nagging and to praise the abuser's efforts to reduce drinking.

7. Some abusers temporarily discontinue or decrease the drinking shortly after the spouse becomes involved in treatment. Recognizing that the spouse is receiving treatment that relates in part at least to his or her drinking, the abuser may become motivated to try to reduce the drinking independently. In any case, such "reactive" effects of the conditions

of measurement are not uncommon although they are not yet well understood.[11] Clearly, any effort to establish a baseline on the abuser's drinking should be extended long enough to obtain a stable, more typical measurement. Clinically, it remains to be seen whether such early and brief positive changes in drinking can be turned to therapeutic advantage.

8. It is already clear that some abusers can be helped to enter treatment or to moderate their drinking through the practitioner's work with the cooperative spouse. Intervention programs can be introduced with the spouse, providing that there is first a careful assessment of relevant factors involving the spouse, the family, and the abuser, and that these interventions are individually tailored. For example, for the ten spouses who participated in five dyadic crossover experiments in the first clinical series (Series I), intervention directed toward facilitation of sobriety for the abuser was carried out through seven spouses when the spouses were receiving unilateral therapy, with either abstinence or moderated drinking being the consequence for four of the seven abusers involved. In contrast, when spouses were in the delayed treatment condition, before receiving treatment, none of the abusers entered treatment and there was no reduction in the high level of drinking. Further analyses with a larger sample of clients has indicated that the unilateral approach used with spouses results in improvement for at least two-thirds of the abusers, when improvement consists of the abuser entering treatment and/or significantly reducing drinking.[12]

9. Because of the diversity of the clientele and the conditions affecting their lives, no one approach to reaching the abuser would appear to be uniformly applicable. Thus, although all of the abusers initially resist treatment, spouse-mediated intervention has succeeded in assisting a few of the abusers to recognize that they have a drinking problem and in inducing them to enter treatment. In addition, some abusers may be candidates for a self-control program, especially if they come to recognize that they have a drinking problem, prefer to proceed more or less independently to try to moderate the drinking, and appear to have the capability of doing so.

Some of the other abusers appear to be particularly tough customers, inasmuch as they are hard to reach otherwise and are particularly steadfast in their heavy drinking. For these abusers, one of the strategies we have employed is programmed confrontation. Patterned, in part, after the Johnson approach but adapted to presentation by an individual spouse, programmed confrontation entails training the spouse to confront the abuser firmly but compassionately in the presence of the therapist concerning the particulars and adverse effects of the abuser's drinking.[13] In addition, the spouse presents the abuser with specific directives to enter treatment and identifies the consequences that the spouse plans to carry out if the abuser fails to take the specified action. Programmed confrontation requires careful assessment, intervention planning, implementation, and follow-up to avoid failure or adverse effects, such as domestic violence. Programmed confrontation is a powerful and extreme induction that can be very successful, but it is one that should be used with great care and when other alternatives are inappropriate.

Programmed confrontation was used with several spouses. For example, in one dyad, the spouse who received unilateral therapy first was carefully trained to confront the abuser compassionately and effectively concerning the amount and effects of his drinking, the actions he must take to stop, and the consequences she would carry out if he did not. Then, the confrontation was carried out as programmed with the abuser in the therapist's presence, with the result that the abuser reduced his drinking, by a program of self-initiated graduated reduction, from a fifth of vodka per day to 6-8 ounces—a result that was the best that could be obtained and one that was maintained through the 18-month follow-up. The abuser in another dyad who was assigned to the condition of delayed treatment did not change his drinking until his spouse later received unilateral therapy. The intervention used with this second spouse was again the programmed confrontation of the abuser, which resulted in the abuser entering treatment for his alcohol abuse and stopping drinking—again a result that has been maintained through the 18-month follow-up.

10. In contrast to the original intervention plan, it appears that intervention need not routinely be focused first on helping the spouse to cope with her or his individual distress, then on family functioning, and finally, when appropriate, on facilitation of sobriety. Yes, many spouses have had difficulties in the area of coping, and most of the families have at least some areas of family difficulty, but in the main, none of these problems has been as pressing or as important as the alcohol problem. Experience to date indicates that the alcohol problem is the one that deserves priority of intervention, whatever role it may play in regard to difficulties in such other areas as spouse coping and family functioning. Thus, assessment and intervention may both be oriented more directly toward facilitation of sobriety for the abuser, with assistance being given for spouse coping and family functioning only as needed and as assistance in these areas contributes directly to fostering sobriety for the abuser.

11. The unilateral approach is very much a method of last resort that should be employed carefully and selectively in families having uncooperative alcohol abusers. Other, less-restrictive alternatives should be pursued first. Most conventional approaches to alcohol treatment would engage the entire family, work with the spouses together, or have the abuser seek individual treatment. Until research establishes which approach is preferable in alcohol treatment, the conventional methods should be considered the desired courses of action. When these fail or are inappropriate, however, the practitioner should consider the unilateral mode.

NOTES AND REFERENCES

1. See, for example, *Alcohol and Health: Report from the Secretary of Health, Education and Welfare* (New York: Charles Scribner's Sons, 1970); and Steven F. Bucky and associates, *The Impact of Alcoholism* (Center City, Minn.: Hazelden, 1978).

2. The estimate is based on the judgment that the combined remedial approaches to the alcohol problem in the United States reach no more than 15 percent of the alcohol population. See C. H. Krimmel, *Alcoholism: Challenge for the Social Work Profession* (New York: Council on Social Work Education, 1971). This leaves 85 percent who are "hidden" and thus are untreated excessive drinkers. If there are some 10 million alcohol abusers, there would be some 8.5 million who are "hidden." If one assumes further that for every alcohol abuser there are five other persons who suffer directly, this yields some 42.5 million individuals in the United States who could potentially benefit from methods of assistance that could reach these abusers. Thomas J. Paolino and Barbara S. McCrady, *The Alcoholic Marriage: Alternative Perspectives* (New York: Grune & Stratton, 1977).

3. Emrick, cited in Paolino and McCrady, *Alcoholic Marriage,* pp. 144–145.

4. For example, see David Berenson, "A Family Approach to Alcoholism," *Psychiatric Opinion,* 13 (1976), pp. 33–38.

5. For additional details, see Joan Ablon, "Perspectives on Al-Anon Family Groups," in N. J. Estes and M. E. Heineman, eds., *Alcoholism: Development, Consequences and Interventions* (St. Louis, Mo.: C. V. Mosby, 1977), pp. 274–283.

6. See, for example, B. F. Corder, R. F. Corder, and N. L. Laidlaw, "An Intensive Treatment Program for Alcoholics and Their Wives," *Quarterly Journal of Studies on Alcohol,* 33 (1972), pp. 1144–1146; and D. P. Howard and N. T. Howard, "Treatment of the Significant Other," in S. Zimberg, J. Wallace, and S. B. Blume, eds., *Practical Approaches to Alcoholism Therapy* (New York: Plenum Press, 1978).

7. Edwin J. Thomas and Cathleen A. Santa, "Unilateral Family Therapy for Alcohol Abuse: A Working Conception," *The American Journal of Family Therapy,* 10 (Fall 1982), pp. 49–60.

8. Ibid.

9. The research is supported, in part, by Grant No. 1 R01 AA04163-02, entitled "Unilateral Family Therapy for Alcohol Abuse," from the National Institute on Alcohol Abuse and Alcoholism, Rockville, Md.

10. For discussion of developmental research and how it differs from conventional research methods, see Edwin J. Thomas, "Generating Innovation in Social Work: The Paradigm of Developmental Research," *Journal of Social Science Research,* 2 (Fall 1978), pp. 95–117; Thomas, "Mousetraps, Developmental Research, and Social Work Education," *Social Service Review,* 52 (September 1978), pp. 468–483; and Thomas, *Designing Interventions for the Helping Professions* (Beverly Hills, Calif.: Sage Publications, 1984).

11. Steven N. Haynes and Wade F. Horn, "Reactivity in Behavioral Observation: A Review," *Behavioral Assessment,* 4 (Fall 1982), pp. 369–387.

12. For further details, see Edwin J. Thomas et al., "Outcomes of Unilateral Family Therapy for Alcohol Abuse: Early Results from a Pilot Study." Unpublished paper, University of Michigan School of Social Work, Ann Arbor, 1984.

13. Vernon E. Johnson, *I'll Quit Tomorrow* (New York: Harper & Row, 1973).

The Role of the Clinician in the Development and Maintenance of Self-Help/Mutual-Aid Groups

Shirley Wesley King and Raymond Sanchez Mayers

S ince the beginning of civilization, human beings have exchanged aid and comfort in an informal manner. From the time of tribes and clans to that of communes and fraternal organizations, people have had to band together to survive. This mutual helping arrangement has been labeled self-help or mutual aid. The groups that comprise this exchange are

> voluntary, small group structures for the mutual aid and the accomplishment of a special purpose. They are usually formed by peers who have come together for mutual assistance in satisfying a common need, overcoming a common handicap or life disrupting problem, and bringing about desired social and/or personal change.[1]

The guilds of the Middle Ages are examples of one type of self-help group, in which artisans banded together to assure existence. These guilds were the precursors of the modern industrial unions that also started as self-help groups but evolved into their current institutionalized form.

Various other forms of self-help/mutual-aid groups have evolved in response to special unmet needs of members of society. For example, the Friendly Societies of nineteenth century England were local groups of workers who set up funds for members in crisis periods, such as illness, death, or other circumstances requiring financial support. By the beginning of the twentieth century, conditions were such that over 27,000 Friendly Societies existed in England.[2] Illustrative of other groups of this nature were consumer co-ops of Europe and America; the ethnically based and services-oriented clubs in the United States, for example, B'Nai B'rith; Sons of Little Italy; League of United Latin American Citizens (LULAC); G. I. Forum; and the hometown clubs found in Puerto Rican, Mexican, and Cuban communities, and the Masons and other fraternities and sororities found in the black communities. Among some of the largest and most successful groups developed in the 1930s were the American Association for Retarded Children; United Cerebral Palsy Foundation; Recovery, Inc.; and Alcoholics Anonymous.

Self-help groups in their current form were virtually unknown some 40 years ago.[3] The transformation of these groups is due to several prevailing societal conditions. For example, after immigration had decreased significantly, many of the self-help and mutual-aid fraternal organizations that had sprung up to serve the needs of the immigrants and their children decreased in importance or became extinct. However, immediately after World War II, there was a large growth in the newer type of self-help groups. Such growth was especially manifest in the social movements of the 1960s.

Other catalysts that gave rise to self-help groups and helped them to spread were based on new needs stimulated by a modern industrialized society. The transition from small-town living, where there is a certain degree of familiarity among the people, to the tremendous degree of anonymity vis-à-vis the bureaucratized mass society has generated a need to recreate a feeling of "community." Moreover, there is a cultural lag between our modern technological age and our ability to deal with the social problems engendered by it. Another significant factor is the uncertain state of funding for the provision of much-needed public services.

These many factors make the resurgence of self-help groups a more viable alternative for the delivery of services to a larger number of people. Self-help/mutual-aid groups, thus, will continue to flourish as a grass-roots response to unmet needs. And although it is clear that the domain of human service agencies does not directly include self-help groups, there remains a role for agencies and their agents (practitioners) in the development and maintenance of these groups.

This article provides a nontraditional course of action for social work practitioners in furthering their professional and ethical goals to enhance the quality of life through work with self-help/mutual-aid groups. Using this perspective, the article (1) defines the characteristics of self-help groups; (2) identifies stages in the process of development and maintenance of the group; (3) outlines the role of the clinician in working with the group and the particular skills necessary for successful outcomes; and (4) discusses practice and policy implications.

SOME CHARACTERISTICS OF SELF-HELP GROUPS

There is great variety in the types of self-help groups. Nevertheless, there are certain characteristics that differentiate them from other small groups. No matter what the purpose and function of the mutual-aid group, it has a character and form different from natural networks and those groups formed by professionals. In self-help groups, peers come together, agree on, and engage in some goal-directed actions. Such behaviors may be directed toward the community, social institutions, or individuals, but there is always an acknowledged purpose in coming together. The group does not exist just for social interaction; it comes to have a life of its own and must satisfy the immediate needs of its members. If it cannot do this it either evolves into another type of group or it ceases to exist.

Some of the characteristics of self-help groups are the following:

1. *Membership Is Limited to Those with Similar Problems.* The impetus for coming together in a self-help group is the recognition that members have common problems or unmet needs; that these problems or needs have not been resolved or met by the traditional human services; and that it is possible for members to help one another. Because individuals are joined together in this way, the members may become a reference group, a point of connection and identification with each other.

2. *Peer Formation.* The group is formed by peers because of the active interest and common needs of the members. Some groups may be formed or sponsored on the initiative of a professional or professional agency, but many groups are formed by people with a common problem precisely because these problems are not resolved by professionals.

3. *Peer Control.* A true self-help or mutual-aid group is controlled by members themselves, that is, major decisions are made by the group as a whole or by duly elected officers of the group rather than by a professional who might claim expertise in the problem area. Even when a group is formed by a professional or professional agency, the professional must eventually relinquish control of the group or it will not be a true self-help group. This is not to say that professionals (that is, clinicians) have no role in mutual-aid groups; they do, but it is a somewhat different type of role.

4. *Immediate Help.* One of the frustrations endured by many human service clients is the long waiting period encountered in receiving services. Self-help groups have no waiting lists and offer immediate aid to those who turn to them for assistance. Usually informal or formal networks of members develop so that the newcomer is enveloped in the new social support system rapidly. And when a new person calls, he or she will usually be referred to a group member immediately or be invited to the next meeting of the group.

5. *Help Is Offered in an Informal Manner.* Although many groups have codified their sets of beliefs and practices (for example, Alcoholics Anonymous, Synanon, etc.), the help offered by one member to another is in an atmosphere radically different from the service offered by most professionals. The social distance and superordinate/subordinate relationship found in professional practice is distinctly lacking in mutual-aid groups. Rather, the relationships are those of peers with common needs or problems.

6. *Help Is Reciprocal.* In the self-help group, the individual is not only

a receiver of services but also a giver of services. This is the basis for what has been called the "helper-therapy principle." Quite simply this principle states that "those who help are helped most."[4] Because all members of the group help each other with similar problems, all benefit. There are many reasons for this. First, by being an active participant in attempting to effect change rather than a passive recipient of aid, the helper becomes less dependent and thus achieves a feeling of mastery and competence. Second, in helping another with a similar problem, the helper is able to view his or her own problems in new ways. Third, the helper acquires a feeling of social usefulness.[5]

7. *Group Activities Are Based on Experiential Knowledge and Expertise.* Experiential knowledge is wisdom gained from personal experience. Experiential expertise refers to competence or skill in handling or resolving a problem through the use of one's own practical knowlege. This approach may be contrasted with professional practice. The professional is more apt to use a systematic, empirically based approach. He or she is trained to maintain a social distance from the client and sees the need for empathy but not identification, for objectivity rather than subjectivity, and for practice based on scientific analysis rather than intuition. Hurvitz has described this dichotomy as the aprofessional versus the professional approach.[6]

Self-help groups have been defined as structures designed for the accomplishment of a specific purpose. Thus, for the clinician, intervention with self-help groups is not only altered by the unique character of these groups, but also by their stages of developmental growth. In this regard, Katz has delineated five stages or periods of growth in self-help groups.[7]

1. *Origin.* The period at which the idea of the group is formulated and preliminary discussions are held with interested individuals.
2. *Informal Organization.* The stage at which a group of individuals with a common problem have agreed to meet occasionally on an informal basis to discuss the problem or need.
3. *Emergence of Leadership.* The stage at which a formal leader may be designated. This may be differentiated from earlier stages in which informal leaders guided the group.
4. *Beginning of Formal Organization.* In this stage, the group becomes solidified and has developed to the point at which its structure becomes formalized. It elects officers, adopts bylaws, follows procedural rules, and may adopt a logo, organizational stationery, and other materials.
5. *Beginning of Professionalization.* In this stage, the formal organization has grown to the point where it may start to hire professionals with expertise in the problem area (see Table 1, p. 146).

Although not all groups pass through all these stages, all self-help groups must go through stages one and two. As groups develop, there is great variation with respect to whether they adhere to each stage in the evolutionary process. For example, some groups explicitly avoid having a formal leader in deference to their members' desire to use rotational leadership or consensus as the preferred decision-making mode (for example, some women's consciousness-raising groups). Some groups never reach stage four. This is especially true of small, non–social action, local-oriented groups. Similarly, many groups never reach stage five because they resist bureaucratic structures and/or the hiring of professionals. The primary aversion to this step rests in the belief of self-help groups that such practices are at cross-purposes to the basic thrust. Elements such as intimacy of interaction, small size, lack of social action focus, and ideology-endorsing consensus have also been cited as reasons for avoiding stage five.[8] Given these identified stages of development, attention must be focused on the role of the clinician with respect to self-help groups' developmental and maintenance processes.

ROLE OF THE CLINICIAN

As suggested earlier, the therapeutic experience under the self-help approach is markedly different from that provided under the professional approach. Consequently, the role of the professional differs as well. For traditional therapists, the circumscribed role of the clinician vis-à-vis the self-help group is ambiguous and may even be perceived as nonessential. The nature of the dynamics of self-help groups dictates a peripheral role at most for the practitioner. In spite of this, clinicians as well as other professionals have distinct roles through which they may interrelate with self-help groups. There are many successful examples of this role, such as the social worker who helped found Parents Anonymous (Leonard L. Lieber) and the psychiatrist who started Recovery, Inc. (Abraham A. Low). Some of the acceptable functions available to those practitioners who wish to work with such groups follow.

1. First, the clinician can serve as a catalyst in initiating groups. There are many successful examples of this role. In some cases, the clinician or professional agency has seen a need and brought peers together and helped them to go through the process of creating an ongoing group. In such cases, the clinician in his or her normal capacity may utilize natural networks and linkages to find people and bring them together. In other cases, a small nucleus of people wanting to start a group have approached professionals for aid, with the understanding that this assistance was of a temporary nature and that control would rest with the members.

2. The clinician may serve as a facilitator or enabler in an ongoing

Table 1
Relationship between the Clinician's Roles and Developmental Stages of Self-Help Groups

Clinician's Roles	Developmental Stages				
	Origin	Informal Organization	Emergence of Leadership	Beginning of Formal Organization	Beginning of Professionalization
Catalyst, Facilitator, Enabler	Worker in central location, direct, primary role				
Enabler/Facilitator		Worker in pivotal location, indirect variable role			
Consultant/Advocate			Worker in peripheral location, indirect facilitator role		
Employee					Worker in central location, direct primary role

group. In this case, the clinician has moved from just bringing people together to guiding them through the problems they must deal with in developing cohesiveness, identifying tasks, and maintaining a functional group to meet the common needs of the members.

3. The clinician may be a consultant to the self-help group. In this case the clinician is brought in for a specific task, when needed. At times, he or she may be called on to address a meeting of the group and be asked to discuss a particular topic of concern. At other times, the clinician may be called on to help the group with specific developmental activities: how to recruit new members, how to involve the membership to a greater degree, how to run a group, how to expand their helping programs, and so forth.

4. The clinician may serve on an advisory or planning board of the group. In this capacity, the clinician has a variety of important functions: He or she gives legitimacy to the group, serves as a link with the larger community and community agencies, and provides input of a professional nature when needed.

5. The clinician may also make referrals to the group. A clinician may work in a human service agency that serves clients with problems similar to the focus of the self-help group. Many times clients have presenting problems that the agency is not equipped or mandated to handle. In these cases, the clinician may refer the client to the appropriate self-help group for support, to supplement services that the client is receiving, or, in some instances, to be the sole service provider for the client. This role is controversial, especially if the self-help group has not gained much legitimacy as yet in the community.

The roles and functions outlined for the clinician represent a departure from the traditional activities known to clinicians in their ordinary group work. However, there is a common foundation in group dynamics that gives the clinician an excellent point of reference in working with self-help groups. Recognizing how self-help groups differ from other groups should also enhance clinicians' abilities to intervene effectively with these groups regardless of the roles the clinicians choose to assume.

INTEGRATION OF THE CLINICIAN'S ROLES AND DEVELOPMENTAL STAGES

Starting with the point of *origin,* there are several roles for the clinician. Henry suggested that as the clinician works his or her way through the various developmental stages of the group, roles vacillate from being direct and central through indirect and variable and back to central as the clinician becomes an employee of the self-help group. Even as an agent of an organization, the clinician is in a strategic position to serve as catalyst, facilitator, and/or enabler to the self-help group at the initial stage. The clinician as catalyst, using facilitative skills, may identify a number of individuals who share similar problems and arrange for them to come together to discuss the feasibility of a group. Thus, the clinician's function and role with respect to the initial stages of the self-help group are similar to his or her customary activities as a group worker. For example, it is the clinician's appointed role and function at the outset of the group experience to identify and select persons to be candidates for the group. Thus the clinician is in a central position as he or she selects the individuals who will comprise the group. In a more defined manner, the clinician uses the primacy of his or her role to "help" or enable individuals to define their problems and approaches for problem resolution.[9]

The second stage of group development, which is labeled *informal organization,* is described by Bales and Strodtbeck as the "orientation" phase.[10] These authors suggested that during this phase or stage, the emerging group concentrates on direct interaction in outlining the problem or potential problem. Moreover, it is during this phase that the participants raise the question of whether the problem can be dealt with effectively by the group. At this stage, the clinician's role is more indirect, yet pivotal as the enabler/facilitator. In the role of enabler, the clinician is process oriented and must allow the group members to express themselves as they work out their differences, problems, and questions in the best manner they can as a collective. The members can only move toward solidification if they are able to work through this phase interdependently as a separate collectivity, distinct from the clinician's involvement. It is essential that the clinician realize at this point that his or her role is determined by the group. However, the clinician's role as facilitator continues to be pivotal and significant in assuring group maintenance and growth with respect to prospective group membership. The clinician must exercise this pivotal, though indirect, function without disrupting the group dynamics.

Emergence of leadership is the third stage of the self-help group's developmental process. The group is now moving into a more cohesive, identifiable entity. The clinician's role is indirect as he or she maintains enabling and facilitating functions with the group. Because groups develop and change over time just as their leadership needs do, the clinician's function must be in tandem with this fact of group life.

The fourth stage addresses the point at which there is a *beginning of formal organization.* The clinician's role at this juncture is clearly outside of the domain of the group and operates *only* at the request of the group. Frequently, the group may require specific knowledge on process and on various topical areas. When this occurs, the clinician may be sought as a *consultant* to share his or her expertise to enhance the effective functioning of the group. Illustrative of this type of exchange is the case in which a clinician as consultant discusses the importance of leadership or types of leadership appropriate for the growth of the group. In other instances, the group may need detailed scientific knowledge about a particular problem facing its membership, such as alcoholism or coping with stress. Although the clinician provides knowledge that is practical and useful for group growth, the involvement remains indirect at all times. This distinction is essential because the group is now autonomous and is working toward formalizing its structure. In the capacity of advocate (one who projects the purpose and function of the group resource), the clinician can share this information with other organizations, other practitioners, the community at large, and prospective members as well.

The fifth and final stage in the group development process is referred to as the *beginning of professionalization.* Specific guidelines are set up under the aegis of professionalization that outline responsibilities, and policies are formulated to protect group members/clientele against unethical practices. Consequently, by moving toward professionalization, the self-help group creates an aura of status that gives legitimacy and credibility. It is at this stage that the group is fully established as an entity with a clear purpose based on a membership nucleus. The group may now deem it prudent to hire practitioners as employees to help it to meet its prescribed functions. In this arrangement, the clinician serves in a central location with direct involvement and functions designated by the self-help group as employer. In other words, the clinician is now an agent of the self-help group. Although the clinician has had direct involvement in earlier phases of the group, the involvement at this stage is perhaps even more direct. As an employee of the self-help group, the clinician has the responsibility to help the group effectively achieve its problem-solving tasks, its leadership functions, and its optimum level of expertise in order to attain group development and maintenance. Some examples of self-help groups that have reached this stage of development are the Association of Retarded Citizens (ARC), Mothers Against Drunk Driving (MADD), and the American Association of Retired Persons (AARP). But therapeutic groups usually do not reach this last stage; they often do not have the needed social and political skills to do so, nor do many have the desire to do so. Groups that move to the professional stage are interested mainly in social action and social change through lobbying and similar activities.

The clinician's role vis-à-vis the various stages of self-help group development is most significant in terms of the clinician's ability to enhance group maintenance and growth. However, the clinician's ability to work effectively with the self-help group is contingent on the following: (1) whether he or she is cognizant and respectful of the self-help group dynamics, (2) his or her own expertise in the group process, and (3) the extent to which he or she understands the appropriate manner of relating his or her skills and the self-help group dynamics. It is tremendously important that the clinician realize that his or her involvement with the self-help group is always governed by the dictates of the group, from the initial phase through the final or professionalization stage. Furthermore, inasmuch as there appears to be a resurgence of self-help groups, it is even more incumbent on practitioners to understand appropriate means of intervention that are applicable to the development, maintenance, and enhancement of self-help groups.

A SELF-HELP GROUP FOR BATTERED WOMEN

Origin. Joan M, a feminist therapist, had been seeing a number of women in her practice who were being physically abused by their mates. Many of them expressed the wish that they had access to other women who could understand what they were going through rather than just those who criticized them for staying in their relationship. She decided to explore the possibility of starting a self-help group for these women. She could see that they needed additional support in attempting to deal with the emotional burdens related to their family problems. Joan asked her clients if they would be interested in joining such a group. Some of them were reluctant to do so, being afraid that their involvement in such a group would endanger the already fragile relationships they were trying to maintain. Others who had successfully left such relationships, but were still trying to deal with their guilt and self-esteem, were eager to form a group. She set a time for the interested women to come together in her office. When they arrived she briefly explained the purpose of the meeting. She wanted the women to discuss whether forming a self-help group for support could be helpful to them. Joan was clearly the catalyst in getting the women together to discuss common concerns.

Informal Organization. Joan knew that some of the women would have to take leadership roles in the development of the group if the group was to be successful. She invited the women to discuss the formation of the group and waited to see what would happen. A few individuals quickly took charge, led the discussion, and helped the group set parameters. Initially the leaders turned to Joan for advice, clarification, and support of their views. At the conclusion of the meeting, the women agreed to meet again to continue discussing the feasibility of a group and what they wanted the group to accomplish. Joan played the role of facilitator in the subtle handling of the group's discussion at this stage.

Emergence of Leadership. The group continued to meet on a weekly basis at Joan's office. Two of the women, Anne and Megan, were very assertive and outspoken; they evolved into the informal leaders of the group. The other women constantly looked to them and seemed to accept their organizational skills in moving the meetings along. Anne was task oriented and tried to have an agenda for each meeting; she was concerned about "using time constructively." Megan was more concerned about the personal lives of the women and about making sure they were getting enough emotional support from the group. She served as mother hen and group clown; she always brought cookies and made coffee for everyone. All the women, however, still looked to Joan as the "expert" and final authority and frequently turned to her for advice or arbitration.

Beginning of Formal Organization. Eventually, the women decided to give the group a name, to set up a formal structure, and to elect officers. Anne was elected President; Megan was elected Vice-President. The women also decided to move their meetings to a local church and to advertise their meetings in the local paper. They asked Joan to continue to be a resource for them and to be a source of referrals to the group. Although Joan had become close to the women in the group, she only attended their meetings when she was asked specifically to come and talk on a topic. Joan noted that the group members had acquired self-confidence and expertise in helping women like themselves, and she did not want to interfere with their development. She let them know that she would always be available to the group collectively and individually; she felt good about her efforts to facilitate independence in women in need. By allowing the group to go off on its own, she had indeed been an effective instrument in the development of a true self-help group.

PRACTICE AND POLICY IMPLICATIONS

The resurgence of self-help/mutual-aid groups finds few human service practitioners trained or prepared to understand and work with such groups. Consequently, many professionals, including clinicians, may be reluctant to work with these groups in the prescribed roles outlined. It is likely that clinicians as well as other practitioners may see the goals, strategies, and assumptions of self-help/mutual-aid groups as aprofessional. These groups may also be perceived as questionable, and thus many professionals may not want to be associated with them. Unfortunately, there are little or no data available on past experiences with such groups to help professionals who do decide to work with them.

In a recent study, in which social workers and other human service professionals were queried about their participation in the planning, development, and maintenance of self-help groups, it was found that social workers were more involved than were other professionals.[11] The study results were based on a representative sample of 43 self-help groups in a four-county area of New York State. The primary reason given by these professionals for starting a group was that at the time they did so, services for members were unavailable or inadequate. The results revealed that 72 percent of the groups had one or more professionals (primarily social workers) involved with them. Customarily, these social workers and other professionals served as expert consultants to the groups—sharing information, knowledge, and resources about the problems experienced by the group members and helping members to develop skills in coping with or changing behavior.

Professionals must view the clients as members of a number of significant groups to which a web of natural support systems is available. This system of support should be identified, recognized, and utilized rather than disregarded. Because there are areas in which natural support systems are incapable of meeting their members' needs, practitioners must be adept and responsive enough to bridge this gap through their relationships with them. This type of relationship contributes to complementarity between members of self-help groups and professionals and also provides reinforcement to self-help groups as natural support systems.

The professional must also be cognizant of the fact that he or she and the client should have a collegial relationship aimed at achieving the same goal—an effective outcome for the client. Professionals must learn that they may assume a number of different functions with respect to these groups. The parameters are set only by the practitioner's inability to be creative, innovative, and flexible in working with self-help groups. It is our professional and ethical obligation to understand, utilize, and strengthen self-help groups as well as other natural support systems in their efforts to enhance the quality of life. After all, is that not a major part of our raison d'être?

NOTES AND REFERENCES

1. A. H. Katz and E. I. Bender, *The Strength in Us: Self-Help Groups in the Modern World* (New York: New Viewpoints, 1976), p. 9.

2. Ibid., p. 17.

3. Ibid., pp. 25–33.

4. F. Reissman, "How Does Self-Help Work?" *Social Policy,* 7 (September–October 1976), p. 41.

5. Ibid., p. 42.

6. See T. Borkman, "Experiential Knowledge: A New Concept for the Analysis of Self-Help Groups," *Social Service Review,* 50 (September 1976), pp. 445–456; and N. Hurvitz, cited by Reissman, "How Does Self-Help Work?" p. 44.

7. Katz and Bender, *Strength in Us,* p. 123.

8. Ibid., p. 123.

9. See S. Henry, *Group Skills in Social Work: A Four Dimensional Approach* (Itasca, Ill.: F. E. Peacock, 1981), pp. 41–42.

10. R. Bales and N. Strodtbeck, "Phases in Group Problem-Solving," in D. Cartwright and A. Zander, eds., *Group Dynamics* (New York: Harper & Row, 1963), p. 391.

11. A. Gartner, ed., *Self-Help Reporter,* 4 (November–December 1980), p. 3.

PART III

Advances in Theory, Ethics, and Evaluative Research

Editor's Comments

Parts I and II are composed of articles on advances in practice and service provision. Such advances depend, in part, on the support furnished by advances in theory development, ethics, and evaluation of effectiveness. The articles in Part III address these issues. The first three articles contribute to the advancement of practice theory through the development and extension of particular practice concepts. The conceptual frameworks and the validity of the practice as established through its usage by practitioners and through outcome studies have the potential to increase practice effectiveness by broadening the scope of services and the range of people served.

In the first article, Middleman, in discussing group work, identifies some of the historical factors that account for the receding of social action as group work's core practice concept and its gradual replacement by the concept of verbal interchange. She then connects contemporary theory concerning the ways that action-in-the-environment influence the development of cognition, sensory perception, motility, learning, competence, and affectual and social functioning to group work's earlier interest in social action. In so doing, she extends and restores the concept of action to a central position—along with verbal interchange—in social work's practice theory.

In any given instance, the differential use of social action and verbal interchange rests on the practice principle of relevance—to the practitioner, client, context, process, and outcome variables—and on the complex interplay among the various parts in the interaction. In taking up the practitioner variable as the critical one, the author describes and analyzes three roles for the practitioner that shape the various uses of action, doing, and experiential activities. As a conceptual framework for understanding the purposes, types, and uses of social action and the relationship of social action to specific practice variables, Middleman's model adds diversity, depth, and richness to practice that might otherwise rely on verbal interchange alone.

In the second article, Callahan develops a framework to evaluate the risk of suicide in clients. Using the framework, he regards ambivalence as a critical, dynamic factor in diagnosis and treatment. The framework is based on five *DSM III* categories of major psychiatric disorders. Within his proposed evaluative framework, Callahan provides clinically based recommendations for the management of potentially suicidal clients and relates these recommendations to the characteristics of each disorder. The proposed framework is buttressed throughout by pertinent research findings and references to the clinical literature. Such a conceptual frame of reference, as a guide to clinical social workers dealing with potentially suicidal clients, marks an important advance in social work practice theory.

Gibbs, in the third article in this series of three, addresses the client-social worker relationship, which has long been the central feature in practice theory. Beliefs and assumptions about its purpose, characteristics, differential use, and desired outcomes may vary among clinical social workers, but few would dispute its significance. However, concepts of relationship have been closer to the realm of value than to that of theory, with the exception of the phenomena of transference and countertransference, ambivalence, and resistance. Witness, for example, the emphasis clinicians have paid to such attitudes as respect, acceptance, self-determination, and nonjudgmentalism. Recently, however, theoretical interest has turned increasingly to the effects on the relationship of differences between the client and the worker, such as those stemming from gender, age, race, ethnicity, sexual preference, religion, disability, and social class.

Gibbs advances this line of theoretical development, with particular reference to treatment relationships of white workers with black clients. Out of their historical and contemporary experiences in a white, racist society, blacks have developed particular interpersonal strategies for dealing with unfamiliar or anxiety-laden situations, including seeking and taking help from society's social service systems. The author gathers these strategies together under two concepts, *interpersonal orientation* (a process focus in relationships) and *instrumental orientation* (a goal/task focus in relationships), to form an interpersonal model of treatment. The model specifies the type of behaviors workers can use during the initial treatment phase to enable a client to move beyond a focus on process to an instrumental focus, which signals engagement in the relationship.

In the next article, Mishne reviews in useful detail the concepts of object relations theory. Her special focus is on the problematic ego development and social functioning of adolescents who suffer from borderline conditions. These adolescents constitute a population well-known to social workers in many different settings and fields of practice. The author relates the psychoanalytic framework of object relations theory, and its concepts about borderline states in particular, to the difficult professional responsibilities involved in the practitioner's work with the systemic triad of adolescent, family, and environment. The practitioner, guided by social work values, must have a working knowledge of psychoanalytic theory and must possess the requisite skills needed to work with the complexities of this population and its significant others. So equipped, and with assessment and treatment closely linked, the social worker can relieve some of the suffering of these young people and their families by helping them to manage stressful internal and external demands and to enhance their coping capabilities. The ultimate objective is the young person's moving forward in the ego development and social growth that had been interrupted early on.

Leaving the realm of theory, the next article, by Joseph, addresses the subject of ethical decision making and ethical problem solving—two topics that underlie all professional activity, including practice, service provision, program development, and research. In this article, the author brings a rapidly changing social context immediately to the fore.

Unanticipated value conflicts and ethical dilemmas are being generated rapidly as the rate of technological development in many fields accelerates. The field of genetics is one exemplar. New forms of human reproduction such as surrogate mothers for the period of pregnancy, frozen embryos, and sperm banks are creating conflicting claims and puzzling new questions concerning basic human relationships. Similarly, in the field of biomedicine, professional commitments confront both the conflicting statutes enacted at the federal, state, and local levels and the conflicting rights and needs generated by judicial rulings. The "Baby Doe" case and the controversial issue of parental versus adolescent rights in the matter of contraceptive assistance for sexually active teenagers are prominent examples.

Fortunately for the profession, NASW has adopted a new and extensive Code of Ethics. But during a period of rapid social change, it is too much to expect that a professional code alone can prescribe appropriate ethical conduct for presently unknown, unforeseen, and never-before experienced ethical dilemmas. Joseph believes that the profession is in urgent need of a model for ethical decision making that will encourage social workers to examine their own value orientations and ethical systems and, in this way, achieve increased objectivity, early recognition and analysis of possible ethical issues, and a base for reaching ethical decisions and undertaking ethical action.

The author makes a strong case for the inclusion of ethical content in the social work curriculum so that practitioners will be prepared—in any field of practice—for ethical decision making in the face of increasingly complex and conflicting rights, obligations, and claims. Such new learning, together with the NASW Code of Ethics and with Joseph's model (and others as they develop), can only advance practice effectiveness and improve service provision.

The final topic in Part III deals with advances in evaluation of effectiveness. Three types of research are fundamental to advances in clinical social work practice—developmental research, basic research in the behavioral and social sciences and in social work, and evaluative research. The usefulness of *developmental research* for the advancement of program planning and service provision was demonstrated in Part II by the work of Thomas and his colleagues. And, although not explicitly mentioned in other articles in Part II, most theoretical advances are generated by findings from *basic research* in the behavioral and social sciences and, less often, in social work. *Evaluative research,* however, is currently receiving the greatest attention, largely because of contextual factors of accountability, fiscal constraints, and the like, and the next two articles deal specifically with evaluative research.

In the first of these articles, Morrison, Rosenberg, and Rehr consider some reasons why evaluative research in social work has been less successful in establishing practice effectiveness than has evaluative research in psychotherapy. Concluding that needed specificity has been missing in social work research on effectiveness, the authors suggest three practice elements—problems being experienced by clients, accuracy of assessments, and outcomes of interventions—as examples of the type of specificity needed. The authors next provide a thorough review of available research methodologies suitable for the study of each of the three elements. The objective of the authors' analysis is to meet the interest of individual practitioners in studying the outcomes of their own practice. But they also observe that an examination of the data across practitioners can yield useful information to the agency about its program outcomes.

Brower and Mutschler, in the second of these articles, take up the challenge posed by computer technology and consider its usefulness in evaluative research to both the clinician and the researcher. The resistance of the clinician to outcome studies and the misunderstanding of practice by evaluators have been noted frequently in the literature. But, for the authors, this problem is more apparent than real. Practitioners *are* concerned about outcomes, and evaluators *want* to understand practice. The real problem has been the lack of a common methodology.

To fill the gap, the authors have devised a computer-assisted method of evaluation designed primarily for practitioners' evaluative concerns, which, at the same time, meets the needs of evaluators. For example, practitioners and evaluators together decide on the questions to be asked; the questions then are operationalized and put into appropriate form for the computer. In this way, the analysis and interpretation of the data produced by the computer are assured of being pertinent to the interests of the individual worker. Brower and Mutschler also indicate, as do Morrison, Rosenberg, and Rehr in the preceding article, that analysis across workers can reveal agency trends, thereby meeting evaluators' needs.

Interaction and Experience in Groups: Doing as Life-Learning

Ruth R. Middleman

The "doings" of groups is an aspect of ordinary life experience, of how people define themselves collectively and individually: We *are* the Stagecrafters; I *am* in Weight Watchers. This doing part of human experience is what led me into social work. I was interested in the fun and games, the arts, and all those other activities that persons engaged in for recreational, socialization, and cultural purposes. By the late 1960s, I had written about these activities and their historical roots within group work.[1] And at this same time, the shifts in the national and professional arenas led group workers away from the small group, and especially from what we knew as "program" in group work. This article deals with some of the factors that have eclipsed and then rekindled interest and repursuit of this doing part of group work within social work and the related helping professions. We shift from past history to a current status review, and some imperatives and projections that may shape our future involvement with action and activities.

PROGRAM, INTERACTION, AND EXPERIENCE

It seems important to begin with certain working distinctions among these terms. Each has special time and place roots, although these words are often used now as if they were interchangeable. We start with *program* with its special meaning, now largely obsolete, in the history of social group work. It did not refer to an organization's broad range of service provisions, nor to any huge initiative (for example, the U.S. aerospace program). It was a rather narrow, specific aspect of group work: the activities—those things participants came to do out of their own interests or the content the group worker proposed in order to pursue professional and agency goals.

In this sense program was like *education,* referring to what individuals do for themselves as well as to the efforts of others in the individual's or the group's behalf. It was the content, but also the process, that is, doing-oriented activities could be used to pursue group purposes (for example, expressing feelings, relating to authority, building ties with others). It was thought of as a tool; and I described it as a "vehicle" through which

159

relationships are made and the needs and interests of the group and its members are fulfilled. And, in a less mechanistic mode of thinking, I urged that one should think of the tool-ness of program more as putty than hammer, that is, a tool that also changes as it is used. It was a product/process or ends/means concept.

What we knew as program is referred to now by both general and specific terms: *Psychodrama, expressive therapies, multimedia, experiential approaches* are the general descriptors. And within sessions, there are *exercises, nonverbals, simulations, games, role plays, tasks* and *encounter techniques*. All of this we used to simply call "program."

Interaction is a concept well known in sociology, communications, and games theory circles. It is a linear, reciprocal term referring to the back-and-forth flow, the stimulating and responding of persons to one another in verbal or nonverbal ways. But in addition to person-to-person interaction, the interaction can be between persons and nature (mountain climbing, jogging), with the random or chancy elements of the world (fishing, playing the stock market or Pac Man), or between persons and the normative aspects of living (taking the ACSW exam, negotiating the airport in Rome). The requisite "doings" in all these types of interactions are learned in childhood through various activities and in more complex versions throughout adulthood. For example, there are the puzzles (abstract versions of person-to-person relations); the games of chance, skill, and strategy that capture certain aspects of experience in which one's control is partial, or interrelated to other elements, and outcomes are dependent and emergent from the interaction. Finally, there are aesthetic events in which cultural elements determine basic interactional possibilities. These types of interactional requirements span all cultures.[2]

Experience is the most general concept in popular, philosophical, and technical vocabularies. It connotes people's living awareness and relationship to self, others, and the larger contextual surroundings. It holds special importance in learning theories. Living and schooling can be thought of as a series of learning experiences. In clinical and educational circles, it links with learning, growth, development, and also with the totality of the outcome of a professional's deliberate helping efforts. And within these ways of helping, the experiential type of learning is often contrasted with the didactic. In this sense, the particular meaning of *experiential* is its emphasis on action and interaction as routes to "whole person" learning. Whole person learning refers to learning experiences that are deliberately constructed to emphasize many sensory, information-receiving systems (touching, moving, visualizing, tasting, and so forth), as contrasted to merely hearing and reading. The experiential orientation acknowledges that thinking and reasoning may happen through diverse modalities, not merely through words.

This brief excursion through the realms of program, interaction, and experiential learning spans a historical period from early group work in settlement houses, through the impetus to in-depth study of communication and helping approaches accentuated by World War II and the subsequent energies of sociobehavioral investigators, to current clinical practice. And the cycle returns us to the doings of groups.

A RE-VIEW OF PROGRAM

The discussion of the doing part of group life is a direct result of my growing alarm—along with that of many other social workers whose backgrounds are in group work—about what had become of the group work of social workers. We formed a loose network, the Committee for the Advancement of Social Work with Groups, began to look more closely at small-group experience and its place within social work education and practice today, and began to stimulate its renewed visibility within ourselves and the broader profession. Since 1979 when we met in Cleveland, we have held six annual symposia on issues and practice with groups in social work. My remarks at the first symposium concerned the disappearance of program, a phoenix that did not die despite our neglect of it, but reemerged in new forms mainly through the simultaneous interest in this area by other professions.[3] I ventured these reflections with considerable advance trepidation—I was going to be hard on social work and on group work. But to my surprise, I had tapped into a common sentiment; and beyond my wildest expectations, I found a welcome there, a shared desire to make better use of our know-how about program and infuse our experiences within that of the whole profession.

I cited the following imperatives for the future:

1. *All* social workers need to become able to use group approaches as comfortably and knowledgeably as individual ones. This involves reviving early group work's focus on normal people and their learning, on wellness, enhancement, competence, and prevention.

2. Specialization (for a master's degree, work in agencies, and private practice) should include special knowledge and skill reflective of group workers' historical contribution to working with groups—a *social* orientation, one concerned with inner *and* environmental forces. Such an orientation distinguishes group work by social workers from that of psychotherapists and other professionals. We have a larger unit of attention: the individual in relation to other group members (communication between members) and in interaction with many impinging outer forces (extragroup situations). Furthermore, I suggest we separate expressiveness from therapy. It seems unnecessary to call the use of nontalking media "expressive therapy." Whether music, drama, dance, etc., *are* therapy or merely natural modes of self-expression would depend on the group's purpose, the orientation of the practitioner, the context of service, and so forth.

3. Theory development in group practice needs to deal with more than the serious, seemingly rational side of group life and begin to account for the nonrational, creative, affective, unexpected, and spontaneous dimensions as well. Our theories of group work have, so far, been partial ones, that is, they dealt with method, and method by definition must exclude the illogical and unplanned aspects of the workings of anything.

4. A cookbook mentality, in which the content of group experience becomes a "thing" again as it was in the early days of recreation, must be avoided. Although a wealth of specifics that bring greater familiarity with structured experiences and diverse interactional, experiential approaches exists in the new literature, this very availability of technique may eclipse the emergent nature of social workers' use of program. Such a mechanistic orientation lines up exercises and may move from activity to activity in a series of half-examined experiences—worker directed and imposed—rather than mutually determined by worker and group, an orientation that social group workers understood.

5. Attention to further research and study on the impact of various activities, of their effects, is imperative. This is more possible now that more practitioners familiar with research methods are leading groups. We need to move beyond a focus on how we do various activities—descriptions of our input—to a sophisticated look at consequences.

6. We also need to use this awareness of experiential approaches within the delivery systems and bureaucracies to humanize *them,* to affect staff meetings and in-service approaches. We need to highlight to others the values of fun and joy, of humor and playfulness, of spontaneity and creativity—a tall order, indeed!

GROUP WORK'S HISTORY WITH DOING ACTIVITIES

There is today within the social work profession a discontinuity so far as group work's tradition and contribution are concerned—a knowledge gap in current students' awareness of the past. They may think the use of expressive media and action experiences was the discovery of Gestalt therapists or growth centers. "Family sculpture" (or use of tableaux) may seem to be the brainchild of family therapists, role play the invention of communication labs or the behaviorists, whereas singing, dancing, games, and crafts may appear to be the "find" of the mental health professionals. Other professions and laypeople have laid claim to these media, have described and refined their use, and put them to special purpose more than social workers have done.

Although group workers were involved years ago with activities, we stopped doing our "homework" and followed the lead of other professions within the very territories we knew so well. For example, in community mental health centers, surveys reveal social work professionals as the dominant service providers (70 percent of personnel) with one-third of the executive directors being social workers.[4] Yet the group worker's special knowledge about activities, group approaches, outreach, partial hospitalization, and group leadership patterns has not influenced the thrust of the programs. This has to do with our lack of influence within the profession, with our small numbers, never more than 6 percent, and with the way curricula and specializations are offered in schools of social work.[5]

Although early group workers were well versed in pursuing all kinds of activities and were knowledgeable and experienced with the contents that expressed the interests of group participants, all the other-than-talking kinds of engagement were gradually abandoned as the American Association of Group Workers (AAGW) merged to help form the National Association of Social Workers (NASW) in 1955. There were many reasons for this: Doing-oriented activities seemed less than professional, were not particularly psychological, were confused with recreation and child's play (trivial and frivolous), and, for some, were even sinful. They were not serious or work-oriented—merely fun and games.

Although group workers gained an identity by joining with the emerging social work profession, they also suffered many losses, such as:

1. They played down involvement with activities and special interests of the group members and became like caseworkers, helpers who talked.

2. They parted company with the early group dynamics movement. They favored an action and service mission more than a study and research interest and thus abandoned an early common exploration of group processes.

3. They gave up their focus on the group in favor of using groups to help individuals grow and change. They adopted new psychological and personality theories to guide their work at the same time that the rest of the profession turned to psychiatry for consultation about groups and about activities. Much of our current approaches could be classified as working with individuals, group watching.[6]

4. They gave up their emphasis on teaching and learning and on members' overt interests as they concentrated on social, "professional" values. It was not unusual to find interracial objectives foremost in the worker's mind and winning at basketball in the members' minds. Like casework in those days, they "social worked others" without their awareness and consent. It did not matter: The loftiness of the goals—democratic decision making, acceptance of others—justified the means.

5. They also gave up the focus on common problems and situations and on the attempt to serve even those with special emotional and personality problems within their natural peer groups.

In short, group workers gave up their focus on normal people, on learning and wellness, on enhancement and competence, and on self-help. All of these directions are now returning to mainstream attention, more from outside influences than from social workers.

The shifts I have enumerated were not necessarily deliberate as much as circumstantial. Many factors contributed. Chiefly, we wanted to "make it" within the profession and with the more powerful influentials: psychiatry and psychology. And we needed to "make it" within the universities —the major sponsors of professional social work education—where nonintellectual matters like activities were especially suspect.

Suffice it to say that group work as one of the three major methods of social work at this time was always more ideation than reality. This tiny specialized minority of practitioners faced many enticements away from continuous energy investment in practice, theory development, and research with the small group. Numbers and economics, the vagaries of funding patterns on a predominantly bureaucratized profession that did not pay professional workers to work with small groups, all figured in these changes. Changing national social policies and the changing social scene, theoretical requirements for community organization and then for a generalist or micropractice in which group work usually survived as something called "individual, family, and groups," demanded intellectual efforts. Also, the special perspectives and talents of group workers led them to broader realms of influence, whereas the simultaneous discovery of "groups" by other professions and their economic advantage for Title XIX and XX payments came to be a force.

My dip into past history should not imply that I have any interest in returning to the good old days, in reviving the social group work we knew, in parting company with or alienating other related professionals and academics who have contributed substantially to the knowledge and use of activities and creative expression. I believe the chances are greater now than ever before for a concerted elaboration of and contribution by our profession using our shared interest in this component of group life. Our work is enhanced by the collaborative deployment of energies, knowledge, and demands for skilled work that far exceed what any single profession could accomplish alone.

I think an analogy exists between the construction of the helping professions' methods of helping and the course of intellectual development at the person level as posed by Piaget, Bruner, and other cognitive theorists.[7] The diverse, sophisticated modalities of communication and the theoretical explanatory systems that support them were contructed in response to practice demands, much as individuals construct their increasingly complex cognitive structures in response to tasks required by the impinging environment.

Looking at the development of group work within social work, I could compare early group work with a *sensory-motor* stage that was preoccupied with doing for the sake of experiencing the doing. Then there was an *intuitive* stage that emphasized hunches, right and wrong ways to do and be, moralistic and magical (or religious) influences. The elaboration of social group work's use of activities might be compared to the stage of *concrete operations* in that concepts were developed for describing the use of activities and particulars and rules were laid down for their use as components of broader theoretical approaches.

Group workers have grown able to deal with increasingly complex tasks with diverse, elaborated, sophisticated responses. However, I think we and other people-helping professions have barely moved beyond this stage (roughly seven to 11 years in the human life-cycle), nor may we ever be able to move to a more formal, abstract stage. We are still caught up with the actual more than the possible. We deal concretely, not abstractly, with specific events. We work inductively, pragmatically, and empirically with reliance on values and ad hoc, partial knowledge rather than on generalizations or laws. This is the uniqueness and appeal of a practice with persons. It demands intuition, creativity, judgment, improvisation, and expressiveness rather than rules, formulas, cause and effect, or logic.

ACTIVITIES IN GROUP WORK TODAY

Since 1979, there has been evidence of more deliberate attention being paid to the doing and action component of groups and of opportunities for us to refine our thinking about the meaning of doing.[8] Let us consider some summary ideas of importance.

1. Action or experiential approaches and groups are big business, not esoterica. The general public is knowledgeable and receptive. Even 2-to-5-year olds are now introduced to self-other social skills through planned approaches.[9] Encounter techniques in public schools are prevalent routes to teaching social-emotional, affective content along with the more academic content. Whole-person approaches to growth and learning have been popularized by the humanistic psychologists and the group movement. Beyond this, Eastern values and different modalities of expression, diverse cultures and lifestyles are directly known or vicariously encountered through television. Moreover, our technological/urban crunch encourages a search for the nonroutine, the new experience and creative outlet, the nonwork-based contacts, and the route to self-improvement— physical, emotional, social, intellectual, and spiritual. There is a receptivity to all sorts of activities, plus more practitioners ready to engage in them unself-consciously, perhaps as a result of their own previous involvement as group participants. Old suspicions and constraints are less binding.

2. The value of talking about—in contrast to doing or encountering as a means of knowing—has been eroded. We now know that nonverbal communication is as important as verbal. Doing is as important as talking.[10] In fact, immersion in activities in which rules, order of perfor-

mance, roles, and expected behavior are known to the participants may be seen as the natural home of speech. What is negotiated and variable is turns at talking.

3. Activities are a language—a form of nonverbal communication in which the verbal component arises around the edges of the activity so as to structure, synchronize, interpret, embellish, and augment the action component. Activities may be considered a component of analogic language that, along with digital (or verbal) language, comprises our communication. In function, the nonverbal or analogic languages convey information, express emotions, regulate social interaction, and convey dominant/submissive relationships.

The analogic languages may be grouped into four categories—two basic and two derived codes—according to how the observable events or markers are produced.[11] The *basic* indicators are actions (performance code) and things (artifactual code)—that is, all actions of the body, and all objects, clothing, food, architecture, and so forth. The *derived* codes make use of the performance and artifactual languages. These two other language codes are the spatiotemporal (or context) and mediatory codes. The mediatory code is of special concern to us. It is an invented or specially constructed arrangement of elements, for example, graphs, pictures, exercises, tasks, that is developed by the people-influencers—us.

Clinicians are knowledgeable about and skilled in using all four codes and are attuned especially to decoding information from clients in the performance, artifactual, and spatiotemporal realms. Since the 1970s, due particularly to the group movement, practitioners also have become skilled in constructing and entering a two-way communication stream using the mediatory code. We encode our communications and structure experiences through various nonverbal pursuits, activities, and *constructed* learning experiences.[12] Here I would include guided fantasy, exercises, all modalities aimed at expanding sensory awareness and perception, what Neuro Linguistic Programming calls "primary representational systems," what Gestalt therapy terms the "sensory contact functions," plus the special techniques of psychodrama, dance, and so forth. All these are mediatory (or person-made) language codes and are essentially analogic approaches to knowing.

4. Activities are their own language, but may be used to express whatever the helper's frame of reference or psychological preference happens to be (ego psychology, family therapy, Gestalt, feminist, behavioral therapy, and so forth). More rarely, as perhaps with psychodrama, does the activity have a particular helping theory of its own. The *meaning* of the activity is only what the helper *thinks* it is. Applying a specific meaning (or interpretation) is a hazardous act, as difficult for the helping person as it is for the artist who must give a name to a painting.

5. At a general level, however, the use of activities is suited to two

major purposes regardless of the practitioner's frame of reference. First, there is mastering the particulars needed to handle oneself with respect to others, to the environment, and to the world of ideas and tasks—learning the rules of the game so to speak. Second, after gaining some facility in this area, one may move beyond this kind of coping-learning to innovation, and the development of one's unique style of living. These are matters of discipline and innovation. They have to do with discovery versus invention.

Discovery is a process of inquiry into what is. It is much of what formal academic work emphasizes. It uses the methods of science, of the experiment, of logic, and of analysis to observe carefully and, via mainly verbal/linguistic and mathematical skills, to make sense out of the world. The discovery process in the activity realm includes learning the rudiments of a particular form, mastering the control of the elements so as to produce the expected product with reliable technique.

Invention is a process of creation of what could be. Involved here is disciplined use of the imagination, often left to chance. Sometimes this is called divergent thinking, that is, entertaining many possible perspectives; or lateral or first-stage thinking, that is, breaking away from known modes of processing information and introducing discontinuities; or intuitive thinking, that is, moving from the inner world to the outer rather than vice versa; or holistic, right-brain thinking. In any event, invention and artistry involve a recombination of elements in a realm in which right and wrong are less important than novelty, new insights, and sometimes a reorganization of elements into a composition never before expressed. I mean here the creative and unique, and not merely the idiosyncratic. Activities and the arts seem especially congenial to risking the new and untried, to suspending critical judgment, and to embroidering the familiar into a new achievement.

6. In the final analysis, how activities are used depends on the intricate interaction of many variables: characteristics of the practitioner (for example, age, sex, theory in use, professional training), context variables (the group and its purpose, size, characteristics of participants, setting), process variables (for example, how the worker and group interact, the particular activity and its demand, the worker's skill), and outcome variables (for example, change, learning, enjoyment, and satisfaction).

CLINICIANS' ORIENTATION

Let us focus on one of the elements just identified—the practitioner's self-view or role orientation, and thus on how controlling a central person he or she will be. This element, beyond all others, affects how activities are used. Three distinguishable roles emerge as possibilities: facilitator, diagnostician-educator, and ecologist. The facilitator designation emerged mainly from the human potential movement (and humanistic psychologies), the diagnostician-educator is linked to the behaviorist tradition, and the ecologist orientation describes a role primarily evolved by social work theorists whose focus was on both persons and environments. The facilitator usually occupies a less central and controlling place within the helping process than the diagnostician-educator, whose procedures and interventions are more exact and prescriptive, or than the ecologist, whose analytic and planning activities shape and focus the ensuing interventions to an extent. All three roles share a long-cherished educational tradition of teacher as arranger of the environment for learning, as specialist in devising the means through which individuals may develop inherent interests and capacities.

Social workers have assumed all three roles in their work with groups. The facilitator and diagnostician-educator, borrowed from humanistic and cognitive-behavioral psychology, characterize much of the group work in community mental health centers, hospitals, halfway houses, and so forth. It is the ecologist orientation that links most closely with the social group work history just sketched.

Ecology aims at more than the environment; it tries to achieve a balance between individuals and environments and has been clarified as a practice orientation in social work by Germain and Gitterman.[13] The social worker as ecologist is concerned with selection and distribution of roles, power, resources, tasks and problem-solving activities. In large part these aims determined the proposal and selection of various activities by social group workers: the encouragement of individuals and group to try to do particular things, the choice of experiences that perhaps filled gaps in members' lives or that participants felt comfortable with and could do with confidence. Certain activities might realign power differentials within the group through modalities that would reveal different talents and skills—that might bring out the silent ones, tone down the dominant ones, encourage cohesion, or involve the group in doing something for others. Mainly, such use of activities evolved from the participants' situations, what they knew and wanted to know and do, the nitty-gritty of their lives. Such program content emerged from the worker-group interaction, with the worker acting as orchestrator or ecologist.

It is this use of activity starting from where the person is that has been obscured of late and that, it is to be hoped, will be renewed. Activities may enhance perceptual complexity (for example, through simulations), encourage discovery (for example, learning to pose and solve problems), stimulate affective complexity (for example, through confronting one's values and feelings), and offer power equalization between group members and the practitioner as well as among members of different gender, class, and ethnicity. The activities may favor the previously unfavored through their skill demands and reveal new dimensions of the self.

CONCLUSION

Bronowski characterized the ascent of man as a brilliant sequence of cultural peaks through which we have culturally evolved by means of our imagination and invention.[14] He said we are not fitted to any environment and have a rather crude survival kit. Yet the paradox of the human condition is that we are fitted to all environments through use of imagination, reason, emotional subtlety, and toughness that make it possible for us not to accept the environment but to change it. From age to age through a series of inventions, we have remade our environment.

We, unlike the insects, are not specialists but are generalists whose major achievement is the ability to build models in our heads by means of arbitrary languages (for example, words, numbers, notes) and by various physical analogues (for example, objects, pictures, images) more closely related to our physical world. It is especially important for both realms to be nurtured and encouraged, for all types of thinking to be valued, and for the activities of groups to be constructed in such a way that participants experience not only what the practitioner has already determined *will do* this or that for the group, but that they may experience activities whose potentials are emergent or even unknown.

We possess at present an unprecedented latitude of tolerance for diversity in individual functioning, now legitimated by science and research. Beyond valuing abstract, logical, rational thinking and the fruits of such actitives, we are now able to appreciate the concrete, the nonlogical, intuitive, artistic, holistic means of knowing and expression. I refer to the research findings concerned with right-hemisphere information processing and with the findings of extensive research on diverse cognitive styles. The practical and political implications of such studies for social workers, educators, and all people-helpers are enormous. We may yet see one of social work's cardinal values operationalized: respect for the infinite individuality and diversity of people. Such helping, teaching, and influencing will, no doubt, be forced to rely more heavily on activities than we can presently imagine.

I remember and I was.
I feel and I am.
I do and I become.[15]

NOTES AND REFERENCES

1. Ruth R. Middleman, *The Non-Verbal Method in Working with Groups* (New York: Association Press, 1968; expanded ed.; Hebron, Conn.: Practitioners' Press, 1980).

2. For elaboration of these folk models, see Omar K. Moore, "Technology

and Behavior," *Proceedings of the 1964 Invitational Conference on Testing Problems* (Princeton, N.J.: Educational Testing Service, 1965).

3. Ruth R. Middleman, "The Use of Program: Review and Update," *Social Work with Groups*, 3 (Fall 1980), pp. 5-23; article also published in Sonia L. Abels and Paul Abels, eds., *Proceedings, First Annual Symposium: Social Work with Groups* (Hebron, Conn.: Practitioners' Press, 1981).

4. "On the Record," *NASW News*, 22 (January 1977), p. 24; and "Inouye Makes Bid in Senate for Social Work Vendorship," *NASW News*, 25 (February 1980), p. 1.

5. Alfred M. Stamm, "1967 Social Work Graduates: Salaries and Characteristics," *Personnel Information*, 11 (March 1968), p. 51, Table 4.

6. For elaboration, see Ruth R. Middleman, "Returning Group Process to Group Work," *Social Work with Groups*, 1 (Spring 1978), pp. 15-26; for a review of current practice with groups in social work, see Catherine Papell and Beulah Rothman, "Relating the Mainstream Model of Social Work with Groups to Group Psychotherapy and the Structured Group Approach," *Social Work with Groups*, 3 (Summer 1980), pp. 5-23.

7. See, for example, Jean Piaget and Barbel Inhelder, *The Psychology of the Child* (New York: Basic Books, 1969); and Jerome S. Bruner, "The Course of Cognitive Growth," *American Psychologist*, 19 (1964), pp. 1-15.

8. Examples include the Conference on Creative and Therapeutic Action in Groups, School of Social Work, Boston University, 1980; The Arts in Social Work conference, School of Social Work, Hunter College, April 1983; and Ruth R. Middleman, guest ed., "Activities and Action in Groupwork," special issue of *Social Work with Groups*, 6 (Spring 1983), which stimulated many submissions on practice with this focus.

9. See, for example, George Spivack and Myrna Shure, *Social Adjustment of Young Children* (San Francisco: Jossey-Bass, 1974).

10. See, for example, Joan M. Erikson, *Activity, Recovery, Growth: The Communal Role of Planned Activities* (New York: W. W. Norton & Co., 1976) for an exciting view of the enhancement possibilities of activities from an Eriksonian perspective; and Eileen T. Nickerson and Kay S. O'Laughlin, eds., *Helping through Action* (New York: Human Resources Development Press, 1982) for a comprehensive array of the other therapeutic modality.

11. For elaboration, see Randall P. Harrison, *Beyond Words* (Englewood Cliffs, N.J.: Prentice-Hall, 1974).

12. Ruth R. Middleman, "The Pursuit of Competence through Involvement in Structured Groups," in Anthony Maluccio, ed., *Building Competence in Clients* (New York: Free Press, 1981).

13. Carel B. Germain, ed., *Social Work Practice: People and Environments* (New York: Columbia University Press, 1979); and Germain and Alex Gitterman, *The Life Model of Social Work Practice* (New York: Columbia University Press, 1980).

14. Jacob Bronowski, *The Ascent of Man* (Boston: Little, Brown & Co., 1973), pp. 19-20.

15. Joan M. Erikson with David and Joan Loveless, *Activity, Recovery, Growth: The Communal Role of Planned Activities* (New York: W. W. Norton & Co., Inc., Copyright © 1976), p. 250. Reprinted by permission of the publisher.

Evaluation of Suicide Risk by Diagnostic Group

Jay Callahan

Many frameworks by which to evaluate suicide potential have been proposed.[1] However, no method has empirically proven itself and, perhaps more important, many clinicians are reluctant to employ any method of lethality assessment that does not primarily depend upon "clinical judgment." This is not very surprising. Clinicians are, however, eager for viewpoints and information that assist them in sharpening their sensitivity to the nuances of evaluation in cases of potential suicide. At the risk of repeating often-quoted generalizations, this article presents some clinical viewpoints both from the literature and from the author's experience. Specifically, it proposes that suicide be considered from the vantage point of overall clinical diagnosis, and that only in such a framework can one make sense of an immense amount of data and anecdotes, many of which are mutually contradictory.

Many studies over the years have had major problems in comparability and external validity due to the lack of explicitly agreed on diagnostic criteria. Until recently each investigator utilized his or her own favorite nosological theory, with the unfortunate result that little could be replicated across studies. However, with the publication of *DSM-III,* one may now see the beginnings of diagnostic comparability.[2]

In the evaluation of suicide lethality, the following aspects have previously been identified as significant:

- suicide ideation vs. suicide intention
- likelihood of impulsive vs. planned attempt
- specificity of impulsive fantasy or plan
- objective lethality of plan
- availability of plan
- subjective lethality of plan
- ego-syntonic vs. ego-alien attitude toward potential attempt
- presence or absence of conscious anger[3]
- conception of death and afterlife
- details of previous attempts
- demographic factors (age, gender, race, marital status, etc.)
- loss of self-esteem
- hopelessness

These items are identified as a basis for suicide evaluation, but will not be discussed here because most clinicians are knowledgeable about their importance.

One aspect will bear repeating, however. It is virtually impossible to overestimate the importance of understanding the suicidal individual's ambivalence toward suicide.[4] An understanding of ambivalence suggests that rating suicide lethality is dynamic, not static, and that it has an effect upon all aspects of the clinical evaluation. It is well understood, for example, that lethality is related to the dangerousness of the method used; one way to understand this factor is in the amount of time provided by different methods in which to effect a self-rescue. Clearly, jumping from a tall building gives one no time, whereas wrist cutting and most overdoses provide ample time. But less clearly understood is the concept that choice of method is not simply a question of availability, but reflects one's ambivalence toward success. That is, a highly ambivalent individual will choose a method that reflects his or her "mixed feelings," such that the method represents both death (the actual attempt) and life (time provided to rescue self).

The dynamic nature of this ambivalence also explains the common occurrence of an individual's suicide attempt and then *immediate* self-rescue, such as taking an overdose and then calling an ambulance. Acting upon the impulse or wish to die itself provokes a temporary increase in the desire to live, tipping the balance back toward life. An understanding of ambivalence has given rise to several provocative technical methods of suicide intervention—for example, "calling the bluff" of a "manipulative" client, or strongly empathizing with the death wish of a depressed one. Needless to say, these are risky maneuvers.

Perhaps ambivalence allows us to understand the precarious balance upon which many suicidal individuals hang. At some points in such an individual's life, the balancing forces of impulse or wish to die versus the desire to live may be quite equal. At such a time the smallest rejection or disappointment, the merest aspect of identification with a dead relative, friend, or celebrity, or perhaps the day's weather may be enough to tip the balance. Furthermore, it is clear that not all highly lethal attempts are successes, and not all gestures are failures. Thus intention is not always a reliable predictor.[5] For these reasons the most accurate evaluation of suicide lethality is to place individuals in general categories of risk: high, medium, low. The assessment of which of the individuals in the high-risk group will subsequently actually complete a suicide attempt is beyond present capabilities.[6]

Suicide attemptors are not a homogeneous group, and thus it is only within specific diagnostic groups that an adequate suicide assessment can be carried out. In this article, five diagnostic classifications from *DSM-III* will be discussed with regard to suicide:

1. Major Depressive Disorder without Melancholia
2. Major Depressive Disorder with Melancholia (including Bipolar Affective Disorders)
3. Psychotic Disorders, including:
   Schizophrenic Disorders
   Major Depressive Disorders with Psychotic Features
   Psychotic Disorders not Elsewhere Classified
   not including: Paranoid Disorders
4. Borderline Personality Disorder
5. Alcohol Dependence.

MAJOR DEPRESSIVE DISORDER WITHOUT MELANCHOLIA

In many publications and discussions of suicide, it is taken for granted that the suicidal individual is depressed. While this is by no means always the case, it is true that the largest number of people at risk for suicide are those with depression.[7] In *DSM-III* the major depressive syndromes are classified as either having or not having "melancholia," as well as with or without psychotic features. This section discusses the problem from the point of view of depressions without melancholia or psychotic features.

The prevalence of depression in the United States today is estimated to vary between 5.7 and 6.8 percent of the population, which places a very large group of people at risk for suicide. One report by Avery and Winokur suggests that as many as 15 percent of clients with affective disorders will someday successfully kill themselves.[8]

In clients with Major Depressive Disorder without Melancholia, treatment is usually outpatient psychotherapy; somatic treatments are usually unsuccessful and inappropriate.[9] In contrast to Major Depressive Disorder with Melancholia, these clients do not lose their capacity to experience or anticipate pleasure, and their affect remains reactive to environmental events. Thus they can usually gain some relief by talking about their difficulties, and they remain able to feel better for brief periods, usually via distraction.

Because they remain able to feel better, if only temporarily, hopelessness is much less likely to develop, and hopelessness has been hypothesized to be an important factor in suicide prediction.[10]

Most of the well-known clinical guidelines about suicide are derived from experience with clients with Major Depression without Melancholia. Once again, the issue of ambivalence is crucial. In reviewing the events of a recent attempt, for example, one can often see evidence of "behavioral" ambivalence, even if the client is unaware of these dynamics. For example, a client's having a full bottle of pills available but only taking some of them, or having a gun available, but using a knife, are significant indicators of the client's ambivalence. The therapeutic task, of course, is to bring this ambivalence to conscious awareness, where it can be examined verbally.

Much published material about one-session mental health emergency work implicitly conceptualizes the process as one of evaluation and disposition.[11] This model ignores a third essential component—that of "intervention," or "emergency treatment." That is, the assessment of suicide should not be thought of as simply an evaluation and then a decision concerning hospitalization versus outpatient treatment, but as a process that also includes some attempt at treatment, some attention to a process of modifying the suicidal ambivalence *right at that time.*

On one level, simply acknowledging and calmly discussing a client's thoughts about suicide will slightly tip the ambivalence in favor of the desire to live. Understanding and a commitment to help, demonstrated by the clinician's time, attention, and energy, will also be therapeutic. In contrast, a surgeon's sarcasm about the superficiality of a wrist-cutting attempt is clearly countertherapeutic, and may precipitate another, more lethal, attempt.

Ultimately, no clinician can "talk" a client out of killing himself or herself. Thus the choice of disposition, at the end of the evaluation and intervention, is based on the relative lethality as it has been assessed, on the overall clinical diagnosis (here it is Major Depression without Melancholia), and on the client's intrapsychic, interpersonal, and social resources. Chief among the intrapsychic resources are judgment and insight.

MAJOR DEPRESSIVE DISORDER
WITH MELANCHOLIA

An important diagnostic distinction is made in *DSM-III* by the use of the subcategory "melancholia." A note in *DSM-III* (p. 205) explains that this word, although somewhat archaic, was chosen because of the unfortunate association of the term *endogenous* with the idea of "unprecipitated." Many endogenous-type depressions do have precipitants. The awkward word *endogenomorphic* was suggested by Klein in 1974 to convey the same meaning—a cluster of specific signs and symptoms, listed below, which are independent of whether a depressive episode was precipitated or not.[12]

This distinction is crucial because of its treatment implications; depressions with melancholia are readily treated by the somatic therapies, such as antidepressant medication and ECT (electroconvulsive therapy), whereas those "without melancholia" do not generally respond to these treatments. In addition, a biological test—still somewhat controversial—termed the *dexamethasone suppression test (DST)* has now been developed to aid in the diagnosis.[13]

The defining signs and symptoms of melancholia are

    A. loss of pleasure in all or almost all activities
    B. lack of reactivity to usually pleasurable stimuli [the person] (doesn't feel much better, even temporarily, when something good happens)
    C. at least three of the following:
        (a) distinct quality of depressed mood, i.e., the depressed mood is perceived as distinctly different from the kind of feeling experienced following the death of a loved one
        (b) the depression is regularly worse in the morning
        (c) early morning awakening (at least two hours before usual time of awakening)
        (d) marked psychomotor retardation or agitation
        (e) significant anorexia or weight loss
        (f) excessive or inappropriate guilt[14]

As is noted in the criteria, two of the defining characteristics of a depression with melancholia are loss of the pleasure capacity ("anhedonia") and lack of reactivity to pleasurable stimuli. Even though depressions of this type are not necessarily more severe than those without melancholia, it is this inhibition of the pleasure capacity that is so experientially powerful. Many depressed individuals are overwhelmed as their ability to experience pleasure slowly drains away, and, combined with the unremitting nature of such a depression—once an episode has begun, the individual's lack of reactivity of mood is persistent—can easily lead to hopelessness.

Because depressions with melancholia are, for the most part, unresponsive to psychotherapy alone,[15] clients are often bewildered to find that they can clarify dynamics, straighten out problematic interpersonal relationships, and set new goals for themselves, but still continue to feel just as bad. This also can lead to hopelessness.

Clients have described such a depression as a "steel curtain that descended on me," and as a "wet blanket that was there all the time." These descriptions capture the "distinct quality of depressed mood" that is common—very often it is a numbness, as opposed to a sadness.

Furthermore, in the vast majority of cases, significant psychomotor agitation or retardation is characteristic only of Major Depression with Melancholia. It is a subgroup of these clients—those with significant psychomotor retardation and severe suicidal thoughts—who are increasingly at risk for suicide as their depression lifts. Whether the depression ends spontaneously, or via treatment, it is typically the motor retardation that yields first, enabling the still-depressed individual to now act on the suicidal thoughts. (This phenomenon is distinct from the statistical finding that the first few months after discharge are the highest-risk period for hospitalized clients.[16])

PSYCHOTIC DISORDERS

Although many clinicians think of depression when considering the issue of suicide, it is important not to forget that a significant number of suicides are completed by psychotic clients.[17] This section considers Psychotic Disorders, including Schizophrenic Disorders, Major Depressive Disorders with Psychotic Features, and Psychotic Disorders Not Elsewhere Classified (not including Paranoid Disorders). Studies in this area are confounded by a lack of diagnostic clarity, as well as by a lack of description of mental status—whether an individual is psychotic or not—at the time of the attempt. In one classic study it was found that schizophrenics had a yearly suicide rate of 167 per 100,000, far higher than a standard (corrected for geography, gender, age, and veteran status) of 22.7 per 100,000 per year.[18] It should be noted that in this same study, the depressed clients had a yearly rate of 566 per 100,000, but again, diagnostic criteria were not well-defined. Probably all sorts of depression were included in the group studied, and it also must be remembered that all clients in this study were ill enough to require hospitalization.

Other studies have reported different rates. A recent report using *DSM-III* diagnostic criteria found outpatient schizophrenics to have a yearly rate of 411 per 100,000, as opposed to only 92 for "all affective disorders." (Interestingly, in this study the bipolar clients had a much higher rate than the unipolars, 318 to 42, each per 100,000.) Another report noted that in a group of clients seen because of at least one prior suicide attempt, male schizophrenics had a subsequent annual suicide rate of 925 per 100,000.[19]

Clinical experience suggests that clients suffering from one of the *DSM-III* paranoid disorders are not as highly at risk as those with the other psychoses. These disorders are characterized by elaborate delusions only, with no disorganization of thinking or personality as is usually found in the other psychoses. Such clients are well-known for their lack of internal distress or subjective discomfort, and, in fact, are more often seen by attorneys than by clinicians, due to their pervasive lack of insight.

One of the most important symptoms of a thought disorder is, of course, hallucinations. In a significant number of psychotic clients, auditory hallucinations may comment on the individual's behavior, or two or more voices may carry on a running dialogue. In a significant number of cases the voices may "command" the client to carry out a particular activity, and in some (but not all) of these cases, the individual may feel compelled to obey. Many chronic schizophrenics have almost continual command hallucinations, which they "ignore," "argue back with," or otherwise disregard. In many acute cases, however, the individual feels powerless to resist the commands, which not infrequently include suicide. In one such case a 27-year-old single male, with an acute worsening of insidious onset schizophrenia spent several hours sitting in a garbage dumpster behind his apartment building; the voices had called him "trash" and "garbage." The next day he overdosed on his antipsychotic medication in a suicide attempt, although he survived. Clearly, his inability to resist the content of the voices was an ominous sign.

A related, equally ominous sign is that of self-mutilation, either real or symbolic. Although not all clients were psychotic, a recent report reviewed 53 cases of male genital self-mutilation, and found controversial, but higher-than-average rates of suicide on follow-up.[20] Symbolic self-mutilation must also be considered, as the following case example shows:

> A 25-year-old chronic schizophrenic came to his clinic one week having impulsively shaved off all of his hair the preceding day. He was unable to explain his behavior, and concerted efforts on the part of his outpatient therapist were equally unsuccessful. He explicitly denied suicidal ideas or impulses. Nonetheless, ten days later, he successfully hung himself in a nearby secluded forest.

Overall, the significant risk factor with psychotic clients is the unpredictableness of their thinking and behavior. It is clear that the prediction of behavior is a highly complex and problematic area, and with individuals whose thinking is disordered, the difficulty is multiplied. The clinician must carry out his or her customary assessment of suicide lethality, and yet must be even less confident than usual that subsequent behavior can be adequately predicted.

Intuitively, depression with psychosis would seem to place an individual at very high risk for suicide. Empirically, the only study that addresses this issue found a suicide rate five times higher in a group of delusionally depressed clients compared to nondelusional ones.[21]

BORDERLINE PERSONALITY DISORDER

A very different set of difficulties is presented by those clients with the diagnosis of Borderline Personality Disorder.[22] Although completed suicides are not uncommon, this group of clients is more often characterized by multiple attempts of low lethality, often wrist cutting. In fact, it is important at the outset to separate out such chronic self-destructive behavior from behavior that is more consciously suicidal. In most cases, these repeated "gestures" are intended to fulfill goals other than suicide, and often the individuals can articulately describe their motivations—to decrease tension, to feel alive, to combat emptiness, and to punish oneself.[23]

At times it is difficult to believe that an individual could be as articulate and (superficially) insightful as these clients often are, and yet be as out of control of their impulses as they are. In many cases the self-destructive behavior takes place in the context of a brief dissociative episode, so that the cutting produces no pain.[24]

In general, it is statistically true that one suicide attempt puts an individual at risk for future attempts, and that a significant percentage of all successful suicides have made previous attempts.[25] However, the implications of this finding are unclear in the situation of chronic "cutting." It is quite possible, of course, for such a client to kill him- or herself "by accident" in one of these "gestures."

Aside from these cutters, clients with Borderline Personality Disorder often present with more serious attempts to kill themselves. Furthermore, they are often very unable to predict their own behavior, so that the common assessment questions regarding future attempts are continually met with "I don't know. . . ." Perhaps due to their propensity to utilize the defense mechanism of "splitting," as well as the pervasive lack of identity and feeling of emptiness, these clients are often acutely responsive to interpersonal and environmental factors.[26] They may appear integrated in their thinking and in good control of their impulses in the office or emergency room, but with a clear sense of terror at the prospect of going home alone. Once there, the controls become weaker, the impulses more powerful, and the client again begins to regress. It is important to take such self-report seriously, as well as to resist the propensity to see such suicidal behavior as conscious and manipulative—it is not, at least not in most cases.

It is equally important to remember that clients with Borderline Personality Disorder often become regressed when positive, hopeful things happen, not just under the stress of loss or threat of loss. The usual cycle is that the beginning of a romantic relationship, the beginning of therapy, or the beginning of a hospitalization inevitably sets up fantasies of fulfillment, all-accepting love, and an end to the never-ending neediness and dependence. Of course, these elusive fantasies are not borne out, and the individual becomes ragefully disappointed. At this point the regression takes place—into psychosis, suicidal acting out, or impulsive violence toward others.

One extremely important therapeutic response to such regression is limit setting. When the regression is taking place, limits must be set, whether the context is an ongoing therapeutic relationship or a single emergency room visit. Limits must be set and enforced, with as much nonjudgmental, nonhostile firmness as possible.[27]

Because of some of the above factors, as well as their already tenuous sense of control, clients with Borderline Personality Disorder are often acutely aware of "control" issues. In addition, these clients' fragile hold on their impulses often elicits frantic efforts at external control on the part of clinicians. The results are power struggles, in which each therapeutic tack on the part of the clinician is met with increased regression, or provocative vagueness, or disturbing "hints" of suicidal behavior on the client's part.

It is thus important not to engage in these power struggles unless absolutely necessary. Limits must be set in specific areas, and in others a neutral position can be taken. It is especially important not to engage in power struggles that are impossible to win, such as (for example) demanding that a "cutter" cease picking at her recent wounds. On the other hand, if or when involuntary commitment is decided upon, on the basis of a particularly serious suicide attempt, it must be pursued without vacillation.

Involuntary commitment to a custodial institution, it must be realized, is basically another limit-setting maneuver. Psychotherapy is rarely provided in such hospitals, but this is their strength—clients with Borderline Personality Disorder often become significantly regressed in highly staffed "intensive" evaluation and treatment units in private and/or teaching hospitals.

The clinician must be firm in setting limits with regard to his or her own involvement, as well. The regression-producing intensity of an intimate relationship is highly alluring to these clients, and so they will in many cases seek that which will invariably make them worse. Some such clients have been known to sleep each night in their cars, parked near their therapist's homes. Well-meaning attempts to "understand," or to "reason with" these individuals will only fuel the fire of further regression and make the necessary limit setting only appear more punitive and contradictory.[28]

When a borderline client is in treatment, or is a regular client of an emergency service, each suicide attempt or risk must be weighed against that client's baseline state of functioning. When the client's usual style of functioning is well-known, reasonably accurate judgments can be made about the seriousness of a particular attempt. Thus in many cases clients can be evaluated and sent home with a minimum of acting out. In some cases this remains true even when borderline clients cannot "promise" they will not make another attempt, as long as this is their usual pattern. On the other hand, with unknown clients of any diagnosis, the inability to plan for their own safety or to be able to reasonably predict their own behavior is an indication for hospitalization.

ALCOHOL DEPENDENCE

Alcoholics kill themselves, and they often do it while drunk. Somewhat surprisingly, not all alcoholics are depressed when they attempt suicide. Much work has taken place in recent years to clarify the relationship between alcoholism and affective disorders. While it is increasingly clear that in most cases alcoholics do not drink "because" they are depressed, but are depressed because they drink, it is still obscure what the source of the depression is. Family and social factors have been postulated, but a recent study identified a "depressive syndrome of chronic intoxication" that may have a physiological basis. In any case, various estimates of suicide rates among alcoholics have been reported. One investigator found the rate to be 133 per 100,000 per year among previously hospitalized male veterans with alcohol dependence, but a later study of male alcoholics with at least one previous suicide attempt found the rate to be an astounding 1562 per 100,000 per year. In a more recent study of outpatients, the rate for "primary alcoholics" was 101 per 100,000, and if clients with a secondary diagnosis of alcoholism are included, the rate climbs to 195 per 100,000.[29]

One study identified two distinct patterns of suicide among alcoholics.[30] The first was termed an "abreactive" syndrome, consisting of an episode of acute intoxication in the context of a problematic, angry interpersonal interaction. The second was described as a "depressive syndrome of chronic intoxication," marked by isolation, depression, and continual drinking for two weeks or more. The latter syndrome produced significantly more potentially lethal attempts.

Another finding was an increased incidence of interpersonal loss among suicidal alcoholics. One-fourth to one-third of two groups of alcoholics who committed suicide had experienced a marital separation or divorce within the last six weeks of their lives.[31]

Complicating factors in the evaluation of and intervention with suicidal alcoholics are amnesia and denial.

> A 52-year-old divorced male with a 30-year history of alcoholism walked out on his front porch one evening, produced a handgun, and proceeded to play "Russian Roulette." A horrified neighbor called the police, who stopped him and placed him in jail after discovering that he was highly intoxicated. When evaluated by mental health staff six hours later, the client denied all memory of the incident, denied feeling at all suicidal, denied the possibility that he would ever behave so recklessly, and denied that he had a drinking problem.

Of course, the only possible therapeutic approach in these cases is to confront the denial. Aggressive attempts to treat the alcoholism must be made, using whatever legal or interpersonal "leverage" that can be brought to bear. This is especially true in light of the evidence that the depression that is commonly present may be a direct result of the drinking per se.[32]

CONCLUDING REMARKS

Assessment of and intervention with suicidal clients is a risky, difficult area that is anxiety producing for all clinicians. In recent years more and more attention has been paid to this serious problem, and it is hoped that viewing the issue of suicide within specific diagnostic groups will be an additional contribution to this effort.

NOTES AND REFERENCES

1. Dan J. Lettieri, "Suicidal Death Prediction Scales," in Aaron T. Beck, Harvey L. P. Resnik, and Lettieri, eds., *The Prediction of Suicide* (Bowie, Md.: Charles Press, 1974), pp. 119–140; George E. Murphy, "Clinical Identification of Suicide Risk," *Archives of General Psychiatry,* 27 (September 1972), pp. 356–359; Peter Sainsbury, "Clinical Aspects of Suicide and Its Prevention," *British Journal of Hospital Medicine,* 19 (February 1978), pp. 156–164; Robert E. Litman et al., "Prediction Models of Suicidal Behaviors," in Beck, Resnik, and Lettieri, eds., *The Prediction of Suicide,* pp. 141–159; Jacob Tuckman and William F. Youngman, "A Scale for Assessing Suicide Risk of Attempted Suicides," *Journal of Clinical Psychology,* 24 (January 1968), pp. 17–19; Avery D. Weisman and J. William Worden, "Risk-Rescue Rating in Suicide Assessment," *Archives of General Psychiatry,* 26 (June 1972), pp. 553–560; Maria Kovacs, Aaron T. Beck, and Arlene Weissman, "Hopelessness: An Indicator of Suicidal Risk," *Suicide,* 5 (Summer 1975), pp. 98–103; Ivan W. Sletten and John L. Barton, "Suicidal Patients in the Emergency Room: A Guide for Evaluation and Disposition," *Hospital and Community Psychiatry,* 30 (June 1979), pp. 407–411; Ari Kiev, "Cluster Analysis Profiles of Suicide Attempters," *American Journal of Psychiatry,* 133 (February 1976), pp. 150–153; and Aaron T. Beck, Roy Beck, and Maria Kovacs, "Classification of Suicidal Behaviors: I. Quantifying Intent and Medical Lethality," *American Journal of Psychiatry,* 132 (March 1975), pp. 285–287.

2. American Psychiatric Association, *Diagnostic and Statistical Manual of Mental Disorders* (3d ed.; Washington, D.C.: APA, 1980).

3. Myrna Weissman, Karen Fox, and Gerald L. Klerman, "Hostility and Depression Associated with Suicide Attempts," *American Journal of Psychiatry,* 130 (April 1973), pp. 450–455.

4. Beck, Beck, and Kovacs, "Classification of Suicidal Behaviors," pp. 285–287; and Donald A. Schwartz, Don E. Flinn, and Paul F. Slawson, "Suicide in the Psychiatric Hospital," *American Journal of Psychiatry,* 132 (February 1975), pp. 150–153.

5. Beck, Beck, and Kovacs, "Classification of Suicidal Behaviors," pp. 285–287.

6. Litman et al., "Prediction Models of Suicidal Behaviors," pp. 141–159; and Carl I. Wold and Robert E. Litman, "Suicide after Contact with a Suicide Prevention Center," *Archives of General Psychiatry,* 28 (May 1973), pp. 735–739.

7. Calvin J. Frederick, "Current Trends in Suicidal Behavior in the United States," *American Journal of Psychotherapy,* 32 (1978), pp. 172–200; and David Avery and George Winokur, "Suicide, Attempted Suicide, and Relapse Rates in Depression," *Archives of General Psychiatry,* 35 (June 1978), pp. 749–753.

8. Myrna M. Weissman and Jerome K. Myers, "Affective Disorders in a U.S. Urban Community," *Archives of General Psychiatry,* 35 (November 1978), pp. 1304–1311; and Avery and Winokur, "Suicide, Attempted Suicide, and Relapse Rates," pp. 749–753.

9. Donald F. Klein, "Endogenomorphic Depression: A Conceptual and Terminological Revision," *Archives of General Psychiatry,* 31 (October 1974), pp. 447–454; Bernard J. Carroll et al., "A Specific Laboratory Test for the Diagnosis of Melancholia," *Archives of General Psychiatry,* 38 (January 1981), pp. 15–22; and

Walter Armin Brown and Iris Shuey, "Response to Dexamethasone and Subtype of Depression," *Archives of General Psychiatry*, 37 (July 1980), pp. 747–751.

10. Kovacs, Beck, and Weissman, "Hopelessness," pp. 98–103; Kenneth Minkoff et al., "Hopelessness, Depression, and Attempted Suicide," *American Journal of Psychiatry*, 130 (April 1973), pp. 455–459; and Alex D. Pokorny, Howard B. Kaplan, and Shih Y. Tsai, "Hopelessness and Attempted Suicide: A Reconsideration," *American Journal of Psychiatry*, 132 (September 1975), pp. 954–956.

11. Sletten and Barton, "Suicidal Patients," pp. 407–410.

12. Klein, "Endogenomorphic Depression," pp. 447–454.

13. Carroll et al., "Specific Laboratory Test," pp. 15–22.

14. APA, *DSM-III*, p. 215.

15. Klein, "Endogenomorphic Depression," pp. 447–454; and Carroll et al., "Specific Laboratory Test," pp. 15–22.

16. Alex D. Pokorny, "Suicide Rates in Various Psychiatric Disorders," *Journal of Nervous and Mental Disease*, 139 (December 1964), pp. 499–506; Pokorny, "A Follow-Up Study of 618 Suicidal Patients," *American Journal of Psychiatry*, 122 (1966), pp. 1109–1116; Joe Yamamoto, Michael Roath, and Robert Litman, "Suicides in the 'New' Community Hospital," *Archives of General Psychiatry*, 28 (January 1973), pp. 101–102; and Ming T. Tsuang, "Suicide in Schizophrenics, Manics, Depressives, and Surgical Controls," *Archives of General Psychiatry*, 35 (February 1978), pp. 153–155.

17. Pokorny, "Suicide Rates," pp. 499–506; Pokorny, "Follow-Up Study," pp. 1109–1116; George Winokur and Ming Tsuang, "The Iowa 500: Suicide in Mania, Depression, and Schizophrenia," *American Journal of Psychiatry*, 132 (June 1975), pp. 650–651; and James R. Morrison, "Suicide in a Psychiatric Practice Population," *Journal of Clinical Psychiatry*, 43 (September 1982), pp. 348–352.

18. Pokorny, "Suicide Rates," pp. 499–506.

19. Morrison, "Suicide in Psychiatric Practice," pp. 348–352; and Pokorny, "Follow-Up Study," pp. 1109–1116.

20. Howard Greilsheimer and James E. Groves, "Male Genital Self-mutilation," *Archives of General Psychiatry*, 36 (April 1979), pp. 441–446.

21. Stephen P. Roose et al., "Depression, Delusions, and Suicide," *American Journal of Psychiatry*, 140 (September 1983), pp. 1159–1162.

22. John G. Gunderson and Margaret T. Singer, "Defining Borderline Patients: An Overview," *American Journal of Psychiatry*, 132 (January 1975), pp. 1–10; and J. Christopher Perry and Gerald L. Klerman, "The Borderline Patient: A Comparative Analysis of Four Sets of Diagnostic Criteria," *Archives of General Psychiatry*, 35 (February 1978), pp. 141–150.

23. Richard J. Rosenthal et al., "Wrist-Cutting Syndrome: The Meaning of a Gesture," *American Journal of Psychiatry*, 128 (May 1972), pp. 1363–1368.

24. Ibid.

25. Avery and Winokur, "Suicide," pp. 749–753.

26. H. George Nurnberg and Ryang Suh, "Limits: Short-Term Treatment of Hospitalized Borderline Patients," *Comprehensive Psychiatry*, 21 (January–February 1980), pp. 70–80; and Barbara Mark, "Hospital Treatment of Borderline Patients: Toward a Better Understanding of Problematic Issues," *Journal of Psychiatric Nursing and Mental Health Services* (August 1980), pp. 25–31.

27. Henry J. Friedman, "Psychotherapy of Borderline Patients: The Influence

of Theory on Technique," *American Journal of Psychiatry*, 132 (October 1975), pp. 1048–1052; and Gerald Adler, "Hospital Treatment of Borderline Patients," *American Journal of Psychiatry*, 130 (January 1973), pp. 32–36.

28. John T. Maltsberger and Dan H. Buie, "Countertransference Hate in the Treatment of Suicidal Patients," *Archives of General Psychiatry*, 30 (May 1974), pp. 625–633.

29. Donald W. Goodwin, "Alcohol in Suicide and Homicide," *Quarterly Journal of Studies on Alcohol*, 34 (1973), pp. 144–156; Joel Solomon, "Alcoholism and Suicide," in Solomon, ed., *Alcoholism and Clinical Psychiatry* (New York: Plenum, 1982), pp. 97–110; Demmie G. Mayfield and Dan Montgomery, "Alcoholism, Alcohol Intoxication, and Suicide Attempts," *Archives of General Psychiatry*, 27 (September 1972), pp. 349–353; George E. Murphy et al., "Suicide and Alcoholism: Interpersonal Loss Confirmed as a Predictor," *Archives of General Psychiatry*, 36 (January 1979), pp. 65–69; Donald W. Goodwin, "Alcoholism and Affective Disorders: The Basic Questions," in Solomon, *Alcoholism and Clinical Psychiatry*, pp. 87–95; Pokorny, "Suicide Rates," pp. 499–506; Pokorny, "Follow-Up Study," pp. 1109–1116; and Morrison, "Suicide," pp. 348–352.

30. Mayfield and Montgomery, "Alcoholism," pp. 349–353.

31. Murphy et al., "Suicide and Alcoholism," pp. 65–69.

32. Mayfield and Montgomery, "Alcoholism," pp. 349–353.

Treatment Relationships with Black Clients: Interpersonal vs. Instrumental Strategies

Jewelle Taylor Gibbs

It is anticipated that minority clients will constitute a disproportionate segment of persons in need of social services in the next two decades due to a number of factors, including population trends, economic changes, and radical revisions of social welfare policies and services. Thus, it is essential for social workers to increase their knowledge of, and enhance their skills relevant to practice with, minority clients in order to improve their effectiveness and to ensure a high level of excellence in the delivery of services to these currently underserved groups.

Since the early 1950s, there has been an increasing number of articles dealing with the issues of engaging black clients in a treatment relationship. These authors have generally focused on several dominant themes that influence the black client-white social worker relationship, for example, differences in expectations, value systems, communication patterns, attitudes toward bureaucratic policies, attitudes toward self-disclosure, mutual stereotyping, status and power issues, and the establishment of mutual trust.[1]

In more recent years, papers have been written about additional factors that impede the development of a relationship between black workers and black clients, such as problems of racial identification, socioeconomic differences, attitudes toward sociopolitical issues, incorporation and projection of majority attitudes and stereotypes, and status issues.[2]

In spite of the growing literature in this field, there has been very little attention paid to the specific dynamics occurring between the worker and the black client in the initial phase of treatment, during which a mutually satisfactory relationship must be established in order to negotiate a contract and proceed with an intervention plan. For the purpose of this article, the "initial phase" of treatment is defined as ranging from one to three sessions, during which the client's problem is assessed, a psychosocial history is obtained, and a treatment plan is formulated.[3]

The goal of this article is twofold: (1) to identify the factors that are especially relevant to the initial phase of establishing a treatment relationship between the social worker and the black client, and (2) to propose an *interpersonal orientation* model that conceptualizes the transactions between the black client and the worker, who can then utilize this information to facilitate the establishment of the treatment relationship.

LITERATURE REVIEW

The need to focus on the initial contacts between the black client and the social worker is clearly indicated by findings from utilization surveys, such as the large-scale survey of community mental health centers conducted by Sue and his colleagues. They found that over 50 percent of the black clients terminated their contact with a community mental health center after one session, as compared to 30 percent of the white clients. Other utilization surveys of outpatient psychiatric clinics and community mental health centers have confirmed the general tendency of black patients to terminate prematurely, and well before a treatment relationship is established.[4]

A second major reason to analyze these early contacts is the frequently reported findings that black clients feel that they are misunderstood, mislabeled, and mistreated by white workers. Although there is considerable evidence that blacks are more frequently assigned to less-experienced mental health professionals and paraprofessionals, more likely to receive more pathological diagnoses, and less likely to be referred for psychotherapy than for somatic or custodial treatment, there is also some contrary evidence that black patients are not discriminated against because of their ethnicity, but due to their low socioeconomic status, the most salient factor in many studies of the mental health delivery system.[5]

The significance of the initial interview in determining the nature of the relationship between the black client and the worker is emphasized by a number of authors, both in the clinical literature and in empirical studies. Griffith and Jones underscored the importance of the initial phase of treatment, as follows: "The race difference appears to have its greatest impact early in treatment, particularly at the first encounter. If the white therapist can establish effective rapport at initial contact and build a therapeutic alliance in relatively rapid fashion, successful outcomes can be achieved with lower-income black clients, usually considered poor risks, and with middle-class black clients despite their initial sense of wariness and consequently slower movement in therapy."[6]

There are three types of studies that bear directly on the issue of establishing a treatment relationship between the social worker and the black client; these are (1) experimental analog studies, (2) clinical studies, and (3) empirical studies of client-worker interactions.

First, experimental analog studies of simulated counseling sessions between black clients and white and black workers indicated that racial similarity is related positively to the client's depth of exploration, that the worker's race is more important than the worker's experience for black clients, that black clients generally prefer black workers, particularly in initial interviews, because the clients feel that they achieve greater rapport and greater empathic understanding with the black workers, and that perceived ethnic similarity is the most important factor in therapist selection for black adults.[7]

In contrast, however, one investigator found that after one interview, a worker's experience was a more important factor than was a worker's race for a sample of black college students; others have found, however, that a worker's race and experience were of equal importance or that race may not be an important factor in therapist preference rating.[8] Findings from these analog studies suggest that racial similarity between worker and client is, on balance, one of the most significant factors in facilitating the treatment relationship, yet experience may be able to offset racial differences in the treatment dyad.

Although analog studies can be criticized because they are simulated rather than naturalistic treatment situations, clinical studies based on observations and case records also have their limitations, owing to the issues of reliability and validity of therapists' reports and records. Nonetheless, reports from a broad cross section of clinicians, working with a variety of black clients, provide further evidence of the problems involved in establishing the treatment relationship.

Studies of the utilization patterns of black college students at integrated universities indicated that the students were reluctant to seek help from traditional sources, were frequently suspicious and hostile in their initial encounters with workers, had difficulties communicating their problems and feelings, and perceived the mental health services as impersonal, inflexible, and inadequate to meet their specific needs. They also generally expressed a preference for black therapists or workers.[9]

Evaluations of clients in private and public outpatient treatment settings have consistently noted symptoms of paranoia and hostility toward therapists, incongruent expectations, guardedness and unwillingness to self-disclose, linguistic and cultural misunderstandings, anxiety about acceptance, fears of being labeled deviant or "crazy," and reluctance to trust.[10] In addition, these studies have reported a persistent tendency of black clients to test their therapists in a number of subtle and overt ways, including verbal abuse, stereotyped mannerisms, canceled and late appointments, and sullen, withdrawn behaviors.

The third and rarest type of study is the empirical investigation of actual black client-therapist treatment relationships. In his study of the effect of racial matching on client-therapist process and outcome, Jones found that, although racial matching did not affect the outcome of therapy, it did affect the process, that is, black clients discussed racial concerns more often with both black and white therapists but also tended to develop a more eroticized transference with black therapists, which apparently facilitated the therapeutic process. In another study by Krebs, black clients had a significantly lower attendance rate at therapy sessions and terminated their therapy with white therapists earlier than with black therapists.[11]

Relevant data from other social science investigations provide indirect evidence of multiple factors contributing to intrinsic problems in the relationship between black clients and white workers. These findings are drawn from historical analyses of the discrimination and prejudice against blacks by the dominant society; sociological accounts of the impact of racism on black-white relationships and the development of a definable black subculture with its own values, behaviors and beliefs; sociolinguistic analyses of black language and communication styles; and psychological analyses of the effect of racism on black self-identity and self-esteem.[12]

All these findings lend support to the clinical data that, owing to the peculiar history of race relations in the United States, blacks have developed a relatively negative set of expectations about receiving help, an attitude of mistrust about accepting help, an anxiety over self-disclosure and self-examination, a fear of being rejected or depersonalized, and an unwillingness to commit themselves to nonfamily relationships.[13]

Given this background, blacks have developed over the years certain interpersonal strategies to cope with situations that are unfamiliar and anxiety provoking. These strategies have been described and documented in a number of sociological and psychological studies of blacks. Jenkins suggested that blacks have a

> tendency to bring personally based affective assessment to learning situations. . . .This reflected a tendency of minorities to rely more than whites on the universal ability to conceptualize situations in terms of their positive or negative valence towards them.[14]

This tendency to relate to others in terms of their interpersonal characteristics rather than their instrumental characteristics has also been noted in a number of clinical and empirical studies of blacks in other interpersonal helping situations including therapist-client, consultant-consultee, and counselor-student.[15]

In a previous paper, the author proposed that black clients place a higher value on the interpersonal competence of the consultant than on the consultant's instrumental competence, that is, clients believe they must be able to establish a satisfactory interpersonal relationship with the consultant and a feeling of mutual trust before they can effectively engage in the instrumental task of consultation. These terms were defined as follows: (1) an *interpersonal orientation* is an individual focus on the process rather than the content of verbal and nonverbal interactions between two people, and (2) an *instrumental orientation* is an individual focus on the goal or the task-related aspects in the relationship between two people.[16]

Table 1
A Model of Interpersonal Orientation to Treatment

Client Evaluation Stages (Themes of Evaluation)	Counselor Behavior Responses (Dimensions of Competence)
I. Appraisal ("Sizing Up")	I. Personal Authenticity ("Genuineness")
II. Investigation ("Checking Out")	II. Egalitarianism (Status Equalization)
III. Involvement (Social Interactions)	III. Identification (Positive Identity)
IV. Commitment (Personal Loyalty)	IV. Acceptance (Empathy, Support)
V. Engagement (Task Involvement)	V. Performance (Task Performance)

SOURCE: Adapted from J. T. Gibbs, "The Interpersonal Orientation in Mental Health Consultation: Toward A Model of Ethnic Variations in Consultation," *Journal of Community Psychology*, 8 (1980), pp. 195–207. Reprinted by permission of the journal.

It is suggested here that this model can be extended to the treatment relationship as another example of an interpersonal helping process. It is viewed as particularly appropriate to the black client–white worker relationship but it is also applicable in many respects to the black client–black worker relationship, as will be noted.

MODEL OF INTERPERSONAL ORIENTATION

The model of an interpersonal orientation to treatment proposes that the initial phase of the treatment relationship can be broken down into five microstages in which the client is evaluating the worker while the worker is attempting to establish a relationship and to assess the client's problems (see Table 1). Each microstage is characterized by a theme that reflects the concerns of the client and his or her ambivalence about the treatment process. Furthermore, the model proposes dimensions of worker behavior that are being evaluated in each stage by the client in terms of his or her needs and priorities in the treatment relationship. The dimensions of worker behavior to be evaluated are similar to those dimensions of counselor competence proposed by Rogers as criteria for effective client-centered counseling, that is, warmth, empathy, congruence, and unconditional positive regard for the client.[17]

Stage I: Appraisal Stage. Stage I is the initial stage of contact between worker and client, during which the minority client "sizes up" the worker, waits guardedly for the worker to initiate the interview, and generally behaves in an aloof, reserved, or superficially pleasant manner. Beneath this reserved facade of the client may be feelings of distrust, suspiciousness, or hostility toward the worker. In this stage the client is evaluating the *personal authenticity* of the worker, that is, the worker's ability to be genuine and approachable.

Stage II: Investigation Stage. Stage II follows closely upon the initial reaction and is characterized by the client "checking out" the worker. In this stage the client may challenge the worker with questions about his or her background, professional qualifications, values, and opinions. This reaction is an attempt by the client to place the worker in an ethnic or social status hierarchy, along an ideological spectrum, or to evaluate the worker's previous professional experience with minority clients. In this stage, the client is judging the worker's ability *to equalize the differences* between himself and clients of a different background.

Stage III: Involvement Stage. Stage III will only follow Stages I and II if the client feels that the worker has "checked out" favorably. Otherwise, the worker will find that the client has terminated prematurely after one or two sessions. If the client is satisfied and makes a *positive identification* with the worker, he or she will begin to open up and to self-disclose. He or she may also, at this stage, attempt to establish a more personal relationship with the worker based on a perceived sense of mutuality and similarity, for example, inviting the worker to lunch or coffee, to attend an ethnic activity in the community, or to contribute to an ethnic cause. This is a form of testing the worker's degree of empathic identification with the client.

Stage IV: Commitment Stage. Stage IV follows Stage III closely if the worker responds flexibly and sensitively to the efforts of the client to establish a more personal relationship. During Stage IV the client becomes committed to the treatment relationship, drops his or her defensiveness, and no longer tests the worker's intentions. However, the client's initial commitment to treatment is expressed in terms of *loyalty and personal regard* for the worker, rather than in terms of a belief in the effectiveness of the treatment process. At this point the client feels that the worker has demonstrated *acceptance* of him or her as a unique individual through empathic and supportive behaviors.

Stage V: Engagement Stage. Stage V is the final stage of treatment during which the client fully involves himself or herself in its task-centered aspects. The client now focuses on identifying problems, defining goals of treatment, and engaging himself or herself in the dynamic process of treatment. In this final microstage, the client has tacitly acknowledged the *interpersonal competence* of the worker as demonstrated in the previous four stages and is ready fully to explore problems with confidence and trust in the worker's *instrumental competence* to utilize professional skills.

The criteria by which the black client evaluates the interpersonal competence of the worker are closely related to the dimensions that have been identified in the literature as major cultural patterns among blacks in terms of expressive behavior and social interactions (see Table 1).[18]

Dimension I: Personal Authenticity. Dimension I is most salient in the Appraisal Stage, when the client is evaluating the worker for his or her perceived "genuineness" and the degree to which he or she projects the qualities of being warm, "real," and "down-to-earth."

Dimension II: Egalitarianism. Dimension II is most salient in the Investigation Stage, when the client is evaluating the way in which the worker relates to a person from a different ethnic or socioeconomic background. If the worker can equalize the status and power differences between himself or herself and the client by using nontechnical language and acting in a democratic, nonauthoritarian manner, he or she will be positively judged on this dimension.

Dimension III: Identification. Dimension III is most salient in the Involvement Stage, when the client evaluates the worker's degree of identification with the client's ethnic background and with the sociocultural milieu of the institution, that is, the degree to which the worker represents the status quo versus the degree to which the worker functions as a change agent. If the client perceives that the worker is committed to helping black clients to resolve their problems as well as to negotiate their social milieu more effectively, without relinquishing their sense of ethnic identity and challenging their basic cultural values, he or she will be positively judged on this dimension.

Dimension IV: Acceptance. Dimension IV is most salient in the Commitment Stage, where the client evaluates the *empathic skills* of the worker and the degree to which he or she demonstrates a comprehension of the sociocultural factors involved in the black client's perception of his or her problems. If the worker can offer the client *nonjudgmental attitudes and support* when the client expresses intrapsychic as well as sociopolitical conflicts, then the worker will be judged positively on this dimension.

Dimension V: Performance. Dimension V becomes most salient in the Engagement Stage, when the client makes his or her commitment to cooperate fully in the treatment process and to address the presenting problems for which he or she initially sought help. This is the final microstage of the initial phase of treatment in which the client shifts his or her dominant orientation from the interpersonal competence of the worker to the worker's instrumental competence.

This entire sequence of five microstages will probably occur within the first two or three sessions, but elements of each stage may be apparent even in the first session. Thus, it is important for the worker to be alert to shifts in each session that reflect the client's movement from one stage to another. Lack of worker sensitivity to these subtle and rapid shifts from stage to stage will result in inappropriate responses to the cues of the client and will increase the probability of premature termination.

DISCUSSION AND CONCLUSION

This model of an interpersonal orientation of black clients to the treatment relationship is derived from a combination of clinical experience, sociopsychological descriptive and theoretical data on blacks, and clinical and empirical findings on black-white transactions in therapy and other interpersonal relationships. This model has a number of significant implications, not only in terms of its heuristic value in explaining the behavior of black clients in establishing a treatment relationship, but also in terms of its applicability to other helping relationships and its relevance to social work education and practice.

First, the concept of an interpersonal orientation among black clients to the treatment relationship contributes to an understanding of the observed differences between blacks and whites in their response to the initial phase of treatment. The interpersonal orientation derives from attempts to personalize relationships that are usually considered impersonal in the dominant culture, that is, to treat a universalistic situation in a particularistic way. This creates communication problems that frequently result in premature termination or continuous client-worker conflict.

Second, the conceptualization of interpersonal competence as a distinct set of skills that can be differentiated from instrumental skills is useful in analyzing the requirements of different treatment situations. If workers are aware that these skills are crucial in order to facilitate communication and mutual trust with black clients, they can then evaluate their own practice and modify their approach so that it will be more congruent with the needs and expectations of their clients. Several authors have suggested that mental health professionals need to be more active, more empathic, and more directive, particularly with low-income black clients. It has also been suggested that preparing black clients for the treatment relationship with more information about the process will result in more successful outcomes, as has been noted for low-income clients generally in a recent review of the literature by Jones and Matsumoto.[19]

Third, a stage-related model of interpersonal orientation and the dimensions of interpersonal competence offer the worker a framework in which to judge his or her relative progress through the initial phase into the active phase of treatment. If conflicts or problems arise during the relationship-building phase, the worker might be better able to identify the sources of the problem and deal with them before the relationship is prematurely terminated.

Fourth, this model is useful for training professionals in the helping professions and for continuing-education programs for experienced professionals, who will then be better equipped to understand the perspectives of black clients and thus be better able to deliver services to them. Conversely, understanding the cultural influences on the behaviors of black clients will also enable workers to point out the inappropriateness of the interpersonal orientation in some situations, so that black clients can learn to be more effective in their dealings with the dominant culture by adopting an instrumental orientation in universal situations.

Finally, the concept of an interpersonal orientation to the treatment relationship may be generalizable to other ethnic minority groups, particularly those who have developed adaptive strategies to cope with their disadvantaged status. For example, studies of Hispanic mental health programs have focused on the importance of professionals understanding the distinctive cultural attributes and interactional patterns of Spanish-speaking clients. A concept very similar to an interpersonal orientation has been described by Abad, Ramos, and Boyce: "Personalismo refers to the inclination of Latin people, in general, to relate to and trust persons, rather than institutions, and their dislike for formal, impersonal structure and organizations."[20]

The model proposed here is tentative and based on theoretical, clinical, and behavioral science data from several disciplinary perspectives. Research designs are needed to test the validity of the model and its applicability to other situations involving blacks in interpersonal helping transactions. For example, audiovisual studies could be conducted of actual treatment sessions involving four racial combinations of client-worker pairings in order to compare intraethnic and interethnic effects in the initial phase of treatment.

For this purpose it might be possible to adapt the system used by Ivey and Authier to analyze the microstages of the initial phase of treatment, particularly since this system recognizes cultural influences in the helping process and focuses on the responses of the counselor.[21] Finally, the applicability of the model to other ethnic groups should be investigated, particularly since demographic trends indicate that minority clients will increasingly comprise a greater proportion of persons served in public social welfare agencies throughout urban America.

NOTES AND REFERENCES

1. See, for example, W. A. Adams, "The Negro Patient in Psychiatric Treatment," *American Journal of Orthopsychiatry*, 20 (1950), pp. 305–310; J. B. Bloch, "The White Worker and the Negro Client in Psychotherapy," *Social Work*, 13 (April 1968), pp. 36–42; D. D. Bowles, "Making Casework Relevant to Black People: Approaches, Techniques, Theoretical Implications," *Child Welfare*, 48 (October 1969), pp. 468–475; H. Rosen and J. D. Frank, "Negros in Psychotherapy," *American Journal of Psychiatry*, 119 (1962), pp. 456–460; C. J. Sager,

T. L. Brayboy, and B. R. Waxenberg, "Black Patient—White Therapist," *American Journal of Orthopsychiatry*, 42 (April 1972), pp. 415–423; and E. Pinderhughes, "Teaching Empathy: Ethnicity, Race and Power at the Cross-Cultural Treatment Interface," *American Journal of Social Psychiatry*, 4 (1984), pp. 5–12.

2. See, for example, M. Calnek, "Racial Factors in the Countertransference: The Black Therapist and the Black Client," *American Journal of Orthopsychiatry*, 40 (January 1970), pp. 39–46; L. Gardner, "The Therapeutic Relationship Under Varying Conditions of Race," *Psychotherapy: Theory, Research and Practice*, 8 (1971), pp. 78–87; and A. M. Jackson, "Psychotherapy: Factors Associated with the Race of the Therapist," *Psychotherapy: Theory, Research and Practice*, 10 (Fall 1973), pp. 273–277.

3. See, for example, B. Compton and B. Galaway, *Social Work Processes* (rev. ed.; Homewood, Ill.: Dorsey Press, 1979); and H. Strean, *Clinical Social Work: Theory and Practice* (New York: Free Press, 1978).

4. See S. Sue et al., "Delivery of Community Mental Health Services to Black and White Clients," *Journal of Consulting and Clinical Psychology*, 42, No. 5 (1974), pp. 794–801; M. Griffith, "The Influence of Race on the Psychotherapeutic Relationship," *Psychiatry*, 40 (1977); pp. 27–40; J. Mayo, "The Significance of Sociocultural Variables in the Psychiatric Treatment of Black Outpatients," *Comprehensive Psychiatry*, 15 (1974), pp. 471–482; J. Yamamoto, Q. James, and N. Palley, "Cultural Problems in Psychiatric Therapy," *Archives of General Psychiatry*, 19 (1968), pp. 45–49; and A. Jackson, "Mental Health Delivery Systems and the Black Client," *Journal of Afro-American Issues*, 4 (1976), pp. 28–34.

5. See, for example, A. Thomas and S. Sillen, *Racism and Psychiatry* (New York: Brunner/Mazel, 1972); C. Willie, B. Kramer, and B. Brown, eds., *Racism and Mental Health* (Pittsburgh, Pa.: University of Pittsburgh Press, 1973), pp. 165–184; S. Sue, "Community Mental Health Services to Minority Groups," *American Psychologist*, 32 (1977), pp. 616–624; O. Baum et al., "Psychotherapy, Dropouts, and Lower Socioeconomic Patients," *American Journal of Orthopsychiatry*, 36 (1966), pp. 629–635; R. Lorion, "Patient and Therapist Variables in the Treatment of Low-Income Patients," *Psychological Bulletin*, 81 (1974), pp. 344–354; and V. Sanua, "Sociocultural Aspects of Psychotherapy and Treatment: A Review of the Literature," in L. E. Abt and B. F. Riess, eds., *Progress in Clinical Psychology* (New York: Grune & Stratton, 1966).

6. See, for example, M. Griffith and E. Jones, "Race and Psychotherapy: Changing Perspectives," in J. Masserman, ed., *Psychiatric Therapies*, Vol. 18 (New York: Grune & Stratton, 1979), pp. 225–235; A. Jones and A. Seagull, "Dimensions of the Relationship Between the Black Client and the White Therapist: A Theoretical Overview," *American Psychologist*, 32 (1977), pp. 850–855; D. L. Jones, "African-American Clients: Clinical Practice Issues," *Social Work*, 24 (March 1979), pp. 112–118; G. Banks, B. Berenson, and R. Carkhuff, "The Effects of Counselor Race and Training upon Counseling Process with Negro Clients in Initial Interviews," *Journal of Clinical Psychology*, 23 (1967), pp. 70–72; W. Banks, "The Differential Effects of Race and Social Class in Helping," *Journal of Clinical Psychology*, 29 (1972), pp. 90–92; and Carkhuff and R. Pierce, "The Differential Effects of Therapist Race and Social Class upon Patient Depth of Self-Exploration in the Initial Clinical Interview," *Journal of Consulting Psychology*, 31 (1967), pp. 632–634.

7. Carkhuff and Pierce, "Differential Effects of Therapist Race"; Banks, Berenson, and Carkuff, "Effects of Counselor Race and Training"; W. Banks, "Differential Effects"; S. Bryson and J. Cody, "Relationship of Race and Level of Understanding Between Counselor and Client," *Journal of Counseling Psychology,* 20 (1973), pp. 495–498; R. Grantham, "Effects of Counselor Sex, Race, and Language Style on Black Students in Initial Interviews," *Journal of Counseling Psychology,* 20 (1973), pp. 553–559; and G. Wolkon, S. Moriwaki, and K. Williams, "Race and Social Class Factors in the Orientation toward Psychotherapy," *Journal of Counseling Psychology,* 20 (1973), pp. 312–316.

8. P. Cimbolic, "Counselor Race and Experience Effects on Black Clients," *Journal of Consulting and Clinical Psychology,* 39 (1972), pp. 328–332; W. Gardner, "The Differential Effects of Race, Education and Experience on Helping," *Journal of Clinical Psychology,* 28 (1972), pp. 87–89; and D. Webster and B. Fretz, "Black and White College Students' Preferences for Help-Giving Sources," *Journal of Counseling Psychology,* 25 (1978), pp. 124–132.

9. See, for example, K. Davis and J. Swartz, "Increasing Black Students' Utilization of Mental Health Services," *American Journal of Orthopsychiatry,* 42 (October 1972), pp. 771–776; J. T. Gibbs, "Use of Mental Health Services by Black Students at a Predominantly White University: A Three-Year Study," *American Journal of Orthopsychiatry,* 45 (April 1975), pp. 430–445; and C. Hammond, "Paranoia and Prejudice: Recognition and Management of the Student from a Deprived Background," *International Psychiatry Clinics,* 7 (1970), pp. 35–48.

10. See, for example, Adams, "The Negro Patient"; C. Block, "Black Americans and the Cross-Cultural Counseling and Psychotherapy Experience," in A. Marsella and P. Pedersen, eds., *Cross-Cultural Counseling and Psychotherapy* (New York: Pergamon Press, 1981); J. S. Gochros, "Recognition and Use of Anger in Negro Clients," *Social Work,* 11 (January 1966), pp. 28–34; W. Grier and P. Cobbs, *Black Rage* (New York: Basic Books, 1968); and Jackson, "Psychotherapy."

11. E. Jones, "The Effects of Race on Psychotherapy Process and Outcome: An Exploratory Investigation," *Psychotherapy: Theory, Research and Practice,* 15 (1978), pp. 226–236; and R. L. Krebs, "Some Effects of a White Institution on Black Psychiatric Outpatients," *American Journal of Orthopsychiatry,* 41 (July 1971).

12. See, for example, L. Fishel, Jr., and B. Quarles, *The Black American: A Brief Documentary History* (Glenview, Ill.: Scott, Foresman, 1970); L. Knowles and K. Prewitt, *Institutional Racism in America* (Englewood Cliffs, N.J.: Prentice-Hall, 1969); K. Clark, *Dark Ghetto* (New York: Harper & Row, 1965); D. Schultz, *Coming Up Black* (Englewood Cliffs, N.J.: Prentice-Hall, 1969); C. Silberman, *Crisis in Black and White* (New York: Random House, 1964); C. Kernan, "Language Behavior in a Black Urban Community," *Monograph of the Language Behavior Research Laboratory,* No. 2 (Berkeley: University of California, 1971); T. E. Kochman, ed., *Rappin' and Stylin' Out* (Urbana: University of Illinois Press, 1972); W. Labov, *Language in the Inner City: Studies in the Black English Vernacular* (Philadelphia: University of Pennsylvania Press, 1972); E. Baughman, *Black Americans: A Psychological Analysis* (New York: Academic Press, 1971); V. Gordon, *The Self-Concept of Black Americans* (Washington, D.C.: University Press of America, 1977); R. Jones, ed., *Black Psychology* (New York: Harper & Row, 1980); and R. Wilcox, ed., *The Psychological Consequences of Being a Black American* (New York: John Wiley & Sons, 1971).

13. See, for example, Block, "Black Americans"; Grier and Cobbs, *Black Rage*; and Thomas and Sillen, *Racism and Psychiatry*.

14. See, for example, Baughman, *Black Americans*; Clark, *Dark Ghetto*; F. Fanon, *Black Skin, White Masks* (New York: Grove Press, 1967); T. Kochman, *Black and White Styles in Conflict* (Chicago: University of Chicago Press, 1981); and A. Jenkins, *The Psychology of the Afro-American: A Humanistic Approach* (New York: Pergamon Press, 1982), p. 162.

15. Gardner, "Therapeutic Relationship"; J. Gibbs, "The Interpersonal Orientation in Mental Health Consultation: Toward a Model of Ethnic Variations in Consultation," *Journal of Community Psychology*, 8 (1980), pp. 195–207; Gibbs, "Black Students/White University: Different Expectations," *Personnel and Guidance Journal*, 51 (1973), pp. 463–469; D. L. Haettenschwiller, "Counseling Black College Students in Special Programs," *Personnel and Guidance Journal*, 50, No. 1 (1971), pp. 29–35; and E. Mackey, "Some Observations on Coping Styles of Black Students on White Campuses," *Journal of the American College Health Association*, 21 (1972), pp. 126–130.

16. Gibbs, "Black Students/White University"; and cf. N. Sundberg et al., "Assessing and Assisting Development of Interpersonal Competence for the Human Services," paper presented at the meeting of the American Psychological Association, Chicago, September 1975.

17. C. Rogers, *Client-Centered Therapy* (Boston: Houghton Mifflin, 1976).

18. See, for example, Jenkins, *Psychology of the Black American*; Schulz, *Coming Up Black*; and Kochman, *Black and White Styles in Conflict*.

19. See, for example, Block, "Black Americans"; M. Kincaid, "Identity and Therapy in the Black Community," *Personnel and Guidance Journal*, 47 (1969), pp. 884–890; Mayo, "Significance of Sociocultural Variables"; Griffith and Jones, "Race and Psychotherapy"; and E. Jones and D. Matsumoto, "Psychotherapy with the Underserved," in L. Snowden, ed. *Reaching the Underserved* (Beverly Hills, Calif.: Sage Publications, 1982).

20. G. DeVos, "Adaptive Strategies in U.S. Minorities," in E. Jones and S. Korchin, eds., *Minority Mental Health* (New York: Praeger, 1982); M. Delgado, "Therapy Latino Style: Implications for Psychiatric Care," in R. Dana, ed., *Human Services for Cultural Minorities* (Baltimore, Md.: University Park Press, 1981); A. Padilla, "Pluralistic Counseling and Psychotherapy for Hispanic Americans," in Marsella and Pedersen, eds., *Cross-Cultural Counseling*; and V. Abad, J. Ramos, and E. Boyce, "A Model for Delivery of Mental Health Services to Spanish-Speaking Minorities," *American Journal of Orthopsychiatry*, 44 (July 1974), pp. 584–595.

21. A. Ivey and J. Authier, *Microcounseling: Innovations in Interviewing, Counseling, Psychotherapy and Psychoeducation* (2d ed.; Springfield, Ill.: Charles C Thomas, 1978).

The Borderline Adolescent

Judith Marks Mishne

In ever-increasing proportion, those of us engaged in child welfare services, and clinical work with children and adolescents, are encountering parents and children who evidence profound psychiatric disorders. This increase in pathology is not simply the result of improved detection and assessment. Rather, societal conditions—notably, increased family disorganization and breakdown—seem to be contributing to a higher proportion of families in crisis whose range of difficulties in response to separation and upheaval may include violence and substance abuse, with resultant alienation and a need for a myriad of services. There has been an increase not only in the overall number of clients, but in the incidence of severe pathologies—specifically, severe character pathology, psychosis, and the borderline syndrome.

The term *borderline* has come into increasing use in the last 20 years to describe a severe form of psychopathology. In clinical practice, however, the concept still is often misused and misunderstood. For example, some see the syndrome as a transitory state between psychosis and severe neurosis, and quickly label clients who give evidence of fleeting periods of psychosis, of intense ego disruption, as "borderline." The borderline syndrome has long had a bad reputation and most frequently has been a "wastebasket" category for those whom we do not know how to label or diagnose. Despite the discomfort of some with diagnosis and labeling, properly used, assessment and categorization can be a kind of empathic shorthand. Such categorization is not pejorative toward clients, but rather, seeks to recognize severe developmental traumata and subsequent ego deficits. In his research on the borderline patient, Knight noted that the ego labors badly and is a feeble and unreliable ally.[1] Clarity about ego strengths and deficits provides guidelines for appropriate treatment planning for the adolescent and the family, plus consideration of environmental interventions via contact with schools, camps, day-care centers, and child-welfare services.

DEFINITION AND ETIOLOGY OF BORDERLINE SYNDROME

The borderline syndrome can best be understood from an ego psychological perspective that embodies a developmental approach. In this view, normal and pathological child and adolescent development are seen on a continuum, with disorders caused by arrests or fixations in normal chronological development. Borderline pathology arises out of a failure of separation-individuation in the course of normal development—just as autism results from an arrest in the normal autistic phase or from neurologic deficit and symbiotic psychosis results from an arrest in the normal symbiotic stage.

Separation-individuation is the third major milestone for the young child, following bonding and attachment, and symbiosis, and it includes the development of object constancy. Separating and individuating describes the maturational step of becoming a separate person with clear self/other boundaries. No longer is there a fantasy of omnipotent control of, merger or union with, or engulfment by, mother. Mother is no longer the all-good or all-bad split object. The normally developing child can love irrespective of frustration and can tolerate ambivalence (that is, simultaneous good and bad feelings) toward the parents. The presence and support of the father (or some additional parental surrogate) is crucial in facilitating separation-individuation. Not only does he provide help and support to mother in the parenting tasks, but he also offers the child security so that the child can surrender mother safely. Moving away from the primary dyad is only possible if there is someone to move toward.

The traditional triadic family structure facilitates the child's entry into a genuine oedipal phase. The parents are permanently introjected by the child on an emotional, as well as pictorial, level. Thus the normal three-year-old can comfortably attend nursery school with a vivid memory of mother's face and ministrations, and the certainty that father also will soon appear. This evocative memory soothes the child during absences from the parents. Borderline children fail to achieve separation-individuation and object constancy and they lack a clear evocative memory. They cannot emotionally recall complete three-dimensional persons and continue to split objects into "all good" and "all bad."

Case Vignette

This lack of separation-individuation, object constancy, and evocative memory, and the use of splitting were exemplified by Karen, a borderline adolescent in a residential treatment institution. She would facilitate and swing, having to love or hate her social worker therapist and the director of her living unit; she could not tolerate ambivalent feelings toward them. Further, when she loved one, she hated the other; she could not love or hate them both simultaneously. This split was graphically illustrated by the bulletin notices she would post, proclaiming "Judy [director] loves me / Betty [therapist] hates me" or vice versa. This phenomenon seemed always to correspond with the psychic state of her borderline mother, whose repeated agitated and suicidal states required numerous hospitalizations. The lack of psychic separation between mother and daughter was striking and, for many years, was unaffected by the physical separation inherent in Karen's residential placement. Karen's lack of object constancy appeared to replicate her mother's lack of consistency and constancy. The symbiotic merger with her symbolic maternal objects was replayed in her wildly fluctuating all-loving or all-hating (split-object) stance toward the therapist and director, and toward herself. This lack of object constancy—the fusion of the good/bad mother—is a hallmark of the borderline state and accounts for the characteristic panic, anxiety, and impulsivity of these patients. The distorted object relations often dictate the optimal plan of long-term treatment for the child, adolescent, or adult borderline patient.

HISTORY OF THE BORDERLINE SYNDROME

In the late 1940s, reports began to appear about a special group of children whose disturbance went beyond neurosis, yet did not meet the criteria of childhood psychosis. Mahler described children who had "a certain kind of benign psychosis" that appeared neurosislike. Weil described "atypical, deviational children with fragmented egos" who had not achieved emancipation from mother; they showed similarities to Mahler's symbiotic cases without obvious psychosis. Others described in similar terms individual cases of perplexing children with "in-between" pathologies. Two major focuses were stressed in describing these children: the nature of their chronic and severe ego disturbances; and the problems in object relations, particularly as manifested in profound separation difficulties.[2]

In the early and mid-1950s, the term *borderline* became widely used for this childhood disturbance. Parallels were drawn between these children and severe borderline states described in the adult literature. This pathology appeared linked to arrests or fixations on a "higher" or more progressed level than that of autism or psychosis. In examining the spectrum of character disorders, Kernberg stressed the term *borderline personality organization* to describe nonchild adolescent patients who demonstrated chronic identity diffusion, primitive defenses, and devaluation concurrent with preserved reality testing.[3]

While disagreement persists even today regarding the developmental stage when the ego defect occurs, since the 1960s there have been marked advances in conceptualizing the criteria, dynamics, and treatment of the borderline patient. There is agreement that the disorder is essentially a preoedipal arrest marked by lack of separation-individuation, object constancy, triadic relationships, and genuine entry into the oedipal phase.

The continuum of this disorder was stressed by Pine, who advised "mapping the borders" of the syndrome and considering the borders "between this domain and neurosis on the one hand and psychosis on the other."[4] The earlier the arrest, the more the adolescent will resemble the psychotic; the later the arrest, the more neurotic he or she will appear. The developmental arrest produces severe defects in ego functioning, for example, persistence of the primitive defenses of the ego and consequent object splitting as a result of a failure to achieve object constancy, and the simultaneous development of a split self-image ("I am all good or all bad").

In the evaluation of the borderline child, it is the whole gestalt, rather than single symptoms, that determines diagnosis. Chronic and conspicuous problems in ego development will tend to indicate the possibility of this disorder, while neurotic children will show a minor range of such developmental deviations. Fundamentally, borderline patients maintain their capacity to test reality and do not evidence the hallucinatory or delusional problems of psychosis.

The application of these conceptions is very difficult with adolescents, given the adolescent phenomena of turmoil states, identity crises, rapid shifts of identity, depressive states, altered and often impaired parent-child relationships, antisocial acting-out behavior, heightened narcissism, and transient or more serious hypochondriacal tendencies or excessive preoccupation with physical appearance. Kernberg reminded us that antisocial behavior in adolescence may be either an expression of normal or neurotic adaptation to an antisocial cultural subgroup, and thus be relatively nonmalignant, or a reflection of severe character pathology and a borderline personality organization masquerading as an adaptation to an antisocial group. For Kernberg, the diagnosis of borderline in the adolescent patient was based on the presence of severe identity diffusion, primitive defenses (for example, denial, projection, splitting), projective identification, and the persistence of reality testing.[5]

For borderline patients, separation-individuation evokes such intense feelings of abandonment that it is experienced as death. To defend against these feelings, borderline adolescents cling to the maternal figure and thus fail to progress through the normal developmental stages of separation-individuation to autonomy. This clinging can be overt or covert—via fight/flight behaviors, substance abuse, delinquent behavior, defiance, and so on. The effect is to retain parental involvement via worry, anger, anxiety, and often-futile attempts to limit, discipline, and control the teenager. Masterson suggested that these adolescents use acting-out behaviors to ward off feeling and facing the abandonment depression they are undergoing.[6]

It is not uncommon for the first breakthrough of severe disturbance to be in adolescence, either early, for example, with the onset of puberty, or considerably later, at stressful times such as those following high school or college graduation, when ever-increasing separate and independent functioning is required. Blos was the first to view adolescence as a second separation-individuation period—involving a replication of the practicing period, the rapprochement for emotional refueling, and the ultimate push for autonomy, separation-individuation, and object- and self-constancy.[7]

The developmental perspective emphasizes that, since nothing appears out of the blue, we must assume earlier vulnerability and unsuccessful negotiation of critical early stages and developmental milestones. A careful, thorough history taking often reveals that the supposedly good earlier adjustment was in fact fragile and/or precocious and that, under the threat of more genuine separation, the earlier unmastered separation fear is overwhelming. Frequently a sexual relationship is used by adolescents to both substitute for, and avoid reunion with and engulfment by, the maternal figure. Having to move away from mother is not the only precipitant. Parental divorce, illness, or unavailability frequently precipitates the adolescent's decline, which might have been avoided prior to this constellation of stresses.

The unavailable father noted by Anderson exacerbates the adolescent's fears and struggles in giving up mother—if there is no one to move toward for nurturance and support.[8] Some adolescents who fear individuation and aloneness merge diffusely with cults and movements, satisfying their intense need for belonging via engulfment. This is an exaggeration of the more normal adolescent's attachment to the peer group, which serves as an appropriate transitional bridge away from the family to the outer world.

DESCRIPTION OF BORDERLINE SYNDROME

Although it is difficult to speak of typical adolescent borderline behavior and symptoms, which vary considerably, some characteristics can be delineated in broad terms.

Borderline adolescents evidence chronic, intense, often diffuse and free-floating, anxiety. Both their defensive system and their sense of reality are inadequate and thus cannot help them bind their anxiety. Often their lack of signal anxiety, which triggers appropriate defense mechanisms to help cope with frightening situations, leads to panic. Dangers from the outside are a constant source of anxiety and, in extreme situations, induce fear of annihilation. These adolescents typically fear separation from parental objects and cling tenaciously to adults who will protect them. They fear disorganization and being overwhelmed by their sometimes uncontrollable impulses.

All borderline clients present symptoms of a hysterical, phobic, or obsessive-compulsive (that is, neurotic) nature; these represent attempted

defenses against more primitive and regressive states. Higher-level borderline adolescents often present a superficial adaptation to the environment
and a pseudoability to maintain some level of object relations. Many
autonomous ego functions are not impaired and intellectual endowment,
cognition, memory, and so on, may be adequate or even superior. However, the neurotic defensive symptomatology is fragile, fleeting, and not
fully structuralized. Thus obsessions can quickly be replaced by multiple
phobias or intense restrictions and inhibitions.

Chronic problems with impulse control, with periods of marked repetitive eruptions of aggression and rage (for example, severe temper tan-
trums), are common among borderline adolescents. These teenagers may
react globally to such potential eruptions by avoiding all social contacts
or by developing intense fantasy involvement that helps to separate them
totally from the frustrating and upsetting environment. Their perception
of reality remains intact, but their investment in it is limited because they
do not abandon the narcissistic pleasure world, as exemplified by the
adolescent drug world. They may evidence major affect constrictions and
a total muting of impulses. However, they do not become psychotic and
do not lose total and prolonged touch with reality.

Severe character pathology, including narcissistic and/or masochistic
elements, is not unusual among these adolescents, who may relieve their
anxiety by self-mutilation. Although one can never predict what will
occur next, one can predict agitation, given these adolescents' severe
responses to change in the environment (for example, family upheaval,
staff change). The masochistic trends are often fueled by harsh superego
precursors. Paranoid aspects are also evident at times. The world is mis-
perceived as a totally threatening and attacking milieu. Oral dependent
features may be prominent. Because of their failure to achieve object constancy, they relate to objects as parts and are unable to evoke the image
of mother when she is not present. Thus borderline adolescents cannot
mourn, and object losses and separations are disastrous. The self-other
components of the borderline client's relationships are often wearing and
draining for those people who deal with them. The real and human characteristics of important people are totally disregarded much of the time,
and these significant adults are instead invested with projected need-
fulfilling characteristics. They must live out prescribed roles for the
adolescent. In this sense the interpersonal relations of borderline adolescents are characterized by an inability to develop empathy.

The phenomenon of merging is often misunderstood and misused with
borderline adolescents. The most primitive form of merging is the fear
that one's bodily characteristics will change to those of another. However,
borderline adolescents' sense of wanting to be *one* relates primarily to the
motive of controlling the independent life of the other, rather than to a
desire for physical merging.

SPECIFIC THERAPEUTIC METHODS

Therapy for borderline patients can be supportive, behavioral, or inter-pretive, all in the context of individual, group, and/or family approaches. Assessment is necessary to determine "(1) the patient's capacity to make a therapeutic relationship; (2) the level of anxiety; (3) the intensity of pain inflicted on self and others; (4) the presence of regressive symptomatology; (5) the conscious motivation for treatment. The failure to make an ade-quate assessment of which type of therapy and frequency can convert a seriously disturbed adolescent into one who is intractably ill."[9]

Schwartzberg noted that most authors emphasize the need for inten-sive, psychoanalytically oriented individual psychotherapy for borderline patients, in contrast to supportive therapy. Kernberg believed such therapy is appropriate for borderline adolescents, but should be "modified by the establishment of parameters of technique required by acting out, or the severity of certain symptoms . . . and the need for external structuring dur-ing minor or major parts of the treatment."[10]

Masterson stressed the need to work through the abandonment depres-sion and split-object relations of borderline adolescents via the therapeutic alliance and transference.[11] He recommended various combinations of individual and family therapy depending on the adolescent's family situa-tion and the severity of the symptomatology. Group therapy is also a fre-quent intervention used in tandem with individual and family therapy, on both an inpatient and an outpatient basis. In general, when an ado-lescent presents severe impulse problems, acting out, and drug abuse, the family cannot provide sufficient support and structure, and hospitaliza-tion or institutional placement becomes necessary.

Deficits in self-esteem, self-reliance, autonomy, and object constancy make many borderline adolescents too fragile for group or family inter-ventions. Such clients frequently cannot share the therapy hour and/or the therapist's attention. Often the parents' personalities act as the primary pathogenic agents; according to Anna Freud, the parents actually "disregard and thereby frustrate important developmental needs of the child." Kohut commented that many such afflicted adolescents present with empty depression and depletion anxiety, and their disturbances in adolescence are often sexualized as they struggle with faulty self-esteem and a missing sense of direction. Because of these characteristics, such teenagers perceive interpersonal communications in group or family sessions as criticisms and assaults. The fragility, narcissistic vulnerabil-ity, and paucity of parental empathy suggest the need for one-to-one interventions that embody empathy rather than confrontation.[12]

Individual treatment is overwhelmingly the major and optimal treat-ment plan for the borderline adolescent. The intractable nature of this severe disorder makes treatment lengthy and draining; severe negative therapeutic reactions to these resistant patients are not uncommon.

Clinical work with borderline adolescents generally requires taxing and extensive work with their families. The goal of establishing empathic relationships within the family is now more generally recognized, as we have moved beyond seeing the disturbed adolescent as the helpless victim of bad parents. We now give greater significance to reality experience, and have increased understanding of parents' unconscious reexperience of their own symbiotic parent/child ties, and thus their engulfing and often damaging bonds to their children. Clinicians in inpatient and outpatient settings must not dismiss parents as irrelevant or irritating obstacles in the treatment of their adolescent patients.[13] The crucial issue in engaging the teenager *and* the parents is the avoidance of a misalliance predicated on old stereotypes, the staff's rescue fantasies, or negative responses to parents, which generally mirror the distorted intrafamilial relationships.

In the past, parents of disturbed youths were often patronized, ignored, or treated with blandness and/or a prejudicial perspective. More keenly recognized currently is the adolescent's loyalty conflict and absolute need to see the parents treated with respect and compassion. Disrespect and conflict are accepted *within* the family system, but are feared and abhorred when coming from the outside. The borderline adolescent, psychically unseparated from his or her parents, most commonly mirrors the parents and needs to experience some adult coalition, such as that between the professionals and the parents, to feel that permission has been granted to move out of the family system and to thereby make new attachments. This movement occurs in the context of the therapeutic alliance, which results from the adolescent's conscious or unconscious wish to accept therapeutic aid in overcoming internal and external resistance.

The patient system—namely, the adolescent, siblings, and parents—presents varying degrees of cognitive, rational approval of the therapist and the therapeutic milieu. Patient and family may evidence fantasies and expectations, as well as distortions and false pretenses, that may enhance or impede the development of a treatment alliance. The therapist may be experienced as a new, real object who is liked and identified with insofar as the patient's ego is intact enough to perceive being helped and understood. The beginning alliance evolves out of trust and satisfaction in the shared work. When the self/other distinction is lacking—more commonly observed in a symbiotic merger, or pseudoalliance—there is a lack of true therapeutic splitting into the self observing and the self experiencing the treatment. Therapists must consistently and repetitively interject their own secondary process and rational behavior into the treatment situation. This process requires patience and respect for the adolescent and the parents—often difficult to sustain in the face of hostility, bombardments of complaints, and distrust. Rarely can one therapist alone handle this barrage from the total patient system.

The importance of a human, rather than institutionalized, contact between the professionals and parents of patients cannot be overemphasized.
Professionals working with borderline patients and their families must be
prepared to be available almost on demand, offering consistency, reliability, concern, and discernible deep involvement in the welfare of the
family. Flexibility and a gradual nonconfrontational approach are recommended. The alliance with the parents of adolescent patients is critical;
without it, or with a negative alliance, major treatment obstacles will
arise.

A clinician's countertransference and counterreactions are inevitable
and can prove to be important assessment tools, giving information on the
degree of primitive regression in the teenager, and the shifts and changes
in tone and emotional attitude in the professional relationship. Such information can be profitably used by the therapist who is aware of the
dangers from within. Kernberg specified (1) the reappearance of anxiety
connected with early impulses, especially those of an aggressive nature,
which now are directed toward the patient; (2) a possible loss of ego boundaries in interactions with specific adolescents; (3) the strong temptation
to try to control the teenager in consonance with an identification with
an object from the therapist's own past; (4) masochistic submission to the
adolescent's aggression; (5) disproportionate doubts about one's own professional capabilities; (6) nihilistic attitudes about the necessary work with
persons and systems in behalf of the adolescent patient. Kernberg noted
that the clinician's capacity to experience ongoing concern for the teenager
helps to overcome and neutralize the aggressive countertransference
responses. Blank stated that the key to management of the countertransference is restraint.[14]

Kernberg noted the therapist's "holding," "mothering," and "emotionally corrective" function in work with borderline patients. The provision of technical neutrality and empathic understanding requires the
patient and clinician to accept their own aggression and trust that this
aggression will not destroy the therapist or the attachment to the therapist;
this achievement grows out of the clinician's trust in the ultimate potential
of the adolescent. The eventually trusted therapist's cognitive formulations strengthen and broaden the patient's self-modulation and object relations. Warmth and availability on the part of the therapist are insufficient by themselves; intellectual clarity, consistent concern for the adolescent, and limits (when needed) are all essential elements in the inter-
pretive psychotherapy of borderline teenagers.

In the treatment of hospitalized borderline adolescents, the family
perspective has become increasingly popular, with a multitude of family-
oriented treatment models. Parents may be seen individually, in marital
therapy, in family therapy, in extended kinship network therapy, and/or
in multiple family group treatment. Sometimes the entire family resides

in the hospital for a period of time. Treatment goals vary and may include the promotion of insight, education and guidance, the discovery of family secrets, and the recognition of faulty familial communication patterns in an attempt to modify pathological behavior. Various treatment modalities may be used concurrently, usually involving more than one therapist. Given the enmeshed family patterns, often work with the immediate family is insufficient and other systems work (for example, with extended family members and with community and social service systems) must be done.

SUMMARY

The clinical ego psychology perspective offered here integrates work with the intrapsychic system, the family, and the environmental systems servicing adolescents. As stated by Fraiberg, psychoanalytic theory is an indispensable component of social work theory and practice.[15] Restoration of functioning requires careful assessment of internal and external motives, relationships, and object representations. Adaptation and maturation require ego regulation of itself by both relationship to the environment and regulation of the internal relationships between the mental faculties. Life transitions, which challenge even normal adaptive capacities, are especially traumatic for borderline adolescents. Professional sensitivity and attention to the demands of age-appropriate transitional tasks can help borderline adolescents to cope with their anxiety and increased vulnerability, to deal with the tasks at hand, and, eventually, to move forward developmentally.

NOTES AND REFERENCES

1. Robert P. Knight, "Management and Psychotherapy of the Borderline Schizophrenic Patient," in Knight and C. P. Friedman, eds. *Psychoanalytic Psychiatry and Psychology* (2d ed.; New York: International Universities Press, 1954), pp. 110–112.

2. Margaret Mahler, "Clinical Studies in the Benign and Malignant Cases of Childhood Psychosis," *American Journal of Orthopsychiatry*, 19 (1948), pp. 295–305; Annemarie P. Weil, "Certain Severe Disturbances of Ego Development in Childhood," *The Psychoanalytic Study of the Child*, 8 (1953), pp. 271–287; B. Rank, "Aggression," *The Psychoanalytic Study of the Child*, 3–4 (1949), pp. 43–48; M. Harley, "Analysis of a Severely Disturbed 3½-Year-Old Boy," *The Psychoanalytic Study of the Child*, 6 (1951), pp. 206–234; A. Maenchen, "Note on Early Ego Disturbances," *The Psychoanalytic Study of the Child*, 8 (1953), pp. 262–270; G. Rochlin, "Loss and Restitution," *The Psychoanalytic Study of the Child*, 8 (1953), pp. 288–309; and A. Alpert, "Reversibility of Pathological Fixations Associated with Maternal Deprivation in Infancy," *The Psychoanalytic Study of the Child*, 14 (1959), pp. 169–185.

3. Otto Kernberg, "Structural Derivatives of Object Relations," *International Journal of Psycho-Analysis,* 47 (1966), pp. 236–253; Kernberg, "Borderline Personality Organization," *Journal of the American Psychoanalytic Association,* 15 (1967), pp. 641–685; Kernberg, "Factors in the Psychoanalytic Treatment of Narcissistic Personalities," *Journal of the American Psychoanalytic Association,* 18 (1970), pp. 51–85; and Kernberg, *Borderline Conditions and Pathological Narcissism* (New York: Jason Aronson, 1975).

4. F. Pine, "On the Context of 'Borderline' in Children: A Clinical Essay," *The Psychoanalytic Study of the Child,* 29 (1974), p. 366.

5. Otto Kernberg, "The Diagnosis of Borderline Conditions in Adolescence," in Sherman C. Feinstein and Peter L. Giovacchini, eds., *Adolescent Psychiatry: Developmental and Clinical Studies,* Vol. 6 (Chicago: University of Chicago Press, 1979), pp. 298–319.

6. J. F. Masterson, *Treatment of the Borderline Adolescent: A Developmental Approach* (New York: John Wiley & Sons, 1972); and Masterson, "The Acting-Out Adolescent: A Point of View," *American Journal of Psychotherapy,* 28 (July 1974), pp. 343–351.

7. Peter Blos, "Character Formation in Adolescence," *The Psychoanalytic Study of the Child,* 23 (1968), pp. 245–263.

8. Robert Anderson, "Thoughts on Fathering; Its Relationship to the Borderline Condition in Adolescence and to Transitional Phenomena," in Feinstein and Giovacchini, eds., *Adolescent Psychiatry,* Vol. 6, pp. 377–395.

9. D. Miller, "Treatment of the Seriously Disturbed Adolescent," in Sherman C. Feinstein and Peter Giovacchini, eds., *Adolescent Psychiatry: Developmental and Clinical Studies,* Vol. 8 (Chicago: University of Chicago Press, 1980), p. 479.

10. A. Z. Schwartzberg, "Overview of the Borderline Syndrome in Adolescence," in Feinstein and Giovacchini, eds., *Adolescent Psychiatry,* Vol. 6, pp. 286–297; and Kernberg, "Diagnosis of Borderline Conditions," p. 318.

11. Masterson, *Treatment of the Borderline Adolescent.*

12. Anna Freud, "Indications and Contraindications for Child Analysis," in *The Writings of Anna Freud,* Vol. 7, *Problems of Psychoanalytic Training, Diagnosis, and the Technique of Therapy* (New York: International Universities Press, 1968/1971), pp. 110–123; and Heinz Kohut, *The Restoration of the Self* (New York: International Universities Press, 1977).

13. Anthony O. McQuinn, "Work with Disturbed Parents," in Eugene Arnold, ed., *Helping Parents Help Their Children* (New York: Brunner/Mazel, 1978).

14. Kernberg, *Borderline Conditions;* and Rubin Blanck, "Countertransference in Treatment of the Borderline Patient," *Clinical Social Work,* 1, No. 2 (1973), pp. 110–117.

15. Selma Fraiberg, "Psychoanalysis and Social Work: A Re-examination of the Issues," *Smith College Studies in Social Work,* 48 (March 1978), pp. 87–106.

A Model for Ethical Decision Making in Clinical Practice

M. Vincentia Joseph

There is an increasing concern about the complexity of ethical dilemmas facing social work clinicians in their various fields of practice. Social workers, as well as other professionals, are becoming more aware of the difficulties and ambiguities in resolving ethical conflicts that involve compelling and competing values and of the limitations of professional codes of ethics in dealing with these. Despite this growing sensitivity to ethical issues, little attention has been given to the systematic reflection of values and analysis of ethics in social work and to the preparation of the practitioner for dealing with ethical problems.

For the practitioner, skills for coping with conflict have consisted primarily of problem-solving models based on role-coping and systems-change theories. Little attention has been given to identifying conflicts in values and ethics or to providing strategies that utilize values-inclusive models for ethical decision making.[1] The author's research supports the need for clinicians to develop skills in this area. The findings indicate that social workers who have no systematic exposure to ethical content approach ethical conflicts in practice terms and utilize practice problem-solving models, whereas those with training in ethical methodology are able to identify and explicate value and ethical dilemmas and utilize ethical principles and models in dealing with these issues.[2] This article considers the importance of tools for ethical analysis as an essential component of the repertoire of coping skills for the clinical social worker and presents a model for ethical decision making.

The model provides an analytical framework for examining value-conflict situations and ethical dilemmas. It suggests a structure and a systematic process for inquiry into ethical issues that emerge in clinical practice and its organizational contexts. This model has been found useful for ethical reflection in a variety of practice situations—in family agencies, and in larger institutional settings—and its effectiveness has been tested through evaluative research in courses in professional social work ethics. Although the model provides a framework for a process for ethical decision making, its limitations should be recognized. A core knowledge of basic ethical concepts and theory is important for a rigorous analysis of ethical options.[3]

For clarity and for our purposes here, *ethics* needs defining. Professional ethics, a branch of philosophy, is concerned with the rightness or wrongness of behaviors of the professional. More generally, it focuses on the morality (the goodness or badness) of individual conduct. Although less attention has been given to social ethics in philosophy, interest is developing. This area is of special interest to social work, as it is directed to the institutional arrangements of society and the social policies that are both explicit and implicit in these. Organizational and collective ethics are areas of growing interest, particularly in medicine.[4] The former is concerned with the morality of organizations and asks such questions as: Is the organization a moral agent? The latter, collective ethics, which deals with the morality of groups and collectivities, is concerned with the distribution of responsibility, for example, team responsibility. Both organizational and collective ethics are especially relevant to contemporary social work.

BACKGROUND

A number of reasons have been suggested for the current broad interest in ethics. Some commentators see this trend as symptomatic of a general malaise in society and a concern about a general drift away from ethical behaviors. Others cite Watergate and the apparent amorality of some political and organizational behaviors as the beginning of serious concerns with value issues. Many emphasize the rapid technological advances, for instance in medicine, that have given rise to new and complex ethical dilemmas as the basic reason for a renewed interest in professional ethics. Many of these dilemmas contain conflicting values that confront us with competing claims and contravening obligations. An example of such a conflict would be the sanctity of life versus the quality of life. Different models of decision making are required to deal with such issues, models that incorporate values and ethical analyses.

Despite the historic and traditional emphasis on values in the profession, little attention has been given to preparation for dealing with value and ethical conflicts. Although there has been a dramatic rise in ethics courses in colleges and universities, with the most striking increase in professional schools, it is estimated that less than 10 percent of schools of social work offer courses, either elective or required, in professional ethics. This is particularly curious since, in the not too distant past, there was concern that values were often substituted for the scientific base of the profession.[5] It is important to note, however, that there is an expanding and broad-based sensitivity to ethical concerns within the profession and a beginning recognition of the need for ethical concepts and models. The revised Code of Ethics, adopted by the National Association of Social Workers (NASW) in 1979, and the process of its formulation evidence this. Workshops on ethics are appearing—at the conferences of the Council on Social Work Education (CSWE) and NASW—and a scholarly literature is emerging.

The developing literature on social work ethics, although minimal at this time, reflects a growing interest in applying ethical discipline and analysis to the various ethical dilemmas that are arising in practice situations. A handful of articles are calling for systematic ethical reflection and two books on social work ethics that utilize ethical methodologies have appeared. Some of these works have identified the limitations of NASW's Code of Ethics in resolving the more complex ethical conflicts and the need for ethical systems to deal with these. Of necessity, codes are framed in general terms. Principles often contradict one another when applied to concrete situations and create conflicting obligations not resolvable in the code alone. This is pointed out very clearly by Abramson in her discussion on hospital discharge planning. The obligation to the organization may conflict with the obligation to the patient. Hence the need for ethical reflection to deal with more complicated issues.[6]

Although a serious literature is developing, journal articles hardly reflect the range of concerns emerging in practice. The articles available focus broadly on areas such as values, confidentiality, client records, malpractice, and the Code of Ethics. Rarely, and only recently, are they treated with a systematic method of analysis. These issues contrast sharply with those arising in the field, which center around deinstitutionalization, deprogramming, biomedical issues of life and the quality of life, suicide, sexual practices with clients, practice models (such as those emerging in family therapy), the rights of the retarded, the rights of adolescents, and societal issues, including the distribution of scarce resources, organizational and team issues, issues related to colleagues, abortion, private practice, burnout, religion in clinical practice, supervision, research, and conflicts emerging with the rise of profit-making organizations in the field of social service, to name only a few. Despite a substantial literature on the management of organizational conflicts, rarely are underlying value and ethical conflicts identified and seldom are ethical tools utilized to deal with these. Thus, the range of ethical concerns and their seriousness highlight, in a striking fashion, the fundamental nature of ethical skills and their relevance to the profession.

CONTEMPORARY ETHICAL THEORIES

Traditionally, ethical theory has been organized around sets of concepts—value, obligation, and moral character traits. These normative components of moral judgment have developed into three major areas of study.

1. Axiology, the study of values, is concerned with what things or states of affairs are important or more important than others.

2. Moral judgments of obligation, the study of obligations, focuses on what ought to be done, through an appeal to rules, norms, principles, and outcomes. Broadly, these are of two types—teleological and deontological. Teleological judgments of obligation derive their rightness or wrongness from the outcomes or consequences of some action. Utilitarianism, which emphasizes the good for the greatest number —a test of consequences—is a teleological approach. Deontological judgments of obligation appeal to principles or rules and hold that actions derive their moral rightness or wrongness from some quality within the act or principle itself (it is intrinsically good or evil).
3. Moral agent theory, the study of virtue or character, is concerned with moral judgments that appeal to moral ideals or models—the kind of person or society it is most appropriate to be or to become.

Considerable work is being done in the field of ethics to develop comprehensive ethical theories to accommodate the complexities that arise with increasing frequency today. Frankena's mixed deontological approach, based on principles of utility and justice, and Becker's methodology, which coordinates the three major theories of morality (value, obligation, and agent morality), are efforts in this direction.[7] They have much to contribute to social work ethics.

There have been, however, few attempts to apply such ethical theories and methodologies to social work practice situations. Recently, Abramson presented a framework for the evaluation of ethical dilemmas in medical settings. The work of Reamer is impressive. He provided a scholarly approach, based on Gewirth's principle of generic consistency, which has considerable applicability to a range of both micro and macro social work situations. Such attempts are significant and suggest the need for further efforts to develop comprehensive approaches appropriate for use in social work situations.[8]

A MODEL FOR ETHICAL DECISION MAKING

The model presented here provides a comprehensive approach that uses ethical methods in analyzing the obligation of the social worker as well as in identifying and prioritizing the values implicit in the dilemma. It utilizes the principle of proportionality, which seeks to prioritize competing goods in conflict situations. This approach has contributed significantly to biomedical problems and has much to offer social work. Specifically, the model has a three-pronged focus. The first is to make explicit our personal ethical decision-making process. As Frankena indicated, people have their own system of working ethics through which they reach ethical decisions.[9] Procedures are often implicit, derived from cultural experiences and previous formal learnings. This is not dissimilar to skills in helping, which are brought to professional social work education from previous experiences, some implicit and others explicit, and are translated into the new learning experience. The second part of the focus is closely related, to explicate not only the underlying dilemma but also our value biases in relation to the situation, in other words, to objectify the situation. And third, the model is intended to provide a guide for ethical decision making.

A basic assumption underlying the model is that value and ethical biases often impede practice competence and coping effectiveness. An awareness of one's own personal value orientation and one's personal ethical system is an important component of self-awareness—one that can contribute significantly to competent practice. This is an aspect of self-awareness that is often overlooked. An important function of the model, therefore, is to help the worker to consider personal values and ethical orientations in relation to the client system, the profession, the agency or service organization, and society. This model is general in the sense that it is useful in dealing with direct practice dilemmas and social policy issues with inherent ethical conflicts.

The ethical model of decision making is a values-inclusive process, one that differs from a generic problem-solving model in that it is geared to surface value and ethical conflicts and to utilize ethical principles in its decision making process. Similar to other problem-solving approaches, it employs rational processes of decision making to reach solutions. Thus, logical processes are utilized in justifying positions—there is a logical arrangement and formulation of the reasons for assuming a particular position. It differs, however, in that values, ethical concepts, and ethical principles are used in evaluating actions and alternate outcomes and in assuming a position in a conflictual situation. This approach, from the outset, requires a clear understanding of the practice situation as well as a precise identification of the central ethical dilemma and related ethical issues that emerge from the situation. The central issue may be related to any one of the client systems or organizational contexts in which social workers carry out their professional responsibilities. The ethical dilemma or problem focus, then, becomes the subject matter or unit of attention of professional social work ethics. It includes an explicit statement of the ethical dilemma and a concise description of the practice situation, the context of the ethical issue. Figure 1 (p. 212) should be helpful in understanding the components of the model and the procedure for analysis.

Essentially, the dilemma is expressed in terms of one good versus a competing good. A case example may be helpful in clarifying this first and important step as well as the other phases of the process. In a clinical situation in which a social worker is counseling a 16-year-old girl on a regular basis around interpersonal relationship problems, the adolescent

Joseph

Figure 1
Ethical Model of Decision Making

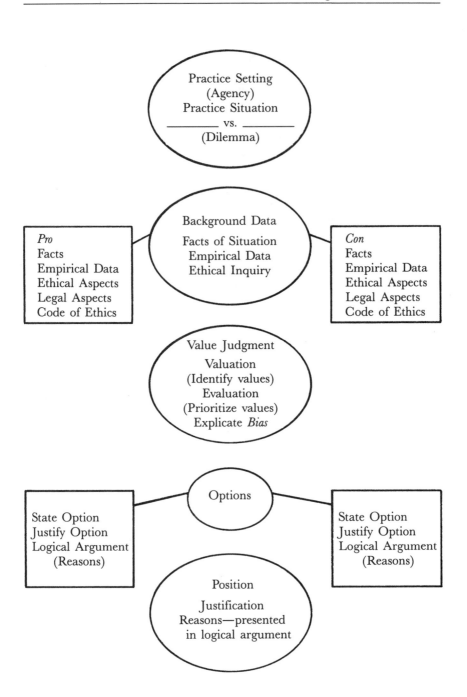

reveals that she has been shoplifting and has stolen a considerable amount of clothing. The initial contract assured confidentiality of all information barring suicidal or homicidal threats. The parents have been seen in treatment regularly by another worker in the agency. In giving this information to the worker, the girl insists that it be kept in strictest confidence. The practitioner faces a dilemma. Does she have a responsibility to maintain confidentiality or does she have an obligation to reveal this information to the parents? What is her obligation to society? Does she have a responsibility to share this information with her colleague?

The NASW Code of Ethics states that the worker should not share confidences revealed by clients without their consent except for "compelling professional reasons." Are the reasons in this case compelling? Furthermore, the worker is obliged to inform clients fully about the limits of confidentiality. Is the promise implicit in the early contract morally binding in this situation? Does Section I of the Code—"The social worker should not participate in, condone, or be associated with dishonesty, fraud, deceit, or misrepresentation"—apply here?[10]

The central ethical dilemma, framed concisely, may be stated as the right of the adolescent to confidentiality versus the right of the family to the information. Closely related is the right of the adolescent versus the right of society. When the dilemma is placed in a context of this right versus that right (pro-con), the varying points of view on the issue become clearer and their arguments are more accessible to scrutiny. Structuring the ethical conflict in this way sharpens the focus of the inquiry.

Background information on the varying positions on the issue is then collected and examined. To assure objectivity, it is essential to gather information about both sides of the issue. This includes the facts of the practice situation, empirical knowledge bearing on the issue (practice knowledge, research), and the ethical criteria or principles utilized in justifying the varying positions represented in the literature. For instance, a utilitarian position, in which the good for the greatest number (the welfare of the community) is used as the main standard to evaluate an action, may be taken to justify the right of the family to this information. A number of ethicists emphasize the importance of factual knowledge and conceptual clarity for the solution of ethical problems. These data, the circumstances of the situation, and relevant theoretical and empirical knowledge have a bearing on the decision-making process.[11] For example, what are the dynamics of shoplifting and how are they expressed in this situation? What is the relationship between this girl and her family? How has she responded to treatment? What is her relationship with the practitioner? Such information often influences the option selected for action.

Values intrinsic to the situation are then identified and prioritized. Becker referred to this as a process of valuation, extracting the values that underlie the dilemma, and evaluation, sorting out these values in rank order or priority listing.[12]

Professional values and ethical standards contained in NASW's Code of Ethics are explicated and personal biases considered. It is of utmost importance for practitioners to become sensitized to any personal biases or prejudices they might have regarding a particular situation. Awareness of one's own personal stance helps to objectify the issue. It dilutes the possibility of decisions generated exclusively from emotional reactions to issues and helps to assure a dialectical process. This phase is especially difficult when one has had personal involvement in the area under consideration. For example, in dealing with ethical issues around death and dying, one's personal experiences with a family member or a client situation may seriously influence the capacity to objectively consider both the pro and con of the issue under study. In such instances, the discipline of the process is useful to the worker in focusing on the issue and managing the affect. Questions such as the following are helpful: Are you aware of any personal bias or preference on this issue? Are you aware of the reasons for this bias?

Finally, alternatives for action are formulated and the reasons (values and principles) justifying each option available for action are logically and sequentially considered. For example, after review of the data, reflection on the values, and analyzing the action alternatives and ethical dilemma (one good versus another good) the dilemma described above might be resolved by concluding that the parents, on the basis of their authority, have a right to the information about their daughter's shoplifting. Justification for this position might be based on the claim that the well-being of the adolescent takes precedence over her right to confidentiality and it may be grounded in the worth of the person. It may also be argued that confidentiality is limited by virtue of age and that the prior right of the long-term well-being of the girl as well as the well-being of society are salient considerations. On the other hand, one might argue in favor of the client's right to confidentiality on the basis of the fiduciary relationship and the contract, a further moral force. Another position might hold, however, that the promise on which the contract was based was superseded by the force of one's professional responsibility to uphold the law. The well-being of society may be argued from a theory of justice that supports the freedom of the person as long as it does not interfere with the well-being of others.

In choosing an ethical position, one must weigh competing claims and the proportional good in these circumstances. This is largely a teleological judgment (based on a proportionate reason, defined by foreseeable consequences for taking action), but one that incorporates deontological considerations (competing obligations) and considers the contextual factors involved. Negative consequences are not directly intended, but are permitted.

It is essential at this phase of the process to justify one's ethical position. This requires that the reasons or arguments that support the position that is taken be laid out in a clear and logical sequence and represent the specific values and set of criteria that guide the ethical judgment and action decision. In the case discussed here, one might assume a position that attempts to maximize the greatest proportionate good—a dominantly teleological approach. If the young woman continues to refuse to discuss the matter with her parents, the practitioner might take the position of maintaining confidentiality on the basis of the contract and the greatest good over evil. She might argue that a breach in confidentiality could interfere with the relationship with the girl, destroy her trust, bring greater harm to her and possibly society. But, on the other hand, through working within the framework of the relationship and a renegotiated contract, greater good could be accomplished. Since empirical data support the therapeutic value of restitution in certain circumstances, the worker might require that the client set up a plan of restitution that would satisfy the requirements of justice and support the client's well-being, of which development of responsibility is a part.[13]

It seems important, at this point, to comment on the interrelationship of practice issues, such as practice knowledge and practice skill, with ethical concerns. One might posit that a skilled practitioner would have contracted more precisely on the boundaries of confidentiality and possibly could have prevented the ethical dilemma that developed later in the treatment process. Perhaps practice skill in handling the issue with the young client would have resulted in her discussing the matter with her parents and planning to deal with the problem responsibly. Contrast this to a less-skilled worker who, on the basis of the parents' authority and/or discomfort with the situation, gives this information to the parents immediately and without reflection with the client. Such situations point up the importance of the interaction of skilled practice and ethical problem solving.

IMPLICATIONS FOR PRACTICE

Implications of the use of ethical systems to cope with ethical dilemmas that arise in practice become evident with their use. Clearly, the quality of practice can be enhanced as competencies in this area are developed. Although such cases as the one described earlier may rarely be reported, as Wilson stated in her work on confidentiality, greater emphasis is being placed on parental authority among family theorists and practitioners and less emphasis on confidentiality within the family system.[14]

In terms of practice models, such issues have an ethical content and need careful consideration.

In the case described here, we may consider the ethical concerns as a significant treatment component. Through engaging the client in clarifying and dealing with the ethical issue, the client may grow in responsibility and manage more effectively some of the issues that led to the conflict. Within a life model and ecological systems approach, a renegotiated contract and work with the ethical dilemma can lead to a greater awareness of the span of the client's responsibility (to self, family, society) as well as enhanced skill in coping and social competency. The modeling of the worker, in terms of concern about the issue, can in itself be therapeutic.

In other situations in which ethical conflicts emerge, such as organizational policies that limit clients' rights or the service quality, ethical analysis may lead to improved service provision and organizational growth. Thus, ethical decision making is related not only to ethical behaviors but also to the enhancement of clinical practice and client service. Also important, ethical skills and competencies can contribute significantly to team decision making. They are useful in helping the practitioner to bring the perspective and value orientation of the profession to many of the complex ethical dilemmas faced in medical settings, mental health facilities, and other institutional settings. At times, particularly with ethical issues related to organizational policies or those involving team decision making, surfacing and clarifying value-ethical conflict and sensitizing all parties involved to the nature of the underlying conflict is sufficient to confront the issue openly and initiate discussion. This important first step often leads to a dialogue and a collaborative decision-making process that deals directly with the ethical concern.

CONCLUSION

Despite a growing sensitivity to ethical concerns, few attempts have been made to utilize ethical reflection in social work practice situations. This article has focused on the importance of applying ethical methodologies to the growing complexities of ethical conflicts arising in clinical practice. An ethical model of decision making has been presented that provides a framework and a process to analyze ethical obligations and to evaluate the values implicit in the ethical dilemma. Such models are suggested as essential components of the problem-solving and role-coping repertoire of the practitioner. Models for ethical analysis, such as the one presented here, need to be developed if we are to deal with pressing ethical issues, both current and emergent, that confront us and if we are to bring our knowledge, perspectives, and resources to bear on them.

NOTES AND REFERENCES

1. Frederic G. Reamer, "Ethical Content in Social Work," *Social Casework*, 16 (November 1980), p. 533.

2. M. Vincentia Joseph and Ann P. Conrad, "Teaching Social Work Ethics for Contemporary Practice: An Effectiveness Evaluation," *Journal of Education for Social Work*, 19 (Fall 1983), pp. 59–68.

3. Research in courses in social work ethics revealed a highly significant difference between students who used the model and those who did not in the effective use of ethical tools and ethical analysis. See Ibid.; see also, William K. Frankena, *Ethics* (2d ed.; Englewood Cliffs, N.J.: Prentice Hall, 1973); Lawrence C. Becker, *On Justifying Moral Judgments* (New York: Humanities Press, 1973); and Andrew C. Varga, *On Being Human* (New York: Paulist Press, 1978).

4. Edmund D. Pellegrino and David C. A. Thomasma, *A Philosophical Basis of Medical Practice: Toward a Philosophy and Ethic of the Healing Professions* (New York: Oxford University Press, 1981).

5. Frederic G. Reamer and Marcia Abramson, *The Teaching of Social Work Ethics* (Hastings-on-Hudson, N.Y.: Institute of Society, Ethics and the Life Sciences, The Hastings Center, 1982); William E. Gordon, "Knowledge and Value: Their Distinction and Relationship in Clarifying Social Work Practice," *Social Work*, 10 (July 1965), pp. 32–39; and Max Siporin, "Moral Philosophy in Social Work Today," *Social Service Review*, 56 (December 1982), pp. 516–538.

6. See Frank Loewenberg and Ralph Dolgoff, *Ethical Decisions for Social Work Practice* (Itasca, Ill.: F. E. Peacock Publishers, 1982); Frederic G. Reamer, *Ethical Dilemmas in Social Service* (New York: Columbia University Press, 1982), particularly the chapter on "Ethical Content in Social Work," p. 533; Marcia Abramson, "Ethical Dilemmas for Social Workers in Discharge Planning," *Social Work in Health Care*, 6 (Summer 1981), pp. 33–42; and M. Vincentia Joseph, "The Ethics of Organizations: Shifting Values and Ethical Dilemmas," *Administration in Social Work*, 7 (Fall–Winter 1983), pp. 47–57.

7. Frankena, *Ethics;* and Becker, *On Justifying Moral Judgments.*

8. See Abramson, "Ethical Dilemmas for Social Workers in Discharge Planning"; and Reamer, *Ethical Dilemmas in Social Service*, pp. 70–80, citing Alan Gewirth, *Reason and Morality* (Chicago: University of Chicago Press, 1978).

9. See Richard A. McCormick, "Ambiguity in Moral Choice," The 1973 Pere Marquette Theology Lecture; and Frankena, *Ethics.*

10. See *Code of Ethics of the National Association of Social Workers* (Silver Spring, Md.: NASW, 1980), Section II, H. 1, and Section I, A. 2.

11. Frankena, *Ethics*, p. 13.

12. Becker, *On Justifying Moral Judgments*, p. 48.

13. Joe Hudson and Burt Galaway, "Undoing the Wrong," *Social Work*, 19 (May 1974), pp. 313–318.

14. Suanna J. Wilson, *Confidentiality in Social Work: Issues and Principles* (New York: Free Press, 1978), p. 123.

How Well Are You Doing?
Evaluation Strategies for Practice

Barbara J. Morrison, Helen Rehr,
and Gary Rosenberg

C linicians are not independent. They are governed by a variety of forces: their professional organizations; insurance and other payment sources; federal and state regulatory bodies; their agencies, where applicable; and, ultimately, their clients. Accountability for the quality and efficacy of service of practitioners is increasingly demanded from each of these arenas. As professionals, practitioners can respond to these demands through a range of service evaluation strategies.

Although the insurance carriers call for a "reasonable, necessary and standard" clinical practice as the factor against which they make reimbursement decisions, others seek more objective and "scientific evidence" of outcomes.[1] These others, such as governmental policymakers, are looking for what they refer to as "real help for people" before underwriting expanded coverage for mental health services.

It has not been easy to confirm the outcomes of psychotherapy and counseling activities. First, the range of social and health problems that cross the thresholds of clinicians is so wide. The problems of today, and certainly tomorrow, are lodged in social diseases deriving from lifestyles that include substance abuse; in social disorders such as person abuse; in social and psychological problems in families; in the stress and anxiety evidenced in those who are the "stabilized sick" or the "worried well"; in the ongoing problems of the chronically ill; and in those individual and family concerns evidenced in the developmentally disabled.[2]

Second, there is no universally accepted treatment for these ailments and no universally accepted terminology for the many kinds of treatment modalities aimed at dealing with these social problems.[3] Americans seeking help cross the threshold of clinicians in a variety of settings, including private practices. When help is offered, it is offered in a face-to-face interchange between a practitioner and one or more clients. The types of therapies currently in vogue include those utilizing verbal, dramatic, or behavioral treatments; biochemical or physical manipulation of the body; and biological interventions through the use of psychotropic drugs and other methods. According to London and Klerman, there are 250 or more forms of psychotherapeutic interventions within these broader categories.[4]

The critical question about any of these interventions relates to their effectiveness in achieving desired clinical outcomes with specific reference to the types of clients served, the types of problems clients present, and the costs of implementation. Studies concerned with this question have been done. For example, Parloff referred to the work of Smith, Glass, and Miller, which analyzed 475 evaluative studies published in the psychotherapy literature and which found the results of treatment to be generally positive. These studies, which represented the collective experiences of 25,000 clients receiving 78 different forms of psychotherapy, reported that the average person who received therapy was better off (according to a variety of outcome measures) at the end of treatment than were 85 percent of the people who did not receive such treatment.[5] These studies, which were for the most part random controlled clinical trials, support the efficacy of the treatments studied.

Studies of social work efficacy, on the other hand, have produced a mixed and less positive picture of clinical outcomes. Thus it becomes important to ask if we are attempting to ascribe clinical outcomes to the social services for those social and health problems lodged in etiological dimensions still unknown, that is for social, physiological, environmental, and psychological dimensions, as well as dimensions with an impact on the workplace, that overwhelm not only the clientele, but also policymakers, planners, and practitioners? The controversies produced by Fischer's studies of social work effectiveness are widely known.[6] What accounts for these differences? Some of them may be explained by the state of the art within the social work profession as it relates to our ability to ask the appropriate evaluative questions and adequately apply available methodologies to answer them.

The problems inherent in social work effectiveness studies appear to be lodged in our global expectations and in the resulting global nature of both the questions we pose and the answers we seek. It has been suggested that movement toward specificity would be a truer stance of the social work services. To be more specific requires us to pose questions about practice and effectiveness by attending to the characteristics of the problems for which we are offering help, with the client's concurrence, and to the outcomes we expect from treatment. These characteristics would include the following:

1. accurate definition of the problem,
2. analysis of the factors creating and maintaining the problem and factors that can help resolve it,
3. assessment of the problem's workability and the setting of goals,
4. negotiation of a contract with the client,
5. preparation of a strategy for intervention,
6. evaluation of clinical outcomes.[7]

In offering these specifics, we have moved from a focus on societal social and health problems to those we deal with withir. an individual client. In noting these components, Wood stated, "not one proposition in this definition of [what she refers to as] good practice is in any way new; each has long been a part of practice theory."[8] These basic and integral components of "good practice" are also the cornerstones of good clinical research. In order to answer the question of effectiveness of casework intervention, one needs specificity to determine the clinician's efficacy in attaining *each* of these components.

Maluccio has provided a more detailed set of guidelines for a scientific approach to practice and the dimensions to be evaluated in assessing its effectiveness. They include:

1. Verbal attempts of the client to describe the problems and of the worker to understand what the client means, as expressed to each other, and mutually agreed upon;
2. Collection of objective and precise information *before* intervention, so as to establish baseline measures of frequency and duration of problems;
3. Continued collection of same data during intervention;
4. Analysis of data regarding the intervention process, that is, to reflect the ongoing course of events in comparison with strategy expectations and to use this feedback information to correct practice as needed, based on both client and therapist perceptions;
5. Follow-up beyond the intervention itself to learn whether the adaptive changes of the service period are being maintained without the worker's assistance;
6. A commitment to professional reporting of evaluation outcomes either in agency records for accountability purposes or in the professional literature as a contribution to the growth of scientific practice.[9]

Our aim in this article is to provide the individual clinician with an overview of available methodologies designed to address each of the specific components in a scientific approach to practice. In so doing, we highlight issues in the use of suggested methodological approaches.[10] We want to state at the outset that this article deals with clinical aspects of care and what the individual practitioner will want to know about his or her clients, the problems clients bring to the treatment encounter, the accuracy of assessments made for guiding intervention, and the outcomes of intervention. Although the individual clinician is the focus of this article, it should be clear that aggregations of data based on the cumulative experiences of individual workers with individual client systems can be used to generate important data. Among these are profiles of client characteristics, client problems, types of services offered, and interventions employed either for groupings of private practitioners or for subunits and whole departments within agencies for purposes of knowledge building, accountability, allocation of personnel, or training directives.

ASSESSMENT AS A BASIS FOR ESTABLISHING PROBLEM-CONTRACTS

Assessment refers to all those activities involved in the selection of information for clinical practice: the actual data collection process and the interpretation of these data in the early stages of intervention. Assessment is the procedure by which the clinician identifies and empirically characterizes the presenting problems and their related situational and psychosocial factors as a basis for negotiating the goals of services with the clients.[11]

Kane noted that

> assessment is a comfortable idea, compatible with social work traditions. Measurement, on the other hand, sounds foreign, mechanical, and anti-humanistic. But when we assess, we also measure. . . . Measurement demands a certain rigor. The definitions used by all measurers must be standardized and the observations made the same way under similar conditions.[12]

A critical component and essential outcome of the assessment process is not solely a clear delineation of the problems in the client system, but an identification of those problems that the client is prepared to work on and for which a contract is to be established. The attempt to evaluate outcomes for all identified problems, rather than contracted problems, has been a major flaw in studies of social work effectiveness. For any given client, multiple problems reflecting broad social need can be identified. We have already noted that many of these are beyond the ability or power of the clinician to change. To identify them as targets for intervention is to predetermine a negative outcome. Social needs require a policy and planning approach that is multidimensional, and in which social work is only one dimension. In our opinion, the outcomes of social work services can only be assessed for those problems that are specified in the contract between the clinician and the client.

Specifying agreed-on contracts with a simple and clear statement of the problem to be worked on achieves several purposes: (1) it helps the client begin to comprehend what he or she needs or wants to change in the life situation, (2) it helps the worker achieve clarity and focus in the treatment process, (3) it delineates the extent of worker accountability, and (4) it sets the parameters for evaluation of outcomes in relation to expectations identified by the parties.[13]

The assessment phase of the clinical process serves to provide baseline data for evaluation of clinical outcomes. Problem-contracts identify which client characteristics or behaviors are to be the focus of baseline assessments and ultimately treatment. Baseline data allow both the practitioner and the client to determine the frequency, severity, and pattern of problem behaviors that are specific to the contract. This is not an unfamiliar component of practice, as the social history and psychological assessment approaches illustrate. Like Maluccio, Gambrill and Barth noted that "the availability of [baseline]...information, together with data collected during intervention, offers continuous feedback to the client and the worker and allows the timely readjustment of efforts toward change."[14]

There are a number of baseline assessment methods. Among these are (1) self-inventories, (2) behavioral interviews, (3) behavioral samples, and (4) behavioral diaries.[15]

Self-inventories are questionnaires that are completed by clients to measure problem behaviors such as anxiety, assertiveness or lack of it, fear, marital dissatisfaction, and so on. Indeed such measures abound in the psychological literature and the individual clinician is likely to find at least one scale purporting to measure the behavior or characteristic of treatment interest. Levitt and Reid have noted a number of self-administered scales that can be given to clients to make rapid assessments of problem behaviors or situations.[16] Clinicians who employ such scales should familiarize themselves with what has been published about the reliability and validity of the instruments. Such measures should be viewed as additive to information gained from the more in-depth psychosocial assessment, rather than as a quick substitute for a skilled clinical assessment.

Behavioral interviews are clinical interviews with the client that allow the worker to observe the client's reaction to certain stimuli, as well as to observe the client's manner of physical and verbal presentation. Such an observation provides "cues as to how the client approaches various life situations and provides the opportunity to gather information about reinforcement preferences, the possible antecedents and consequences that control behaviors chosen for modification, how motivated the client is to change, and finally who would be the best mediators of change."[17] Reporting these behaviors requires standardization in observations that remains a current research objective.

Behavioral samples are actual observations of the client in situ. These are used in residential settings, psychiatric facilities, and other predetermined places, like the home. Such observational evidence can be used alone or as corroborative information for client reports of behaviors. What is to be looked for during the observation should be clearly specified and standardized across observations and across observers, where applicable. Such observations can be fostered by the use of videotapes. Limitations to this approach are evident—when clients know they are being observed, there is an alteration in the behaviors that are targets of observation. Other problems relate to the extent of observations required for the objectives. This can be a costly approach, but valid for certain types of situations.

Behavioral diaries can be used when direct observation is not possible. Clients or significant others can be asked to keep a diary or log of information concerning the pattern of behaviors of interest, their antecedents, and consequences that may be suggestive of points of intervention. Often the worker will have to help the client structure the diary by establishing a contract as to what to look for, when to look for it, and how to observe and how to annotate the observation.

An issue to be considered in baseline methodologies is interobserver reliability, which can be determined by correlating independent observations of two or more observers. Such interjudge reliability would also be used when baseline data are obtained from written records or drawn from behavioral interviews or client-prepared behavioral diaries. When behavior occurs in different contexts, baselines may be secured for various contexts; these might indicate whether the dynamics or the behavior is similar or different, depending on the context.

CLASSIFICATION OF PROBLEM-CONTRACTS

Problem-contracts identified and assessed during the baseline period lend themselves to classification. Developing a classification scheme is a research endeavor in itself. Major issues focus on agreement of definition, clarity and simplicity of language in defining and labeling problems, and production of categories that are mutually exclusive while being both general enough and specific enough to capture the nature of identified problems. A problem profile can be delineated for each client or client system. A single worker or workers in relevant clusters can aggregate problem-contract data across sets of clients to get a broader view of problems that bring clients into treatment.

There are numerous problem-oriented classification schemes in the practice literature. They may focus on problem behaviors and personality disorders, as does the *Diagnostic and Statistical Manual of Mental Disorders* (Third Edition), as well as on broad psychosocial problems and environmental needs, as does the Berkman/Rehr Problem Classification Scheme developed for hospital inpatients and their families.[18]

Problem classification schemes allow clinicians to:

1. examine modal patterns for different types of problems,
2. cross-examine client characteristics by problem types,
3. determine through problem-to-problem outcome studies which problems they are having the most and least success with.

PROCESS STUDIES: EVALUATION OF CLINICAL PERFORMANCE

Another shortcoming of evaluation studies reviewed by Wood was the failure of the investigators to adequately describe the nature of the intervention process or service component. The lack of descriptive clarity made it difficult for the consumer of the research to ascertain whether the intervention was actually implemented.[19]

Gambrill and Barth noted the difficulty of clearly describing interventions and the problems posed for replication efforts by poor descriptions. They stated,

> It is true that producing a clear description requires effort, but it can be done. The clear description of the interventive procedures is a critical aspect for the delivery of service, and for this reason, it is increasingly stressed in discussions of ethical and legal concerns related to practice.[20]

The wide range of modalities employed for what may be comparable problem-contracts makes for another difficulty in describing interventions.

Clarity is required for evaluation purposes. As Kane indicated, methods need to be tested, but first, they, as well as practice, need to be described in "reproducible units." Specifically,

> The innovator should be responsible for detailing anything considered essential to the intervention. Once the practice is so described, another reasonably competent social worker should be able to perform the technique.[21]

She continued,

> Once practice is described with this kind of detail, it can be tested. The detail grows out of the careful observations of the social worker who has developed the technique. Eventually, when enough experience is accumulated, that worker has an obligation to write it down, leaving out aspects that are considered incidental or trivial...but including anything that is pivotal to the method.[22]

Detailed descriptions also make it possible to ascertain the appropriateness of an intervention employed and to make some judgments about clinical performance. Process studies of clinical performance are sparse in the evaluation literature of social work, but there are many of psychotherapies in the mental health literature. Frequently, studies move from problems to outcome with no attention to the clinical interventions.

Some strides toward assessment of clinical performance can be illustrated by the peer-review methodologies developed in social work. Although peer review is an internal quality-monitoring system in which, typically, workers within the same agency system review and monitor each other, the methodology can be extended to other evaluation-oriented situations. For example, the private practitioner may ask one or more colleagues who are also in private practice to join in forming a peer review network. At the other end of the spectrum, workers from different agencies may join to review work across settings as a basis for establishing criteria for acceptable standards of practice for a cluster of agencies with similar mandates or even for the profession as a whole.

Defined as a method for evaluating the quality of service provided by an individual practitioner, peer review operates on a number of assumptions: that good social work practice is substantially different from bad, that social workers know and can recognize the difference, that written records of clinical sessions can serve as an indicator of the quality of practice, and that social workers can monitor and evaluate the work of their colleagues.[23]

Chernesky and Young noted that as an evaluation method, peer review differs from and complements other approaches that are helpful in assessing the effectiveness of services provided. They characterized the peer-review system as follows:

1. determines professionally recognized standards of care for acceptable and nonacceptable behavior against which performance and services are compared,
2. provides an ongoing and systematic process by which practicing professionals monitor the quality of care given by their colleagues to determine whether practice is in accordance with the designated standards and criteria,
3. permits compilation of review results in order to identify patterns and trends in the quality of service provided, and
4. establishes corrective mechanisms to deal with deficiencies identified as related to individual performance and to organized system problems.[24]

The critical feature of the peer-review process is the feedback loop to the worker that carries the expectations of accountability, follow-up, and corrective action when indicated.

Much more work needs to be done to develop evaluation methods involving process, performance, or interventions. Tools such as audiovisual equipment and tape recorders will aid us in critically examining samples of clinical practice other than written case material. A critical issue in the development of process studies is, and will continue to be, the willingness of workers to risk exposing their practice skills to scrutiny by others.

OUTCOME STUDIES

Several methodologies are available for evaluating the outcomes of practice. End points or points for repeated measurement over the course of treatment might include the following: (1) changes in client behavior as measured by self-report or observation, (2) client satisfaction with service, and (3) follow-up as to the long-term effects of treatment.

The outcome evaluation methods described here are a few of those available to social workers and include the following: (1) goal attainment scaling, (2) controlled clinical trials including single-subject designs, and (3) client follow-up studies.

Goal-Attainment Scaling

In this evaluation method, treatment goals are established *prior* to the intervention as part of the worker-client contract. Goals are clearly and simply stated in a manner that facilitates gathering evidence as to their attainment. Typically, each goal is assessed along a five-point scale with values ranging from a low of -2 to a high of $+2$. The zero point represents the expectation of a client's posttreatment level of functioning, and it is in relation to this zero point (that is, the expected outcome) that the observed end points are compared. The scale is used to assess where clients are at the end of treatment for each specified goal, and, ideally, the scoring is done in a private session with a skilled clinician who was not involved in the provision of the service or treatment.

Guy and Moore described a goal-attainment strategy that they devised at the South Carolina State Hospital, a psychiatric hospital with a daily census of 1,310 patients, 70 percent of whom were schizophrenics.[25] The task of the hospital staff was to develop an instrument tailored to meet the needs of a chronic psychiatric population. The psychology staff first developed an inclusive list of the 37 most frequently observed problem behaviors. The staff then divided into task forces and defined each problem into increments of behavior, ranging from the most to the least problematic. Definitions were modified through an iterative process in which each task force reviewed what other groups had written until all were satisfied that increments of behavior were so defined that any therapist could use the scale and be able to identify a particular patient's level of functioning as it related to problems in the problem classification list. Each problem area is considered to be independent of all others when scoring is done.

Goal-attainment scaling can be done on the individual level between one clinician and his or her client as part of the contracting agreement. As with other methodologies, it provides data that can be aggregated across workers for purposes of program evaluation. As Guy and Moore explained, by collecting premeasures and postmeasures from all therapists in a specific treatment program, an evaluator can aggregate the data and compute the amount of goal attainment per therapist, per problem, or per specific therapeutic modality. This information allows the evaluator to find, given the criterion of maximum goal attainment, which therapists can produce an improvement in patients' behaviors, which problems are amenable to improvement, or which therapeutic modalities are successful at producing positive change.

Controlled Clinical Trials

Controlled experimental trials of treatment interventions are sparse in the annals of social work research. A central issue relates to the ethics of denying service to people in order to have randomly selected control groups. This issue remains an unresolved dilemma for social workers today.

Kane suggested that until we, as a profession, are willing to subject our clinical interventions to experimental tests of efficacy, we will be hard put to demonstrate that what we do makes a real difference:

> The ethics of experimentation in social work have been questioned. Critics say that we cannot withhold a service that we believe to be helpful. My own position is the opposite. I perceive an ethical imperative to support experimental studies within the profession so that social work, a scarce resource, may be used most effectively. . . .Why is it that the ethics of random selection are questioned, but the ethics of responding to referrals or problems that we happen to notice are not? Both approaches leave persons unserved, but one permits us to understand the ultimate utility of the service we give.[26]

Experimental methodologies exist that can be used to test the efficacy of interventions with groups of clients or with an individual client. All of the methodological complexities of experimental designs, especially those using several groups, are beyond the scope of this article, but the reader is encouraged to explore the literature in this area.[27]

Since the individual clinician is the central focus of this article, we will, however, take a closer look at some of the single-subject experimental designs.[28] Single-subject designs follow the general rigor of experimental designs for groups. Typically, all the elements in the research model that we have described thus far are involved. The problem-contract must be clearly identified. Baseline measures of problem behaviors with respect to frequency, duration, and intensity are taken prior to the intervention. Usually the client is involved in taking baseline measures of his or her own problem behaviors. Treatment is given and the posttreatment measures of behavior are compared to baseline measures to assess the direction and degree of change. This is the classical before and after experimental design.

One could also have a repeated-measures design in which several measurements are taken over the course of the treatment process, allowing not only comparisons to baseline measures but comparisons between interim measures over the course of treatment. Reversal designs can also be used; here baseline measurement is followed by intervention, followed by a measurement, at which point the intervention is withdrawn. If a postwithdrawal measure indicates a return to baseline functioning, or at least functioning below that occurring during treatment, the evidence is stronger that the treatment is associated with observed improvement in functioning.

Single-case experiments highlighted in the literature tend to emerge most frequently from a behavior modification framework. Often the behaviors to be changed are less complicated to observe and measure. Social workers deal with a wide range of complex human behaviors, and the utility of the single-case experiment for testing interventions with more complex behaviors is an area needing much more work.[29]

Gambrill and Bart stated that

> no single-case experimental study, no matter how well controlled, can demonstrate that an intervention will always have a given effect on selected dependent variables. Replication is necessary to increase confidence in a study's original findings, and follow-up data are required to determine the longevity of effects. The AB design, consisting of baseline followed by intervention phase and often used in the context of practice, provides a weak basis for believing that a given intervention was responsible for observed changes.
>
> However, replication across different clients or occasions decreases vulnerability to some types of confounding effects.[30]

Some of the confounding variables in the single-case designs are related to the idiosyncratic features of the client, the therapist, and/or the setting in which the treatment takes place. Replication across clients, therapists, and settings tends to "wash out" the effects of these confounders, and treatment effects that can be demonstrated across several domains inspire greater confidence.

Client Follow-Up Studies

The practice literature in social work has increasingly placed greater emphasis on the client as a partner in the treatment process and an important participant in the evaluation of treatment outcomes. Client follow-up studies are descriptive studies, usually of the survey type, that focus on (1) client satisfaction with services rendered, (2) worker-client agreement on service outcomes, and (3) maintenance of improved behaviors after the completion of treatment. The methods of data collection in client surveys may include face-to-face interviews, telephone follow-up, or self-administered questionnaires (usually with a mail distribution return).

There are a number of issues that can be raised about the validity of data derived from client follow-up studies. Sample bias can be an issue if one relies on voluntary feedback from clients. For example, are clients who readily respond to the request for feedback more likely (or perhaps less likely) to be satisfied with the service? Most follow-up methodologies suffer sample loss due to the inability to locate clients. If the inaccessibility is nonrandom (that is, related to factors such as social class, lifestyle, etc.), sample bias will be an issue.

Guy and Moore suggested that client surveys aimed at measuring client satisfaction rest on a number of assumptions: (1) that the consumer population is capable of describing and evaluating the quality of service, (2) that satisfaction is a valid indicator of the effectiveness of service, and (3) that consumer evaluation of treatment efficacy, appropriateness, and outcome is equivalent to professional and/or objective appraisal of these factors.[31]

Maluccio highlighted some of the methodological limitations in client follow-up studies:

1. Research designs of follow-up surveys, especially questionnaires, involve fixed alternatives, thus precluding the client from freely evaluating the service and expressing his or her own areas of concern;
2. The studies tend to be simplistic in methodology and superficial in scope, with a lack of emphasis on *why* clients express the level of satisfaction that they do;
3. Studies tend to stress perceptions of worker-client interaction, with little attention to other factors in clients' life situations that may influence their use and perception of services; and
4. Sample bias may exist.[32]

It is important to recognize openly these limitations and, if possible, to use them as a guide in developing better client follow-up methodologies. In spite of these limitations, there is clearly a place for consumer evaluation of services as a corollary to other evaluation evidence. As Maluccio noted,

> The growing interest in client perception of services is related to an emphasis on consumerism throughout our society, persistent criticism of social work effectiveness, and increasing demands for accountability emanating from consumer groups, funding bodies, and social workers themselves.[33]

Our research center, the Murray M. Rosenberg Applied Social Work Research Center, Division of Social Work (Community Medicine), Mount Sinai School of Medicine, City University of New York (CUNY),

New York City, assumes responsibility for conducting both self-administered questionnaires and telephone follow-up with patients served by our hospital. The methods used in the Patient Questionnaire are described in detail in the quality assurance literature.[34] Our experience has suggested that a random sample telephone follow-up yields better response rates and greater variance on service ratings than the self-administered questionnaire. Allowing space for voluntary comments and carefully recording verbal comments about services that patients make during the telephone follow-up tends to reduce the superficiality noted by Maluccio. Often the comments are quite detailed and very explicit as to areas needing correction, as well as commendation. A critical feature is designing a good feedback loop so that practitioners know how to use client input as a basis for improving service.

Although this example derives from an institutionally based effort at assessing client satisfaction, individual clinicians can also use questionnaires and telephone follow-up to ascertain client satisfaction with treatment. The same issues of bias and appropriate methodology pertain.

NOTES AND REFERENCES

1. Morris Parloff, "Psychotherapy Research Evidence and Reimbursement Decisions: Bambi Meets Godzilla," *American Journal of Psychiatry,* 139 (June 1982).

2. Helen Rehr, "More Thoughts on American Health Care," in Rehr, ed., *Milestones in Social Work and Medicine* (New York: Prodist, 1983).

3. Perry London and Gerald Klerman, "Evaluating Psychotherapy," *American Journal of Psychiatry,* 139 (June 1982), p. 710.

4. Ibid.

5. Parloff, "Psychology Research Evidence and Reimbursement Decisions," p. 721, citing Mary L. Smith, G. V. Glass, and T. I. Miller, *Benefits of Psychotherapy* (Baltimore, Md.: Johns Hopkins University Press, 1980).

6. See, for example, Joel Fischer, *Effective Casework Practice: An Eclectic Approach* (New York: McGraw-Hill, 1978); and Fischer, ed., *The Effectiveness of Social Casework* (Springfield, Ill.: Charles C Thomas, 1976).

7. Katherine M. Wood, "Casework Effectiveness: A New Look at the Research Evidence," *Social Work,* 23 (November 1978), p. 451.

8. Ibid.

9. Anthony Maluccio, *Learning from Clients* (New York: Free Press, 1979), pp. 178–179.

10. Numerous references are made throughout this article to books and articles that provide more detailed examples of evaluation methodologies.

11. Gary Rosenberg, "Practice Roles and Functions of the Health Social Worker," in Rosalind S. Miller and Helen Rehr, eds., *Social Work Issues in Health Care* (Englewood Cliffs, N.J.: Prentice-Hall, 1983).

12. Rosalie Kane, "Knowledge Development for Social Work Practice in Health," in Gary Rosenberg and Helen Rehr, eds., *Advancing Social Work Practice in the Health Care Field* (New York: Haworth Press, 1983), p. 65.

13. Laura Epstein, "Short-Term Treatment in Health Settings: Issues, Concepts, Dilemmas," in Rosenberg and Rehr, eds., *Advancing Social Work Practice in the Health Care Field.*

14. Maluccio, *Learning from Clients;* and Eileen D. Gambrill and Richard P. Barth, "Single-Case Designs Revisited," *Social Work Research and Abstracts,* 16 (Fall 1980), p. 18.

15. See John Wodarski and Dennis Bagarozzi, *Behavioral Social Work* (New York: Human Sciences Press, 1979), in particular chap. 3, "Essentials of Behavioral Assessment," pp. 62–88.

16. See John L. Levitt and William J. Reid, "Rapid-Assessment Instruments for Practice," *Social Work Research and Abstracts,* 17 (Spring 1981), pp. 13–19; and Richard B. Stuart, *Helping Couples Change* (New York: Guilford Press, 1980), in particular chap. 4, "Assessing Troubled Marriages," pp. 61–132.

17. Wodarski and Bagarozzi, *Behavioral Social Work,* p. 75.

18. American Psychiatric Association, *Diagnostic and Statistical Manual of Mental Disorders* (3d ed.; Washington, D.C.: APA, 1980); and Barbara Berkman, "Psychosocial Problems and Outcome: An External Validity Study," *Health and Social Work,* 5 (August 1980), pp. 5–21.

19. Wood, "Casework Effectiveness."

20. Gambrill and Barth, "Single-Case Designs Revisited," p. 18.

21. Kane, "Knowledge Development," p. 62.

22. Ibid, p. 63.

23. Roslyn Chernesky and Alma T. Young, "Developing Peer Review Systems," in Helen Rehr, ed., *Professional Accountability for Social Work Practice* (New York: Prodist, 1979), pp. 74–91.

24. Ibid, pp. 77–78.

25. Mary Guy and Linda Moore, "The Goal Attainment Scale for Psychiatric Inpatients," *Quality Review Bulletin,* 8 (June 1982), pp. 19–29. See also James R. Seaberg and David F. Gillespie, "Goal Attainment Scaling: A Critique," *Social Work Research and Abstracts,* 13 (Summer 1977), pp. 4–9.

26. Kane, "Knowledge Development," p. 64.

27. See, for example, Donald T. Campbell and Julian C. Stanley, *Experimental and Quasi-Experimental Designs for Research* (Chicago: Rand McNally, 1963); and Fred N. Kerlinger, *Foundations of Behavioral Research* (2d ed.; New York: Holt, Rinehart & Winston, 1973), in particular chap. 23, "Laboratory Experiments, Field Experiments and Field Studies," pp. 395–409.

28. For an overview of single-subject research in clinical practice, see the special issue of the *Journal of Social Service Research,* 3 (Fall 1979), entitled, "Single-System Research Designs."

29. See Judith C. Nelsen, "Issues in Single-Subject Research for Nonbehaviorists," *Social Work Research and Abstracts,* 17 (Summer 1981), pp. 31–37.

30. Gambrill and Barth, "Single-Case Designs Revisited," p. 16.

31. Guy and Moore, "Goal Attainment Scale," p. 20.

32. Maluccio, *Learning from Clients,* p. 21.

33. Ibid, p. 16.

34. B. J. Morrison, H. Rehr, G. Rosenberg, and S. Davis, "Consumer Opinion Surveys: A Hospital Quality Assurance Measurement," *Quality Review Bulletin,* 8 (February 1982), pp. 19–24.

Evaluation Systems for Practitioners: Computer-Assisted Information Processing

Aaron M. Brower and Elizabeth Mutschler

The debate over adding evaluation and monitoring systems to social work practice has raged almost since the inception of the profession. This issue has been forced by the increasingly tight economy of the past decade, and particularly of the past few years, to the extent that systematic documentation of practice has become a prerequisite for external funding. However, the reality of these systems in social service agencies has not caused practitioners and evaluators to come together to create evaluation systems to meet both their needs; instead these two parties remain at odds.[1]

For the most part, practitioners have not enthusiastically embraced current evaluation systems, and, as a result, they are seen by evaluators as not wanting their practice evaluated at all. The authors believe that responsible practitioners, those who are sincerely interested in providing the best services possible, do want to be evaluated and, in fact, already evaluate their work through qualitative methods such as supervision, talking with colleagues, and attending case conferences. Because these qualitative methods cannot be easily quantified, practitioners get no credit for the evaluation they do. Furthermore, because of current limits in the technology of objective evaluation, the systems are seen by practitioners as not addressing their evaluation questions.[2]

The gap between the evaluative concerns of the practitioner and the technology of most evaluation systems can be seen as a methodological problem and not as an intrinsic incompatibility between the evaluation goals of practitioners and evaluators. No one could deny that both parties state they want to be able to provide the best—the most effective and efficient—services to their clients.[3] It is only the lack of a common methodology that keeps this goal disguised. This article, therefore, presents a method to develop computer-assisted evaluation systems that are useful to practitioners by describing a prototype system. It is our hope that the methodology we propose is not perceived as advice to practitioners on how to do their work from moralistic researchers. The method was designed primarily *for* the practitioner's use and secondarily to meet the administrative (accountability and external funding) needs. This strong and admittedly one-sided approach is taken—with the knowledge that the majority of evaluation systems are designed for administrators— to facilitate the work that needs to be done to narrow the gap between evaluative methods that are acceptable to both practitioners and evaluators.

INITIAL CONSIDERATIONS

The relevant literature contains many descriptions of how practitioners view present evaluation systems in their agencies.[4] What follows represents a summary of these descriptions in the form of a list of concerns that must be addressed by evaluators in creating evaluation systems.

1. *Relevance*—An evaluation system has to generate information that will be relevant to the work that practitioners do in order for practitioners to use it. Criteria that will help make a system relevant are as follows:

   A. its ability to generate immediate feedback: since a case may change radically from session to session, the feedback time must be shorter than the session-to-session time;

   B. its ability to be useful to practitioners even as the system is administered: ideally the system should force practitioners to operationalize and articulate their assumptions about the problem assessment and treatment plan.

2. *Involvement*—Practitioners must be involved in the actual planning of the system to make it address their particular concerns. They must also remain involved in system modifications and updating to assure the continued evaluation of their changing concerns.

3. *Trust*—Practitioners have to be able to trust the intentions of the evaluator before they can participate in the evaluation process. They need to know why they are being evaluated, according to what criteria, and where the information will eventually go.

4. *Confidentiality*—Practitioners need to be able to assure maximum confidentiality to their clients. This concern is related to the issue of trust. Both the practitioner and the client need to know, from the outset of their relationship, who will have access to the information generated in their meetings.[5]

5. *Time Consumption*—An evaluation system has always been seen as something "extra" that takes time away from the real work that the

practitioner is paid to do. The system must be kept as simple and as "user friendly" as possible. Furthermore, practitioners need to receive credit commensurate to the time they spend attending to the evaluation system.

In general, current evaluation systems are seen by practitioners as not addressing their evaluative concerns. Because evaluators have brought the system into the agency and function as its representative, they have taken the blame for this system failure. However, instead of resting the blame on the evaluators themselves, complaints should instead be directed to the state of the art of evaluation research. The problem is not that the systems are trying to do something contrary to what practitioners do, it is that the systems are trying to process the information in a different way. Most computer-assisted systems have concentrated on collecting information that is easily concretized, such as client demographics and case dispositions. This "case flow" information has not been of great interest traditionally to the individual practitioner. And because evaluation systems are limited to collecting concrete bits of information, the task of developing relevant systems becomes one of concretizing the "right" information.[6] Collecting the right information, however, forces one to confront two important issues that typically are never thoughtfully resolved when an evaluation system is created.

Issue Number 1: Evaluation Systems Are *Not* All Created Equal

Leviton and Hughes have categorized evaluation systems according to how the information that is generated can be used:[7]

1. instrumental use—using information for the purpose of decision making or problem solving;
2. conceptual use—using information to influence one's own thinking about an issue, without putting the information to any specific use;
3. persuasive use—using information to influence someone else's thinking to support a specific opinion or defend it from attack.

Weiss distinguished differences in systems according to the part of the agency to which they are applied; her distinguishing variable is the level of an organization that is the target of the evaluation. Schkade and Schoech nicely identified the kinds of decisions that need to be made at each level of an agency's hierarchy. They also suggested appropriate decision support systems for each level.[8]

Combining the Leviton and Hughes typology of evaluation system utilization, the Weiss typology of system target, and the Schkade and Schoech typology of decision-making demands at different agency levels defines the following methodological dilemma confronting those creating an evaluation system:

1. Evaluation can be done on the case level for the purpose of making a practitioner's work more effective and efficient. For this to happen, the evaluation system must ultimately be individualistic (since one is now forced to choose between a system being flexible for the case or standardized to generate aggregated data) and under the control of the practitioner. This kind of system generates case-by-case information that may have limited generalizability to other clients.

2. Evaluation can be done on the agency level for the express purpose of meeting the needs of the evaluators—be they third-party funding sources, administrative personnel, or community resources. For this, the evaluation system must ultimately be standardized and under the control of the evaluator. This kind of system generates information that is relevant at the macrolevel. It may not produce recommendations for the practitioner, nor necessarily measure what in fact goes on during the treatment sessions.

Issue Number 2: Task Demands in Social Work Are a Mixed Bag

There are at least two kinds of task demands generated by the work done at an agency that are placed on practitioners and evaluators. Carter and Newman have identified this situation as one in which there is a distinction between evaluating client outcomes versus service costs. Simpson described different emphases that evaluators and practitioners place on evaluative research. Simpson stated that, roughly speaking, evaluators concentrate on treatment outcomes while practitioners are more interested in the strategy and the experience of the treatment intervention.[9] For our purposes, the distinction between these demands can be recognized in terms of the following:

1. The practitioner and evaluator must respond to the demands that are intrinsic to the practitioner's work. Essentially, these demands take the form of questions such as, What is troubling my client? What am I doing about it? How well is it working? These demands are always present for the responsible practitioners, regardless if they work for a community mental health agency, are under contract to an industry, or are in private practice.

2. The practitioner and evaluator must respond to the demands that are intrinsic to the work setting. Questions such as, Who do I see? How do I spend my time? What services do I provide? will vary more closely according to where the practitoner works and what resources are available.

Both kinds of demands are important for both parties. For the practitioner, however, the first kind is of primary concern; for the evaluator, it is the second that is paramount.[10]

Current Conditions of Evaluation Systems

Ideally, a system should address the needs of the practitioner and evaluator. Issue number 1, "evaluation systems are *not* all created equal," recognizes the technological gap that currently exists, forcing a choice between creating a system that is either ultimately flexible and practitioner oriented or ultimately standardized and administrator oriented. To bridge this gap is no mean task. But by not recognizing this gap explicitly, evaluators accuse practitioners of not following through with the system and of not wanting to be evaluated; practitioners accuse evaluators of creating a system that is too time-consuming and irrelevant to the actual work that is done. Thus, each party faults the other for the system's limitations. With this issue clearly stated, however, both parties can focus their attention on resolving this largely technological problem.

Issue number 2, "task demands in social work are largely a mixed bag," clarifies for practitioners the legitimate interest that external evaluators must have in their own work. For evaluators, it makes plain the sincere evaluative concerns of practitioners. Again, by not acknowledging the importance of both task demands, both parties can easily misunderstand the priorities of the other and not recognize the overlap. Practitioners accuse evaluators of being over concerned with "cost" factors, and evaluators see practitioners as irresponsibly hiding their work behind unmeasurable client "outcomes." Therefore, the two parties can become polarized. With the recognition of the duality of concerns, both considerations can be seen as compatible.

A PRACTITIONER-ORIENTED EVALUATION SYSTEM

To address the concerns raised in the previous section, a laboratory to develop a practitioner-oriented evaluation system was set up in conjunction with the basic research course in interpersonal practice for graduate social work students. As a result of being taught techniques to articulate and operationalize clinical questions, and of being taught the rudimentary skills necessary to use a computer, each student was given the opportunity to create an evaluation system to help in the work each would do in his or her field placement.[11]

The process by which these practitioner-useful evaluation systems were developed can be conceptualized as a four-step model.[12] To illustrate the methodology, the remainder of this article is devoted to using one specific evaluation question to work up a simulated evaluation system.

Step Number 1: Identify the Relevant Evaluative Questions

The way to begin to conceptualize an evaluation system is to identify the specific questions that practitioners and evaluators want to answer. To elicit these questions, practitioners should examine the two kinds of demands, identified in issue number 2: that is, those demands intrinsic to the practice per se and those intrinsic to the practice setting.

Demands intrinsic to one's practice elicit the question succinctly put by Bergin and Strupp, "What specific therapeutic interventions produce specific changes in specific patients under specific conditions?"[13] These demands elicit questions directly concerned with how to maximize treatment for the client.

Demands intrinsic to one's practice setting elicit such questions as How am I using my time? What tasks do I do? and How much time does each take? Who do I see? What kinds of problems do they have? What services do I provide? These demands elicit questions concerned more directly with the client "raw material" and the resources available to serve the client population.[14]

Some questions are relevant to *both* parties, and these are the key questions that the evaluation system should center around. For example, one could ask, "What services am I *currently* providing to specific clients or for specific problems? Is this a bias of mine, or are my colleagues doing the same thing?" This two-part question could produce answers that address the concerns of the evaluator—by providing "time-cost" data for the agency—as well as produce a first clue to specifying practice outcomes—by identifying for the practitioner *what* he or she does with clients when they meet.[15] This question will be the one we use as we work our way through the model.

Step Number 2: Operationalize the Questions

Once the questions that the evaluation system is to address are clearly identified, the second step is to translate these questions into a form that can be understood by a computer. One must first identify all the information needed to answer the questions, in essence operationalizing them.

Tables 1, 2, and 3 (pp. 240–244) list the information we chose to collect to answer our questions. One should take note of two important points. First, nothing is sacred about the information we collected, nor is the form in which it is arranged. For example, Fortune discusses using Hollis and Reid's typologies to codify verbal communication. The information presented here was chosen by a committee of evaluators and practitioners in our lab as being the information most vital to the specific question we posed. Second, one should note that each cluster of variables (referred to in the tables as fields) is organized around a specific aspect of the treatment process. "Clientdata" contains typical intake information. Information in the field is collected only once. "Episodedata" is our attempt to document what transpires within each client-practitioner contact. The information contained within the field is collected each time a contact is made. "Evaluationdata" provides ongoing evaluation ratings. Because in our labs the mean length of treatment is approximately three months, we decided that it would be most efficient to collect Evaluationdata at monthly intervals. Again, this decision was made by the committee, based on what would be most clinically relevant to us.[16]

Step Number 3: Analyze the Data

After collecting information on an appropriate number of cases, we are in a position to answer the questions stated earlier. Notice that some of the variables (or fields) are duplicated in more than one dataset. These variables become the "linking" variables allowing us to join the information collected in two or more separate datasets.[17] By having the computer create an output that summarizes the client demographics (age, sex, race, and so forth) in Clientdata for each service provided in Episodedata, we can look for trends in the services distributed. By selecting cases for workers individually or by summarizing across workers, we can see if these trends represent idiosyncratic preferences or biases of the agency. By creating an output coupling services provided with the evaluation ratings in Evaluationdata, we can see if there are differences in these ratings depending on the specific services provided. In general, we can discover if these outcomes depend more on client characteristics—meaning some clients will get better simply because of who they are when they walk in the agency's door—or on the services we can provide to them once they are inside.

At step number 3, our task is easy; a computer can take any variable or cluster of variables and show its relationship to any of the others. The key is that we devoted most of our energy to developing the questions that we wanted an evaluation system to address and to identifying the specific information we needed to collect.

Step Number 4: Interpret the Results

Step number 4, that of interpreting the outputs obtained earlier, is crucial to the evaluation system. Computers can only provide information in a form that can be likened to raw material. We, as the users of the system, must interpret the output received in such a way so that we can apply it to answer our initial questions. For the question posed, "What services am I currently providing?" one should be careful not to make causal statements, or prescriptions, from these largely descriptive data. Likewise, Gingerich and Feyerherm have discussed the often-neglected distinction between a statistically significant finding and a clinically significant one.[18] Only the users of the system can make this distinction.

CONCLUSION

Developing an evaluation system relevant for practitioners has to be a continuing process. Once the initial questions are answered with the information obtained through the system, it is inevitable that more knowledgeable and clinically sophisticated questions will arise. For example, it may have been found that clients from higher socioeconomic levels remain in treatment longer than those from lower levels, although there are no mean differences between the types of problems presented by these two client groups. Were they actually in greater need, or did the practitioners tailor their treatment plans to meet the client's ability to pay for service? Is there anything wrong with this? One would have to adjust a system to document the process that the practitioners go through when they develop their treatment plans. Or, it might have been found that the variables measuring the evaluation ratings were not sensitive enough to pick up observable and/or felt differences in the clients. These variables, then, would need to be redesigned.

The critical point of this four-step model is that energy has to focus *primarily* on creating, and re-creating, questions vital to the practitioner. This view is not a new one, yet it cannot be emphasized enough.[19] Without doing the work needed to tap practitioners' curiosity and practice experience, the evaluation system can never be made useful but will become yet another target of the complaints leveled at the mountains of paperwork that have become a staple of social service agencies.

The concept of creating a practitioner-oriented evaluation system may not be a new one, but its realization still elicits excitement. In at least one agency, practitioners enthusiastically made use of the evaluation techniques offered by their system, because they found the techniques improving their work.[20] Unfortunately, the system could not keep pace with their ever-increasing need for more sophisticated techniques, and as the system became more and more outdated, their interest in it decreased.

Nevertheless, practice demands in these times of limited finances and increased accountability call for a more sophisticated and knowledgeable practitioner. If the current trends continue, computer-based evaluation systems will be a mainstay of even the smallest agency. Rather than being swept along by the rush of data that will pour from these systems, practitioners can, and should, learn the skills now to create the kinds of systems that can be useful to their practice.

Table 1
Representative Dataset Called **CLIENTDATA**

FOR: CLIENTDATA
DATA SET DESCRIPTION:
CLIENT DEMOGRAPHIC INFORMATION

FIELD NO.	FIELD NAME	ABBREVIATION	VALUE	DESCRIPTION
F(1)	CLIENT	ID		CLIENT IDENTIFICATION NUMBER
F(2)	AGE	AGE		CLIENT AGE
	CATEGORIES (ONLY)			
	CHILD	CH	1	UNDER 10 YEARS OLD
	TEEN	TN	2	11–19 YEARS OLD
	YOUNG	YG	3	20–29 YEARS OLD
	ADULT	AD	4	30–39 YEARS OLD
	MAGE	MG	5	40–49 YEARS OLD
	OADULT	OA	6	50–59 YEARS OLD
	RETIRE	RE	7	60–69 YEARS OLD
	OAGE	OG	8	70+ YEARS OLD
	MISSING	MISS	0	MISSING DATA
F(3)	RACE	RACE		CLIENT RACE
	CATEGORIES (ONLY)			
	WHITE	WH	1	WHITE
	BLACK	BL	2	BLACK
	ASIAN	AS	3	ASIAN
	HISPANIC	HP	4	HISPANIC
	NAT. AMER.	NA	5	NATIVE AMERICAN
	OTHER	OT	6	OTHER RACE
	MISSING	MISS	0	MISSING DATA
F(4)	INCOME	INCO		CLIENT INCOME
	CATEGORIES (ONLY)			
	ZERO	ZERO	1	0–4,999 DOLLARS
	FIVE	FIVE	2	5,000–9,999 DOLLARS
	TEN	TEN	3	10,000–14,999 DOLLARS
	FIFTEEN	FTN	4	15,000–19,999 DOLLARS
	TWENTY	TWTY	5	20,000–24,999 DOLLARS
	TWENTY-FIVE	TWFV	6	25,000–29,999 DOLLARS
	THIRTY	THRY	7	30,000–34,999 DOLLARS
	THIRTY-FIVE	TRFV	8	35,000+ DOLLARS
	MISSING	MISS	0	MISSING DATA
F(5)	SEX	SEX		CLIENT SEX
	CATEGORIES (ONLY)			
	MALE	MALE	1	MALE CLIENT
	FEMALE	FEMA	2	FEMALE CLIENT
	MISSING	MISS	0	MISSING DATA

Table 1
(Continued)

FOR: CLIENTDATA

DATA SET DESCRIPTION:
CLIENT DEMOGRAPHIC INFORMATION

FIELD NO.	FIELD NAME	ABBREVIATION	VALUE	DESCRIPTION
F(6)	TX-HISTORY	HX		MOST RECENT TREATMENT
	CATEGORIES (ONLY)			
	IN-PATIENT	INPT	1	IN-PATIENT TREATMENT
	OUT-PATIENT	OTPT	2	OUT-PATIENT TREATMENT
	GRP-HOME	GPHM	3	GROUP HOME
	SUB-ABUSE	SBAB	4	SUBSTANCE ABUSE TREATMENT
	NONE	NONE	5	NO PREVIOUS TREATMENT
	OTHER	OTHR	6	OTHER TREATMENTS
	MISSING	MISS	0	MISSING DATA
F(7)	PAYMENT-TYPE	PAY		PAYMENT TYPE
	CATEGORIES (ONLY)			
	MEDICAID	MCAD	1	MEDICAID
	MEDICARE	MCAR	2	MEDICARE
	PRIV. INSUR.	PRIN	3	PRIVATE INSURANCE
	SELF	SELF	4	SELF PAYMENT
	NONE	NONE	5	NO PAYMENT
	MISSING	MISS	0	MISSING DATA
F(8)	WORKER	WKID		WORKER IDENTIFICATION NUMBER

Table 2
Representative Dataset Called **EPISODEDATA**

FOR: EPISODEDATA

DATA SET DESCRIPTION:

EPISODE (EACH CLIENT-WORKER CONTACT) INFORMATION

FIELD NO.	FIELD NAME	ABBREVIATION	VALUE	DESCRIPTION
F(1)	CLIENT	ID		CLIENT IDENTIFICATION NUMBER
F(2)	DATE	DATE		DATA OC CONTACT
F(3)	SESSION	SESS		LENGTH OF SESSION
	CATEGORIES (ONLY)			
	15-MIN	FIF	1	15 MINUTES
	30-MIN	THIR	2	30 MINUTES
	60-MIN	SIX	3	60 MINUTES
	90-MIN	NIN	4	90 MINUTES
	120-MIN	OTWT	5	120 MINUTES
	NO-SHOW	NS	6	CLIENT DID NOT SHOW
	CT-CAN	CC	7	CLIENT CANCELLED
	TH-CAN	TC	8	THERAPIST CANCELLED
	MISSING	MISS	0	MISSING DATA
F(4)	WORKER	WKID		WORKER IDENTIFICATION NUMBER
F(5)	SERVICE	SERV		SERVICE PROVIDED AT CONTACT
	CATEGORIES (ONLY)			
	CRISIS	CRIS	1	CRISIS INTERVENTION
	INDIVIDUAL	IND	2	INDIVIDUAL TREATMENT
	MARITAL	MAR	3	MARITAL TREATMENT
	FAMILY	FAM	4	FAMILY TREATMENT
	GROUP-TX	GPTX	5	GROUP TREATMENT
	GROUP-HOME	GPHM	6	GROUP HOME
	FOSTER	FSTR	7	FOSTER PLACEMENT
	CONC. SERV.	CNSV	8	CONCRETE SERVICES
	OTHER	OTH	9	OTHER SERVICES
	MISSING	MISS	0	MISSING DATA

Table 3
Representative Dataset Called **EVALUATIONDATA**

FOR: EVALUATIONDATA

DATA SET DESCRIPTION:
EVALUATION INFORMATION

FIELD NO.	FIELD NAME	ABBREVIATION	VALUE	DESCRIPTION
F(1)	CLIENT	ID		CLIENT IDENTIFICATION NUMBER
F(2)	TIME	TIME		TIME OF EVALUATION RATING
	CATEGORIES (ONLY)			
	INTAKE	INT	1	INTAKE SEVERITY RATING
	ONE-MONTH	ONE	2	SEVERITY RATING AT ONE MONTH
	TWO-MONTHS	TWO	3	SEVERITY RATING AT TWO MONTHS
	THR.-MONTHS	THR	4	SEVERITY RATING AT THREE MONTHS
	FOUR-MONTHS	FOUR	5	SEVERITY RATING AT FOUR MONTHS
	TERMINATION	TERM	6	SEVERITY RATING AT TERMINATION
	FOLLOW-UP	FOL	7	SEVERITY RATING AT FOLLOW-UP (ONE MONTH AFTER TERMINATION)
	MISSING	MISS	0	MISSING DATA
F(3)	DATE	DATE		DATE OF ADMINISTRATION
F(4)	PROBLEM	PROB		PROLEM IDENTIFIED
	CATEGORIES (ONLY)			
	INDIVIDUAL	IND	1	INDIVIDUAL PROBLEM
	MARITAL	MART	2	MARITAL PROBLEM
	FAMILY	FAM	3	FAMILY PROBLEM
	SUB. ABUSE	SUB	4	SUBSTANCE ABUSE PROBLEM
	DEVEL. PROB.	DEV	5	LIFE-STAGE DEVELOPMENTAL PROBLEM
	SEXUAL	SEX	6	SEXUAL PROBLEM
	ECONOMIC	ECON	7	ECONOMIC PROBLEM
	LEGAL	LAW	8	LEGAL PROBLEM
	HEALTH	HLTH	9	PHYSICAL HEALTH PROBLEM
	EDUCATION	ED	10	EDUCATIONAL PROBLEM
	OTHER	OTHR	11	OTHER PROBLEM
	MISSING	MISS	0	MISSING DATA
F(5)	RATING	RATE		SEVERITY RATING (FROM 0 TO 100)
F(6)	SCALE	SCL		NUMBER OF SPECIFIC HUDSON RATING SCALE
	CATEGORIES (ONLY)			
	CONTENTMENT	CONT	1	GENERALIZED CONTENTMENT SCALE
	SELF-ESTEEM	SELF	2	INDEX OF SELF ESTEEM
	MAR. SAT.	MAR	3	INDEX OF MARITAL SATISFACTION
	SEX SAT.	SEX	4	INDEX OF SEXUAL SATISFACTION
	PAR. ATT.	PAR	5	INDEX OF PARENTAL ATTITUDES
	ATT. MOTHER	MO	6	CHILD'S ATTITUDE TOWARD MOTHER
	ATT. FATHER	FA	7	CHILD'S ATTITUDE TOWARD FATHER
	FAM. REL.	FAM	8	INDEX OF FAMILY RELATIONS
	PEER REL.	PEER	9	INDEX OF PEER RELATIONS
	OTHER	OTHR	10	OTHER INDEX
	MISSING	MISS	0	MISSING DATA

Table 3
(Continued)

FOR: EVALUATIONDATA

DATA SET DESCRIPTION:
EVALUATION INFORMATION

FIELD NO.	FIELD NAME	ABBREVIATION	VALUE	DESCRIPTION
F(7)	KAS1	KAS1		FIRST BEHAVIORAL INDICATOR OF IDENTIFIED PROBLEM SELECTED FROM THE KAS BEHAVIOR INVENTORIES
	CATEGORIES (ONLY)			
	NEVER	NEVE	1	ALMOST NEVER
	SOMETIMES	SOME	2	SOMETIMES
	OFTEN	OFTE	3	OFTEN
	ALWAYS	ALWA	4	ALMOST ALWAYS
F(8)	KAS2	KAS2		SECOND BEHAVIORAL INDICATOR OF IDENTIFIED PROBLEM SELECTED FROM THE KAS BEHAVIOR INVENTORIES
	CATEGORIES (ONLY)			
	NEVER	NEVE	1	ALMOST NEVER
	SOMETIMES	SOME	2	SOMETIMES
	OFTEN	OFTE	3	OFTEN
	ALWAYS	ALWA	4	ALMOST ALWAYS

NOTES AND REFERENCES

1. For a good historical perspective on this issue, see Aaron Rosenblatt, "Research Models for Social Work Education," in S. Briar et al., eds., *Research Utilization in Social Work Education* (New York: Council on Social Work Education, 1981), pp. 17-20; Joseph W. Eaton, "Science, 'Art,' and Uncertainty in Social Work," *Social Work*, 3 (July 1958), pp. 3-10; M. B. Heineman, "The Obsolete Scientific Imperative in Social Work Research," *Social Service Review*, 55 (September 1981), pp. 371-397; Florence Hollis, *A Typology of Casework Treatment* (New York: Family Service Association of America, 1968); I. L. Hottman, "Research, Social Work, and Scholarship," *Social Service Review*, 30 (January 1956), pp. 20-32; Yeheskel Hasenfeld, "The Implementation of Change in Human Service Organizations: A Political Economy Perspective," *Social Service Review*, 54 (December 1980), pp. 508-520; E. Flaherty and C. Windle, "Mandated Evaluation in Community Mental Health Centers," *Evaluation Review*, 5 (October 1981), pp. 620-638; and Ludwig L. Geismar and Katherine M. Wood, "Evaluating Practice: Science as Faith," *Social Casework*, 63 (May 1982), pp. 266-272.

2. See Aaron Rosenblatt, "The Practitioner's Use and Evaluation of Research," *Social Work*, 13 (January 1968), pp. 53-59; J. M. Arsenian, "Research in Psychiatric Social Work," *Social Service Review*, 26, No. 1 (1952), pp. 15-29; W. Filstead, "Using Qualitative Methods in Evaluation Research: An Illustrative Bibliography," *Evaluation Review*, 5, No. 2 (1981), pp. 259-268; B. G. Glaser and A. L. Straus, "Discovery of Substantive Theory: A Basic Strategy Underlying Qualitative Research," *American Behavioral Science*, 8, No. 6 (1965), pp. 5-12; R. A. Ruckdeschel and B. E. Farris, "Assessing Practice: A Critical Look at the Single-Case Design," *Social Casework*, 62 (September 1981), pp. 413-419; Margaret Blenkner, "Obstacles to Evaluative Research in Casework: Part I," *Social Casework*, 31 (February 1950), pp. 54-60; and Malcolm G. Preston and Emily H. Mudd, "Research and Service in Social Work: Conditions for a Stable Union," *Social Work*, 1 (January 1956), pp. 34-40.

3. Numerous writers have discussed parallels between the research process and the treatment process, cf. Joel Fischer, *Effective Casework Practice: An Eclectic Approach* (New York: McGraw-Hill, 1978); Harris K. Goldstein, "Making Practice More Scientific Through Knowledge of Research," *Social Work*, 7 (July 1962), pp. 108-112; and Srinika Jayaratne and William Daniels, "Measurement Cross-validation Using Replication Procedures within Single-case Designs," *Social Work Research and Abstracts*, 17 (Fall 1981), pp. 4-10. See also S. N. Sheinfeld and G. L. Lord, "The Ethics of Evaluation Researchers: An Exploration of Value Choices," *Evaluation Review*, 5, No. 3 (1981), pp. 377-391.

4. The literature is replete with descriptions, examples, complaints, and cautions about the use of evaluation systems in agency settings. The following list is meant to illustrate the range of these writings, both in the focus of their concerns and in their longevity: Arsenian, "Research"; Blenkner, "Obstacles: Part I"; Margaret Blenkner, "Obstacles to Evaluative Research in Casework: Part II," *Social Casework*, 31 (March 1950), pp. 97-105; L. H. Boyd, Jr., John H. Hylton, and Steven V. Price, "Computers in Social Work Practice: A Review,"

Social Work, 23 (September 1978), pp. 368–371; Flaherty and Windle, "Mandated Evaluation"; Wallace J. Gingerich and William H. Feyerherm, "The Celeration Line Technique for Assessing Client Change," *Journal of Social Service Research,* 3 (Fall 1979), pp. 99–113; George Hoshino and Thomas P. McDonald, "Agencies in the Computer Age," *Social Work,* 20 (January 1975), pp. 10–14; M. W. Howe, "Casework Self-Evaluation: A Single-Subject Approach," *Social Service Review,* 48 (March 1974), pp. 1–23; Verne R. Kelley and Hanna B. Weston, "Computers, Costs, and Civil Liberties," *Social Work,* 20 (January 1975), pp. 15–19; E. Mutschler, "Using Single-Case Evaluation Procedures in a Family and Children's Service Agency: An Integration of Practice and Research," *Social Service Review,* 3 (January 1979), pp. 115–134; Mildred M. Reynolds, "Threats to Confidentiality," *Social Work,* 21 (March 1976), pp. 108–113; H. Rodman and R. Kolodny, "Organizational Strains in the Researcher and Practitioner Relationship," *Human Organization,* 23 (1964), pp. 171–182; Rosenblatt, "The Practitioner's Use and Evaluation of Research"; W. H. Yeaton and L. Sechrest, "Critical Dimensions in the Choice and Maintenance of Successful Treatments: Strength, Integrity, and Effectiveness," *Journal of Consulting and Clinical Psychology,* 49, No. 2 (1981), pp. 156–167; and W. H. Yeaton and L. Sechrest, "Estimating Effect Size," in P. Wortman, ed., *Methods for Evaluating Health Services* (Beverly Hills, Calif.: Sage, 1981).

5. The potentially dangerous abuses of well-organized information systems have attracted the attention of legislators. For a summary, see A. F. Weston, "Home Information Systems: The Privacy Debate," *Datamation,* 28 (July 1982), pp. 110–114.

6. See Richard L. Simpson, "Is Research Utilization for Social Workers?" *Social Service Research,* 2 (Winter 1978), pp. 143–157; Boyd, Hylton, and Price, "Computers in Social Work Practice"; and D. Schoech and L. Schkade, "Computers Helping Caseworkers: Decision Support Systems," *Child Welfare,* 59 (November 1980), pp. 566–575.

7. L. C. Leviton and E. F. X. Hughes, "Research on the Utilization of Evaluations: A Review and Synthesis," *Evaluation Review,* 5 (August 1981), pp. 525–548.

8. C. Weiss, *Evaluation Research* (Englewood Cliffs, N.J.: Prentice-Hall, 1972); L. Schkade and D. Schoech, "Decision Support Systems for Human Services: Prospects and Problems," in *Software, Hardware, Decision Support Systems,* Special Topics: Proceedings of the 15th Hawaii International Conference on System Sciences, Vol. 2 (North Hollywood, Calif.: Western Periodicals, 1982), pp. 629–639.

9. D. E. Carter and F. L. Newman, "NIMH, A Client-Oriented System of Mental Health Service Delivery and Program Management: A Workbook and Guild," Publication No. (ADM)76-307 (Washington, D.C.: Department of Health, Education & Welfare, 1976); and Simpson, "Is Research Utilization for Social Workers?"

10. Schoech and Schkade, "Computers Helping Caseworkers."

11. Use of computers by agencies for evaluation has been on the rise. See Boyd, Hylton, and Price, "Computers in Social Work Practice," for a review. Teaching students the beginning skills necessary to use a computer, in spite of widespread "technology anxiety," was not as difficult as one might imagine. See P. S. Nurius and E. Mutschler, "Use of Computer Assisted Information Pro-

cessing for Social Work Practice," unpublished manuscript, University of Michigan School of Social Work, 1982, for an elaboration on this topic.

12. With our refined four-step model and teaching strategies, we have begun to develop and implement full-scale computer-assisted evaluation systems in area social service agencies. See A. M. Brower et al., "Computer Assisted Evaluation and Decision Making in Human Service Organizations" (Ann Arbor: Center for Research on Learning and Teaching, University of Michigan, 1982).

13. A. E. Bergin and H. H. Strupp, *Changing Frontiers in the Science of Psychotherapy* (Chicago: Aldine-Atherton, 1972).

14. C. Perrow, *Organizational Analysis: A Sociological View* (Monterey, Calif.: Brooks/Cole, 1970).

15. Norman L. Bonney and Lawrence H. Streicher, "Time-Cost Data in Agency Administration: Efficiency Controls in Family and Children's Service," *Social Work,* 15 (October 1970), pp. 23–31.

16. Anne E. Fortune, "Communication Processes in Social Work Practice," *Social Service Review,* 55 (March 1981), pp. 93–128; and A. M. Brower, "The Uses of Global Rating Scales to Tap an Agency's Practice Norms" (Ann Arbor: University of Michigan, 1982).

17. This is a property of *relational datasets,* allowing us to maximize the computer's efficiency. See D. Kahn et al., *MICRO Reference Manual, Version 5.1* (Ann Arbor: Institute of Labor and Industrial Relations, University of Michigan, 1982).

18. J. Hankins, "A Conceptual Model for the Integration of Management Information Systems and Program Evaluation in Social Service Agencies" (Ann Arbor: University of Michigan, 1982); G. Wood, *Fundamentals of Psychological Research* (2d ed.; Boston: Little, Brown, 1979); and Gingerich and Feyerherm, "The Celeration Line Technique for Assessing Client Change."

19. Martin Bloom and Stephen R. Block, "Evaluating One's Own Effectiveness and Efficiency," *Social Work,* 22 (March 1977), pp. 130–136; M. Bloom, P. Butch, and D. Walker, "Evaluation of Single Interventions," *Journal of Social Service Research,* 2 (Spring 1979), pp. 301–310; R. D. Brodie, B. L. Singer, and M. R. Winterbottom, "Integration of Research Findings and Casework Techniques," *Social Casework,* 48 (June 1967), pp. 360–366; Wallace J. Gingerich, "Procedure for Evaluating Clinical Practice," *Health and Social Work,* 4 (May 1979), pp. 104–130; Florence Hollis, "The Coding and Application of a Typology of Casework Treatment," *Social Casework,* 48 (October 1967), pp. 489–497; James R. Seaberg, "'Case Recording by Code," *Social Work,* 10 (October 1965), pp. 92–98; Seaberg, "Systematized Recording: A Follow-up," *Social Work,* 15 (October 1970), pp. 32–41; and C. B. Traux and R. R. Carkhuff, *Toward Effective Counseling and Psychotherapy* (Chicago: Aldine, 1967).

20. Mutschler, "Using Single-Case Evaluation Procedures."

EPILOGUE

Editor's Comments

The term "epilogue" denotes "a concluding section that rounds out the design of a literary work."[1] The following article by Cooper serves that function, even though it is adapted and shortened from her plenary address, which actually opened the 1982 Clinical Conference. Cooper offers a prefigured set of conditions that she believes must be met for clinical practice to achieve the status of excellence in the 1980s and beyond. This offering is especially fitting as a conclusion to the reviews of advances in clinical social work provided by the contributors to this volume.

Cooper views the achievements of clinical social work with pride, while demanding that its practice and its education for practice confront emerging conditions with courage and commitment. It seems probable that those conditions, like those for achieving excellence, will include contextual changes, redefinitions of population groups, recognition of new responsibilities and opportunities for service by clinical social workers, as well as continued attention to theory and knowledge development, ethics, and research.

So, it might be said that the epilogue to this volume is a prologue to the future of clinical social work.

---

[1] *Webster's Seventh New Collegiate Dictionary* (Springfield, Mass.: G. & C. Merriam Co., 1967).

Concepts and Practice Issues in Clinical Social Work

Shirley Cooper

The practice of clinical work involves changing hope—ours and our clients'—into aspiration and action. This grasping of potentiality and exercise of choice constitute an important aspect of human freedom. To do our work well, however, we clinicians must concern ourselves with both actualities and potentialities. Realities shape the conditions and constraints of clinical work, whereas a grasp of potentialities, if guided by the values that have sustained social work, permits us to seek new opportunities. Failure to address both, realistically and relentlessly, creates illusions of omnipotence or despair. As individual clinicians and as a profession, we must resist these two pitfalls. We dare not compromise our aspirations, even while we realistically struggle to alter those conditions that burden, impoverish, and constrict human beings and their potential. Gould has written:

> We pass through this world but once. Few tragedies can be more extensive than the stunting of life, few injustices deeper than the denial of opportunity to strive or even hope.[1]

There are three conditions that, I believe, are the most critical in dictating clinical work. These are (1) the realities that serve as our surround and context, (2) the knowledge, skill, talents, timidities, values, and limits of clinicians, and (3) the clients' wishes and capacities as they seek our help. This article discusses some aspects of the first two of these conditions. Failure to make careful and painstaking differentiation and assessment of them distorts the clinical process, whether this involves a therapeutic intervention, a program design, teaching, or the formulation of clinical theory or social policy. As one may note, the first two of these three variables parallel the person-situation or ecological paradigm that is increasingly winning acceptance in social work.

REALITIES

Perhaps the most glaring factor in current reality is the pace of change. For the first time in human history, each individual in the course of one lifetime must adapt to and survive fundamental and radical changes in reality. And for the first time in human history, we can destroy all of human civilization. This hurtling pace of change creates hazards *and* opportunities. The short-range view of the realities in which we practice are grim and sharply at odds with the humanistic values of social work, while the pace of change itself can add a perspective of transition, unpleasant as instability may be.

How can one characterize the present reality? Bell wrote: "The foundation of any liberal society is the willingness of all groups to compromise private ends for public interest."[2] Recently there has been a merciless erosion of such values; great inequities are now rationalized by straitened circumstances. Steinfels has characterized these times as manifesting

> the widespread distrust of institutions among all classes, the anomie and hostility of inner-city youth, the abandonment of the vulnerable to bureaucratic dependency; the casual amorality of the business world, [and] the retreat from civic consciousness and responsibility.[3]

It seems that we are becoming a nation of skeptics, turning inward toward what some have characterized as a culture of narcissism, while simultaneously, dogma, cults, and sects of all kinds proliferate with leaders who often combine "charisma and hustle" as they promise new ways to salvation. What is particularly important about these groups for social work is that they reveal once again that people struggle to combat a sense of alienation and that basic human needs for intimacy and attachment are so powerful that they lead some to exchange personal freedom for them.

For many, the present is bleak. Unemployment is still high. One person in seven has fallen below poverty standards, while almost one of every five children in the United States is classified as poor. The purchasing power of all families has been declining; in 1982 it was less than a decade earlier. Blacks and women account for the largest increase in poverty rates, representing over one-third of those below poverty levels in 1981.[4] Full-time women employees earn about 60 percent of the income earned by men. Despair has many statistical faces in a nation growing ever more dichotomized into the affluent and the poor.

And what of the spirit? Fried has asserted that the most prominent factor in endemic, as opposed to acute, stress is economic deficiency, leading to a pervasive sense of helplessness and hopelessness. The poor experience a sense of futility, too often contracting their belts *and* their expectations. Fried has remarked: "The striking effects [of endemic stress] emerge in the subtle, ominous, subclinical manifestations of apathy, alienation, withdrawal, affective denial, decreased productivity, and resignation."[5]

Pilisuk has convincingly pointed to the pervasive relationship between "social marginality" and ill health, suicide, alcoholism, hypertension, multiple accidents, and unpredictable violence.[6] Increasingly, this social isolation marks the poor, the disabled, the elderly, minorities, and single parents—more dramatically so as social programs for such groups are curtailed or destroyed.

Thirty billion dollars has been slashed from domestic spending through fiscal 1985, the largest proportion of these cuts being made in those programs that concern social workers and our clients most directly.[7] Still more cuts are being asked for. Neither state nor local agencies can offset these enormous reductions, and the callous view that private donations will fill the void created by federal budget slashes is refuted by every study of private philanthropy.

However, if we do not like what we see and know to be true, there is a simple solution. In October, 1982, the *New York Times* reported that the Reagan Administration had eliminated or reduced at least 50 major statistical programs that measure the state of the economy, the health of the nation, and the effectiveness of federal programs—vital information for social planning. A report approved unanimously by Democrats and Republicans alike commented that these cuts "have raised serious questions over the future of the federal statistical system."[8] But, the *reality* of experience cannot be eliminated so easily.

Doing away with statistical programs is not the only way that knowledge and information are being reduced. In 1981, Hamburg estimated that federal dollars formerly available to social scientists were being cut between 65 percent and 80 percent.[9] These reductions not only impair research in progress; they drastically curtail our investment in the future, vitally affecting the capacity to train young social scientists. The same constraints apply to education, in general.

Thomas Paine, writing of our nation's struggle for independence, said "T'is not the concern of a day or of a year or of an age; posterities are involved in this contest." It is not the poor alone who need social work knowledge and skill. Mobility; changing relationships between men and women; attitudes about sex, class, race, marriage; and economic and other factors have sharply influenced human affairs and family life. In the 1970s, for example, the rate of divorce tripled, and the percentage of children living in single-parent families doubled.[10] At present, adolescent suicide, child abandonment, and child abuse are on the rise.

The problem of child abuse is a particularly illustrative one for our times and for the state of clinical social work. Paradoxically, at a time when essential resources diminish, the study of abuse has begun to yield solid data about how to predict, prevent, and treat abusing families. We have come a long way since Kempe's landmark 1962 report on the battered child syndrome.[11] Early programs focused largely on identifying and reporting abused children. Interventive styles were often crude and focused largely on environmental tinkering—a different matter from paying sufficient and balanced attention to environmental factors.

In the last 15 years, there has been a dramatic advance in knowledge and skill in the field of child abuse. There is convincing evidence from various sophisticated studies that, given sufficient knowledge and resources and *if* we get to such families soon enough, we clinicians can make an important difference to abusive families.[12] To be deterred from implementing knowledge and skills that we have come to acquire gradually and painstakingly is a national disgrace.

Even closer to home, social workers are, along with many of our clients, bearing the brunt of this madness to cut services and programs.[13] Increasingly we work in settings that are more concerned with mass production and units of service than with autonomy and quality of services. Management is ever more present, whereas teaching, supervision, and opportunities for young clinicians to learn their craft shrink. Rules, procedures, and regulations proliferate, while interest in creativity, craft, and care slip away. The separation between technology and values is a central problem of our time. The history of social work is marked by our commitment to the integration of values with methods. We dare not become acquiescent to this growing trend to separate the two.

One could go on citing further statistics and data that delineate the nature of other threadbare realities in our national social fabric, but it is not my intent to engender depression and despair. Instead, I bring these data to the fore because the realities are *one* critical determinant in shaping the nature, style, and limits of all clinical work. We must know them, face them, and persist in the never-ending struggle to alter them as citizens and professionals. I would like to turn to some issues related to the second of the three conditions that I asserted shape clinical work.

KNOWLEDGE, SKILL, VALUES, TALENTS, TIMIDITIES, AND LIMITS OF CLINICIANS

I have stated with respect to child abuse that social workers know a great deal more than we have the resources or capacities to implement. This holds true in other areas of clinical work, as well. However, to lament externally imposed constraints and to struggle with these is one thing. When our own shortcomings hold us back, that is another matter. Which brings me to a warning: I intend to address and to take full responsibility for our share of some clinical failures. My intent is not to cast blame; rather I would hope to enhance responsible behavior. I do not want to create dichotomies; rather, I would assert the need for respectful collaborations in our field, which cries out for an appreciation of its diversity and the plurality of all our processes.

In spite of its shortcomings, we can all be proud of our profession's purposes, perspectives, processes, values, heritage, and struggles.[14] What, then, are my indictments?

Expedience

We clinicians have sometimes surrendered too readily and too compliantly in the face of external constraints. Faced with setbacks and too few resources, we have, at times, permitted our methodology and styles of intervention to conform to outside limits. I am well aware that no single clinician, nor the profession as a whole, can function apart from the realities. It would be as stupid to suggest, for example, that teachers stop educating the young because their educational institutions are less than desirable. We, like they, do not totally control our work. But when necessity dictates compromises, we must know what they are and the impact they have, and resist expedient temptations to rationalize the rightness of compromised clinical processes. We must persist in finding ways to convey what we know and value, *and* what is amiss with the services we deliver. It does not automatically follow that theories and methodologies must be redesigned to fit bad policy or bad programs. I think it is not altogether accidental that many agencies and workers have become enamored with case management rather than with casework. It is inconceivable to me that a client can be properly treated without case management—but this does not substitute for casework.

Let me give another illustration: Natural helping networks, mutual support, and self-help groups have properly become a recognized and valued set of ideas and practices in assisting people. However, you will notice immediately that such premises back up the assertions of right-wing prophets who insist that government need no longer concern itself with the needy and that self-help is both sufficient and good for the soul. It must be affirmed that these systems cannot substitute for careful professional help.[15]

Pilisuk, an advocate for and student of natural helping networks, commented:

> The frail elderly and the developmentally disabled child are not about to plant organic gardens or build their own solar-heated homes from recycled materials. Most people cannot provide support for all their own needs.... Self-help must be distinguished from a ruthless social Darwinism.[16]

Are we, as a profession, teasing out and pointing out where self-help can be productive and where it cannot? I think not enough.

To point to the role of expediency in dictating methodology and agency program development one could use other examples: the undifferentiated and sometimes ruthless pressure to deinstitutionalize, ill-considered and hastily drawn permanency planning programs, the insistence on brief clinical work under all circumstances, or other fashionable modes.[17] My message is simple: Necessity may sometimes become the mother of invention; it may, as well, be the parent of irreparable damage.

Professional Affairs

A second issue is the conduct of our own affairs. Practicing clinicians have too often, too readily, and too despairingly yielded their convictions to the "brain trust" in our field—the academics. This happens in a variety of ways too numerous and too complicated to review in depth here, but three interrelated worrisome factors in this process include:

• a misjudgment of the nature of science, and the theory and knowledge it generates;

• a belief—sometimes explicit and sometimes implicit—that the academics in our field are indeed more able than the clinicians to study, teach, and evaluate practice; and

• a far too complacent view that the knowledge explosion that surrounds our field and from which we draw practice principles is beyond the grasp or time of the practitioner. This results in a resistance to any attempt to stay abreast of current knowledge, not infrequently accompanied by the practitioner's defensive sense of doubt, or conversely to an overattachment to beliefs, rather than to critical thought.

Gould has warned against the view that science is an objective enterprise:

Science must be understood as a social phenomena, a gutsy human enterprise, not the work of robots programmed to collect pure information. . . . Science progresses by hunch, vision and intuition. . . .Theories, moreover, are not inexorable inductions from facts![18]

He stated that science must learn to accept that

some topics are invested with enormous social importance but blessed with very little reliable information. When the ratio of data to social impact is so low a history of scientific attitudes may be little more than an oblique record of social change.[19]

I submit that this is *precisely* the state of affairs in which clinicians work.

To quote again from Gould: "Many questions are formulated by scientists in such a restricted way that any legitimate answer can only validate a social preference."[20] Once again, the study of clinical work seems to be precisely in such a state. For example, in an article about studies of practice largely conducted by social work academics, Reid and Hanrahan have observed:

Research on the methods of clinical social work suggests that earlier pessimism about the effectiveness of these methods is no longer warranted... based on the developments of new forms of practice and better designed experiments.[21]

Quite rightly and carefully, they acknowledged that most of the studies in their review were "often of limited scope" and that "the practical importance and durability of...change have yet to be fully demonstrated."[22] Although three or four of the studies reviewed addressed significant experiences, the writers reported that most did not concern important life functions or adaptation, nor could the outcomes be shown to be durable or transferable to real-life events.

Effectiveness. I know that I bring my own subjective impressions about clinical effectiveness to my work. No one can be satisfied with this alone, although I am sure that I do not distort the fact that clinical processes are effective, under certain necessary conditions. However, I am no more satisfied with my perceptions as being good enough proof than I am with the honest efforts of Reid and Hanrahan. We may not yet be skillful enough to capture ways of distilling appropriate clinical questions precisely enough and to find proper instruments to truly assess effectiveness, but those who practice must go on trying. And we must find our own "gutsy" way to phrase the questions and methods that suit the nature of clinical processes, undeterred by overestimates of scientific objectivity.

My own special clinical interest has been in the treatment of children and their families. My students and I have had our share of unsuccessful or partially successful outcomes. However, I have also seen teased and rejected children learn to make friends; children who could not learn become curious and competent; children with terrible nightmares who learned instead to dream; children who mastered their own tyranny; and deeply troubled children who had torn at themselves, their playrooms, and the social workers, who learned to respond to newly won internal signals and to apply their own "brakes." I have heard a child say as he pointed to his chest pridefully, "I found a happy place inside"; I have heard another say, "I don't always want a choice, I want a chance"; a 7-year-old report that he can now find his hidden feelings just as he can find the hidden pictures in those puzzles. Recently, a formerly angry, depressed, and volatile 18-year-old patient told me that he had come on a wondrous discovery in the course of tuning his piano: The middle-range notes were the hardest to tune and that any slight deviation in tuning one string influenced the way the other notes sounded. The patient said, "This piano tuning is exactly like what we've been doing here—working on the middle range."

Teaching and Learning. Two problems result from leaving the teaching (along with the study) of clinical practice largely to the academicians.

Years ago those who taught in schools of social work came to the university with considerable practice experience. This is no longer so. Many teachers of method no longer have a vast reservoir of practice experience to draw on, and too few teachers remain part-time practitioners. It is my impression—often repeated—that a great many methods courses are more concerned with teaching *about* practice than with the stuff of it. I do *not* think that clinical practice can be taught by either teaching theory alone *or* by focusing exclusively on minute case-method transactions. The direct translation from a theory to an intervention is not yet possible, whereas exclusive concern with method strategies does not lead to solid accretions of transferable concepts.

One way to think about the teaching of practice involves the development of middle-level conceptualizations derived from parts of various more abstract theories. These middle-level conceptualizations may have the capacity to guide day-by-day or even minute-by-minute transactions with clients, while permitting the clinician to be led back to the theories from which they are derived. Our finest social work thinkers and teachers understood this well.[23]

Let me try to make these notions a bit more concrete. In an illustration elsewhere I have tried to suggest that every client communication contains two elements: the *content* the client presents and the *form* in which this is offered.[24] The content conveys information about the when, the where, the what, and the why of ideas and experiences. The form of the communication conveys different, but no less important, information. How a client tells something can add to the meaning of the content, change the meaning of the content, and provide more general and vital information about the person. The form of communication is related to personality organization and thus will change less readily and less frequently than the content.

It is possible that a content-focused practice may be the most effective way to help when a client presents delineated problems. In contrast, a client who wants help with less clearly focused and limited problems may require more attention to form issues. I am talking about degrees here— not about absolutes—these ideas are, as yet, untested. I am sure, however, that this distinction helps many of my students learn to listen in a many-layered way, providing them with a systematic, comprehensive, and manageable form to order their observations with clients. In short, the distinction attempts to partialize the broad and elusive ideas subsumed under the art of listening.

The ways in which "intercurrent events" shape experience can be used as another illustration. Intercurrent events are those highly colored events in human experience that punctuate a lifetime, such as losses, moves, graduation, and so on. These events have the capacity to organize a person's subjective reality and behavior. Through their connections to earlier

related experiences, intercurrent events have both filtering and magnetiz-
ing qualities. For some people, such events touch on existing vulnerabilities; others may experience the event in ways that create the opportunity for new or reworked mastery. Both types of people may be drawn
toward earlier similar experiences—to repeat and/or to master them. It
is in this sense, then, that images of filters and magnets come to mind.

Obviously these brief examples of middle-level conceptualizations need
extensive expansion and elaboration. Although now fragmentary, such
ideas can lead, ideally, to a coherent body of concepts that would bring
theory and practice closer together. Such arrangements of ideas have the
additional virtue of making it possible to draw from diverse theories and
bring to practice a sense of immediacy and vitality.

I believe such principles will come from the field of practice, ultimately,
if we practitioners take the time and effort to conceptualize our work.
It can come from a closer and equal collaboration between practitioners
and academicians. It will not come from educators who have not been
close to practice.

Which leads directly back to the realities. Full-time practitioners, with
exceptions, have neither the time and sometimes not the skills to devote
to the work of developing practice theory. Academics, responding to the
different mandates of their settings, tend less to have the desire or the
fresh and well-developed practice experience to move in this direction.

This point struck me with fresh awareness at a meeting of practitioners
and teachers in which the concept of teaching the use of transference by
social workers was briefly under discussion.[25] A young man rose to suggest that perhaps one of the difficulties lay in the fact that some ideas
are more *caught* than *taught*. What a wonderful distinction, I thought, and
"caught on" anew to why the teaching of casework method is such a difficult endeavor and requires teachers whose practice experience is fresh.
Perhaps that was why Whitehead wisely taught, "Knowledge does not
keep any better than fish. . . . It must come to the students as if it were
drawn out of the sea and with the freshness of immediate importance."[26]

I repeat that the freshness and vitality of practice cannot readily be
conveyed by teachers whose practice is limited or old. A caveat to this
is, there are rare and inspired teachers who do not practice and many
superb clinicians who cannot teach. The two skills are different.

So how can we resolve this problem, knowing that prescriptions without
means lead to paralysis, not progress? The problem cannot be resolved
by individual practitioners. It is the business of the entire profession, and
clinicians must press to have the profession assume responsibility. Is it
unrealistic to insist that our profession as a whole press unswervingly for
guidelines to certify and accredit schools of social work by ensuring that
a proportion of the methods faculty be engaged in the practice of clinical
work and have equal academic standing as other colleagues? The pro-

fession of law operates its education system in this way and, learning from social work and medicine, is extending the use of legal clinical internships.

But changing the requirements for teachers is only one way. Clinicians with greater levels of practice experience must return to the schools to get advanced degrees and insist that the curriculum be relevant to their needs. Schools must be pressed by the profession to accept a portion of their doctoral candidates from those who have solid and extensive practice experience. Too few practitioners are getting their advanced training in schools of social work. Instead, they seek advanced training in largely non–social work institutions that seem more relevant to practice. Each arm of the profession must seek ways of relating to the others effectively and relevantly. We dare not permit drift by default.

A FINAL WORD

A final word on clinicians' responsibility in determining our own destiny, as fully as conditions permit. We clinicians cannot allow ourselves the "luxury" of sloppy, flabby thinking. This is no luxury; ultimately it stunts the capacity for a relentless and inquiring curiosity about what we know and what we must yet come to learn. Sloppiness in thought keeps what is as yet unknown out of sight, obfuscating complexity and curiosity without discomfort. We must learn with greater precision what conditions and interventions will be helpful in solving what kinds of problems directed toward what outcomes sought by clients. We must do this with all the passion and commitment that infuse knowledge with immediacy, vitality, and a sense of rightness and timeliness.

As Toffler has reminded us,

> The recognition that no knowledge can be complete, no metaphor entire, is itself humanizing. It counteracts fanaticism. It grants even to adversaries the possibility of error.[27]

Discovery and dogma do not walk comfortably together. The question is, can we face the future in our own work and for our profession, armed with the impulse to discover, taking inspiration from those things we hold to be of value?

NOTES AND REFERENCES

This article is a shortened version of a plenary address given at NASW's Second Clinical Practice Conference, "Clinical Social Work: Practice Excellence for the 80s," Washington, D.C., November 18, 1982.

1. Stephen V. Gould, *Mismeasure of Man* (New York: W. W. Norton, 1981), pp. 28–29.

2. Daniel Bell, as quoted by Michael Walzer in a review of Peter Steinfels, *Neo-Conservatives: The Men Who Are Changing American Politics* (New York: Simon & Schuster, 1979), in *The New York Review of Books,* 26 (October 11, 1979), p. 5.

3. Ibid., p. 8.

4. Bureau of Labor Statistics, as reported in *New York Times,* July 20-21, 1982, and *San Francisco Chronicle,* September 15, 1982.

5. Marc Fried, "Endemic Stress: The Psychology of Resignation and the Politics of Scarcity," *American Journal of Orthopsychiatry,* 52 (January 1982), p. 6.

6. Marc Pilisuk, "Delivery of Social Support: The Social Innoculation," *American Journal of Orthopsychiatry,* 52 (January 1982), pp. 21-31.

7. Report by the House Government Operations Committee, *New York Times,* October 5, 1982.

8. Ibid., p. 12.

9. David Hamburg, MD, Director of the Health Policy Program at Harvard University, as cited in *San Francisco Examiner and Chronicle,* September 27, 1981, p. 23.

10. The number increased from 3.3 million children to 6.6 million according to the *San Francisco Chronicle,* September 15, 1982. Americans aged 15-24 are hurting themselves at a rate three times higher than 25 years ago. Suicide among males of this age is the third leading cause of death, according to a Harvard University study by Leon Eisenberg, October 21, 1979.

11. C. Henry Kempe et al., "The Battered Child Syndrome," *Journal of the American Medical Association,* 181 (July 1962), pp. 17-24.

12. See, for example, Byron Egeland et al., "A Prospective Study of the Antecedents of Child Abuse," *National Institute of Mental Health Report* (Washington, D.C.: U.S. Government Printing Office, September 1979); Egeland and Don Brunguell, "An At Risk Approach to the Study of Child Abuse," *Journal of the American Academy of Child Psychiatry,* 18 (1979), pp. 219-235; and Egeland, M. Breitenbucher, and D. Rosenberg, "Prospective Study of the Significance of Life Stress in the Etiology of Child Abuse," *Journal of Consulting Clinical Psychology,* 48, No. 2 (1980), pp. 195-205.

13. Federal cuts hit social service providers hardest. According to the *San Francisco Chronicle,* September 26, 1982, 41 percent of cuts are represented in all charitable organizations.

14. See, for example, the entire section entitled "Human Ecology and the Mental Health Professions," *American Journal of Orthopsychiatry,* 52 (January 1982), pp. 109-160, and in particular the introduction by Edmund W. Gordon. This section of the journal testifies to the growing acceptance of the ecological perspective by all mental health disciplines and acknowledges that social work understood it sooner than other professions.

15. A useful and balanced study of self-help groups and their relationship to professional involvement is presented in Ronald W. Toseland and Lynda Hacker, "Self-Help Groups and Professional Involvement," *Social Work,* 27 (July 1982), pp. 341-346.

16. Marc Pilisuk, "The Future of Human Services Without Funding," *American Journal of Orthopsychiatry,* 50 (April 1980), pp. 202-203.

17. A thoughtful and important critique of the pressure to develop permanency planning programs for all children is offered by Malcolm Bush and

Harold Goldman, "The Psychological Parenting and Permanency Principles in Child Welfare: A Reappraisal and Critique," *American Journal of Orthopsychiatry*, 52 (April 1982), pp. 223–235. Although I would agree with the authors that Joseph Goldstein, Anna Freud, and Albert Solnit, *Beyond the Best Interests of the Child* (New York: Free Press, 1980), have rested their recommendation for permanency planning on their reading of psychoanalytic theory, I believe that this remains a poor reading of that theory and has become a rationalized and poorly reasoned acceptance of the "theory" by the field of child welfare for long-standing deficiencies in the institutions and programs that deliver such services. It illustrates perfectly the point I wish to emphasize—that social work dare not use undigested, undifferentiated theory nor constricting social policy to guide programs or methods of intervention, even under pressure.

18. Gould, *Mismeasure of Man*, pp. 21–22.

19. Ibid., p. 22.

20. Ibid., pp. 22–23.

21. William J. Reid and Patricia Hanrahan, "Recent Evaluation of Social Work: Grounds for Optimism," *Social Work*, 27 (July 1982), p. 328.

22. Ibid., p. 338.

23. See, for example, the work of Annette Garrett, Bertha Reynolds, Florence Hollis, Charlotte Towle, Gordon Hamilton, Helen Harris Perlman, and many other great teachers who recognized and taught concepts in the helping relationship long before object theory, attachment theory, communication theory, self-psychology, and developmental thinking were as advanced as they are today. See also Shirley Cooper and Leon Wanerman, *A Casebook of Child Psychotherapy: Strategies and Techniques* (New York: Brunner/Mazel, 1984), pp. 5–12, for a fuller discussion of middle-level conceptualizations.

24. Shirley Cooper, "Social Work: A Dissenting Profession," *Social Work*, 22 (September 1977), pp. 360–367.

25. Second International Conference on Clinical Work, School of Social Work, Smith College, Northampton, Mass., July 27–August 1, 1982.

26. Alfred North Whitehead, *The Aims of Education* (New York: Macmillan Co., 1929), p. 147.

27. Alvin Toffler, *The Third Wave* (New York: Bantam Books, 1981), p. 6.

Contributors

Denise Bronson, MSW, is Research Associate, School of Social Work, University of Michigan, Ann Arbor.

Aaron M. Brower, MSW, is a doctoral candidate in social work and psychology, and is Senior Counselor, Counseling Services, University of Michigan, Ann Arbor.

Jay Callahan, MSW, is Unit Supervisor, Psychiatric Emergency Services, Washtenaw County Community Mental Health and Department of Psychiatry, University of Michigan Hospital, Ann Arbor.

Jane F. Charnas, DSW, is Clinical Social Worker/Consultant, Associated Mental Health Professionals, College Park, Maryland.

Shirley Cooper, MS, is Clinical Professor of Social Work, Department of Psychiatry, University of California, San Francisco, and is in private practice.

Robert P. Dunleavy, MSW, is Sexual Abuse Specialist, Children's Bureau of Delaware, Wilmington.

Leatrice A. Endlich, MSW, is Day Treatment Therapist, Gillis Home for Children, Kansas City, Missouri. She was formerly Teaching Associate, Department of Child Psychiatry, University of Kansas Medical Center, Kansas City.

William S. Etnyre, MSW, is Co-Director, Social Workers Northwest, Seattle, Washington.

Edith Fein, MA, is Director of Research, Child and Family Services, Inc., Hartford, Connecticut.

Don R. Fuller, MSW, is Division Director, Office of Human Development, Department of Health and Human Resources, State of Louisiana, Baton Rouge.

Dianne Gerard, Ph.D., is Director of Counseling Services, Personal Assistance Center, Naval Station, Pearl Harbor, Hawaii.

George S. Getzel, DSW, is Professor, School of Social Work, Hunter College of the City University of New York, New York.

Jewelle Taylor Gibbs, Ph.D., is Acting Associate Professor, School of Social Welfare, University of California, Berkeley.

Joyce Hamilton-Collins, MSW, is Social Worker, Mt. Sinai Hospital, Hartford, Connecticut.

Thomas Hlenski, MSW, is Supervisor, Family Therapy, CoPay Inc., Great Neck, New York, and is a doctoral candidate, School of Social Welfare, Adelphi University, Garden City, New York.

M. Vincentia Joseph, DSW, is Associate Professor, National Catholic School of Social Service, Catholic University of America, Washington, D.C.

Shirley Wesley King, Ph.D., is Assistant Professor, Graduate School of Social Work, University of Texas at Arlington.

Janet H. Lowrey, MSW, is Assistant Director, Gillis Home for Children, and Clinical Social Worker, Communicative Disorders Department, Research Medical Center, both in Kansas City, Missouri.

Abraham Lurie, Ph.D., is Professor, School of Social Work, Adelphi University, Garden City, New York.

Rosemary Masters, MSW, JD, is former Director, Families of Homicide Victims Project, Victims Service Agency, New York, New York, and is now in private practice.

Raymond Sanchez Mayers, Ph.D., is Assistant Professor, Graduate School of Social Work, University of Texas at Arlington.

Ruth R. Middleman, Ed.D., is Professor, Kent School of Social Work, College of Urban and Public Affairs, University of Louisville, Louisville, Kentucky.

Mary Lou Misci, MSW, is Clinical Social Worker, Medical Center of Delaware–Christiana Hospital, Newark.

Judith Marks Mishne, DSW, is Professor, School of Social Work, New York University, and in private practice, New York, New York.

Barbara J. Morrison, DSW, is Director, Program Development Unit, New York State Office for the Aging, Albany. She was formerly Co-Director, Murray M. Rosenberg Applied Social Work Research Center, and Assistant Professor, Community Medicine, both at Mount Sinai School of Medicine, City University of New York, New York.

Elizabeth Mutschler, Ph.D., is Associate Professor, School of Social Work, University of Michigan, Ann Arbor.

Arleen B. Nelson, MSW, is Co-Director, Social Workers Northwest, Seattle, Washington.

Kathleen A. Olmstead, MSW, is Chief of Social Work, Child and Family Services, Inc., Hartford, Connecticut.

Helen Rehr, DSW, is Edith J. Baerwald Professor of Community Medicine, and Director, Murray M. Rosenberg Applied Social Work Research Center, both at Mount Sinai School of Medicine, City University of New York, New York.

Joy C. Rich, MS, is a consultant and in private practice, Great Neck, New York.

Gary Rosenberg, Ph.D., is Director, Department of Social Work Services, Mount Sinai Hospital, and Associate Professor, Community Medicine, Mount Sinai School of Medicine, City University of New York, New York.

Janette B. Russell, MSW, is Assistant Professor, School of Social Work, Grambling State University, Grambling, Louisiana.

Cathleen Santa, MSW, is Clinical Social Worker, Department of Psychiatry, University of Michigan Hospital, Ann Arbor.

Bella H. Selan, MS, is Clinical Assistant Professor, Department of Psychiatry, Mount Sinai Medical Center Clinical Campus, University of Wisconsin Medical School, Milwaukee.

Lawrence Shulman, MSW, is Vice President for Social Work, St. Luke's–Roosevelt Hospital Center, New York, New York.

Edwin J. Thomas, Ph.D., is Professor of Social Work and of Psychology, School of Social Work, University of Michigan, Ann Arbor.

Anne Weisenborn, MSW, is Clinical Social Worker, National Institutes of Health, Bethesda, Maryland.

Joan Wheeler, MSW, is Project Coordinator, Psychotherapeutic Program for Cancer Patients and Their Families, Nassau County Department of Mental Health, Mineola, New York. She is a doctoral candidate in social work at Adelphi University, Garden City, New York.

Joanne Yaffe, MSW, is Instructor, School of Social Work, University of Wisconsin, Milwaukee.